First published in Great Britain in 1992 by
Bellew Publishing Company Limited
8 Balham Hill, London SW12 9EA

The collection copyright © Bellew Publishing 1992

All rights reserved. No part of this publication may be reproduced, stored in a retrieval system or transmitted, in any form or by any means, electronic, mechanical, photocopying, recording or otherwise without the prior permission of the publisher

ISBN 1 85725 044 3

Phototypeset by LDA, Taplow, Berkshire
Printed in Great Britain by
Hartnolls Ltd

Royalties will go to The Canterbury Oast Trust

MANY MANSIONS

Interfaith and Religious Intolerance

Preface by the Archbishop of York

Edited by Dan Cohn-Sherbok

Bellew Publishing
London
1992

Many Mansions

OTHER TITLES IN THE CANTERBURY PAPERS SERIES:
Series Editors Dan Cohn-Sherbok and Kenneth Wolfe

ESSAYS ON RELIGION AND SOCIETY
Edited by Dan Cohn-Sherbok

TRADITION AND UNITY:
Sermons Published in Honour of Robert Runcie
Edited by Dan Cohn-Sherbok
Foreword by Lord Hailsham

USING THE BIBLE TODAY:
Contemporary Interpretations of Scripture
Edited by Dan Cohn-Sherbok

FUNDAMENTALISM AND TOLERANCE:
An Agenda for Theology and Society
Edited by Andrew Linzey and Peter Wexler

RELIGION: CONTEMPORARY ISSUES:
The All Souls Seminars on the Sociology of Religion
Edited by Bryan Wilson

Contents

Preface *John Habgood* — vii
Setting the Scene *Christopher Lewis* — ix

Part I Christianity and Other Faiths

1 Toleration — 3
   George Carey
2 Christianity and World Religions — 18
   Robert Runcie
3 Christianity and Other Religions — 31
   Gavin D'Costa
4 Christ and Interfaith Worship — 44
   Andrew Linzey
5 Evangelization and Other Faiths: the Motivation for Mission — 53
   Michael Barnes
6 Christ and the Scandal of Particularities — 61
   Alan Race
7 Dialogue in an Age of Conflict — 73
   Michael Nazir-Ali
8 The Case for Religious Pluralism — 82
   Paul Badham

Part II The Challenge of Interfaith

9   The Meeting of Religions Today — 95
    Geoffrey Parrinder
10 Models of Interreligious Communication: Reflections on Interfaith Dialogue — 107
    Ursula King

11	A Religious Understanding of Religion: a Model of the Relationship between Traditions *John Hick*	122
12	Religion after the Enlightenment *Keith Ward*	137
13	Interfaith Prayer *Marcus Braybrooke*	149
14	The Concept of Interfaith Dialogue *Bhikhu Parekh*	158
15	Christian–Muslim Dialogue in the Twentieth Century *Shabbir Akhtar*	169
16	Ranking Religions *Dan Cohn-Sherbok*	176
	Notes and Acknowledgements	187
	List of Contributors	199

Preface

Other faiths used to belong to other lands. At home rival religious claims could safely be ignored. Or, if not ignored, patronized. The superiority of one's own faith was so evident that the alternatives could somehow be brought within its purview without posing any real theological or social threat.

Today things are different. Different faiths are practised cheek by jowl in most parts of the world. It is less easy for one to dismiss another as manifestly inferior, particularly when, as in Britain, minority faiths are usually lived with a much greater degree of devotion than the majority ones. Ignorance, suspicion and condescension, are slowly giving way to mutual respect. The need for social harmony reinforces the desire to take each other seriously, and there is in some quarters a willingness to share not just ideas, but occasions of worship.

This change of perspective, however, is not without its problems. Social harmony is one thing, but to devalue Christian claims about the uniqueness of Christ and the finality of his work is another. How far can Christians afford to recognize other paths to transcendent reality without undermining their own faith? How should the call to evangelism be interpreted in a context where other faiths are acknowledged and respected? How can serious dialogue between faiths be commended without accepting the possibility that in the process faith itself will be changed?

These are worrying questions for many Christians, as recent sharp reactions have demonstrated. Some of the answers given to them have provoked sharp reactions from communities which feel they are being targeted. There is a danger of withdrawal into separate enclaves, superficially friendly maybe, but anxious to avoid any real encounter.

This book is timely, therefore. I hope it will help to demonstrate, not only the high significance of interfaith encounter in today's world, but also the possibilities of entering into it with integrity and strength of commitment.

JOHN HABGOOD
Archbishop of York

Setting the Scene
Christopher Lewis

There is a story, perhaps apocryphal, of the school head faced with Christmas in a multi-faith area who decided to include all the oxen, asses and shepherds but to leave Jesus out of it. Do the central tenets or figures of a faith have to be played down in order that there may be creative contact with other faiths? It is a question which has recently led to controversy, especially over events in cathedrals. Yet it is no new question, having been asked in the inter-church context of the ecumenical movement since its origins in the nineteenth-century missionary endeavours. There the question was asked in the form: 'Does what is essential in the beliefs of a particular church have to be diluted or omitted in order for there to be greater unity?' And what is asked in religious circles can also be debated in all belief-systems: to what degree can fervent socialists consort with others without compromising what they hold to be their most crucial beliefs? To what extent can a vegan get together with a liberal vegetarian when faced with ecological disaster?

Significantly it is new circumstances and purposes which provide the context for new opportunities. In the case of the ecumenical movement, the missionaries who were inspired to convert people to faith in Christ found that many of their fellows from other churches, far from being beyond the pale, shared the same Christian vision and many of the same beliefs. Co-operation which had looked impossible at home in the light of historic divisions, was now seen to be not only desirable but essential for the sake of the people among whom they were working. As missionaries sought to export those insights to their home countries, so the ecumenical movement grew. Many who were initially suspicious and who had cried 'compromise!' in the initial stages came to see the value of meeting other Christians for dialogue and even of worshipping together. Many who started out with the wish to convince others of the rightness of their own position eventually acknowledged that those others had also been in receipt of God's grace and that truth was something best sought with their aid and in their company.

Christians are rather nearer to the beginning of a similar experience with the great world faiths. The ecumenical movement leads directly into the interfaith movement. The uncertainty of knowing what stage we are at and what words and actions are appropriate for that stage, creates conflict. What do people actually do when faced with particular decisions? Recently the debate about relations between Christianity and other faiths has been focused on specific events in Britain such as the Commonwealth Day Observance in Westminster Abbey and various services held in cathedrals, for example in Winchester, Bristol and Coventry. One event which attracted considerable attention was held in Canterbury in September 1989 and it may be illuminating to examine the circumstances briefly.

The threats to the environment are now very well documented and indeed have contributed to a more global consciousness. Christian theology has perhaps been slow in assimilating this change, but since the mid-1970s there has been an attempt to grapple with the newly perceived ecological threats in the light of a Christian doctrine of creation. Yet the threat is plainly not something which can be faced by any one section of humanity, nor by any one religion acting on its own. It is a shared crisis: impending disaster for the whole human race is something which requires of us an unprecedented degree of co-operation and which especially challenges the world religions to discover together what resources they can offer to humankind.

In 1989 the British Council of Churches together with the World Wide Fund for Nature (WWF – formerly the World Wildlife Fund) arranged a conference at Christ Church College in Canterbury with the title 'Christian Faith and Ecology'. This event was part of a wider 'Festival of Faith and the Environment' organized by the WWF Network on Conservation and Religion which invited 'members of different faith communities to join us in Canterbury to show us something of their work and to share with us their concern for the environment'.[1] The festival was arranged for WWF by the International Consultancy of Religion, Education and Culture (ICOREC), an organization which produces educational material about a number of religions. The purpose of the festival was to highlight the link between the faiths and environmental concerns. Some of the inspiration for this and other similar events originated in the Day of Prayer for Peace in Assisi in 1986, attended by representatives of the major faiths; among the Christian representatives were the Pope and the Archbishop of Canterbury.

From an early stage in the planning of the events at Canterbury they became the object of criticism. The cathedral received a large quantity of mail which concentrated its attack on three events which were to take place in the cathedral building itself. In particular the letters were encouraged by the organization 'Action for Biblical Witness to Our Nation' (ABWON). The cathedral was taken to task for hosting 'interfaith worship' and for implying that all faiths are going the same way when it should have been proclaiming salvation through Jesus Christ alone. Demonstrations were planned and leaflets were printed by ABWON and by a Cheltenham organization called 'Save Another Soul'.

The three events were: a service of welcome of pilgrims from a number of the world's great faiths, a concert with the title 'The Forest – a Celebration of Trees' and a eucharist on the Sunday morning at which the Archbishop of Canterbury was the preacher. Each occasion was, of course, different. The service of welcome drew on Christian resources (for example, the prayer of St Francis) and did not use material from other faiths, in so far as the Psalms and the Book of Proverbs can be said to belong to Judaism. It was criticized for 'leaving Jesus out', although the name of Christ was mentioned in the address and the whole context of the cathedral is heavy in Christian symbolism. The theme of the service was the creation, understood as belonging to God and therefore worthy of respect and care. It concluded with a visit to the site of the martyrdom of Thomas à Becket.

The concert, like all concerts, was not vetted word for word beforehand and contained some words which would not have been suitable for Christian worship. In particular there were songs from a musical about ecology called *Yanomamo*, one of which contained the chorus: 'The trees have power. We worship them. With their strength we grow. We live because they give us life. Yanomamo.' The event was, however, unambiguously not worship and was seen by most people as equivalent to the many other concerts and events which take place in Canterbury, as in other cathedrals.

Then, thirdly, the eucharist was celebrated on the Sunday, using the customary Church of England rite, with prayers and readings on the theme of the doctrine of the creation. People from other faiths and none were present at the occasion, as they are free to be at any service. At the back of the service booklet were printed some passages for reflection written by members of a number of faiths on the subject of the world of nature.

The criticisms took various forms, but most objected to any 'multi-faith' worship taking place in the cathedral or its immediate surrounds. Canterbury events were seen as especially significant on account of the cathedral's position within the Church of England and the Anglican communion. The worship was alleged to treat all religions as equally valid, equally worthy of respect and thus to deny the finality of Christ. As the focus of the festival was environmental it became associated in the minds of many with 'New Age' thinking and therefore with a pantheistic blurring of the distinction between the Creator and his creation. From there it was a short step to associate the festival with occult practices.

The correspondence in private and in the press continued for some time after the festival. In the *Daily Express* John Selwyn Gummer, Cabinet Minister and member of the General Synod, having said that Westminster and Canterbury accounted Buddhists, Hindus and Muslims equal to the faith of Jesus, observed: 'What a mercy that St Augustine did not take the same ecumenical view of the Druids!'[2]

Eventually, in December 1991, an Open Letter addressed to the Leadership of the Church of England was published in the press, signed by numerous Church of England clergy and supported by lay office-holders and some clergy of the Church in Wales. The text of the letter was as follows:

> Believing that Jesus Christ the incarnate Son of God, is both God and man, the unique revelation of God, the only Saviour and hope of mankind – we, the undersigned members of the Church of England, are concerned that his Gospel shall be clearly presented in this Decade of Evangelism.
>
> We desire to love and respect people of other faiths. We acknowledge and respect their rights and freedoms. We wholeheartedly support co-operation in appropriate community, social, moral and political issues between Christians and those of other faiths wherever this is possible. Nevertheless, we believe it to be our Lord's command that his Gospel be clearly proclaimed, openly and sensitively, to all people (including those of other faiths) with the intention that they should come to faith in him for salvation.
>
> In this we affirm no more and no less than the Apostolic and Anglican tradition. Article XVIII says: 'Scripture doth set out unto us only the Name of Jesus Christ, whereby men must be saved.'
>
> In consequence we are deeply concerned about gatherings for interfaith worship and prayer involving Christian people. These include the Interfaith Commonwealth Day Observance in Westminster Abbey and other such events in some of the cathedrals and churches of England, whether they refer to Jesus Christ or whether such references are minimal or excluded.
>
> We believe these events, however motivated, conflict with the Christian duty to proclaim the Gospel. They imply that salvation is offered by God not only through Jesus Christ but by other means, and thus deny his uniqueness and finality as the only Saviour.
>
> These events are frequently deeply hurtful to those in this country who have come from other religions into the Christian faith, and also to Christian minorities in other lands, both of whom have frequently experienced persecution from the other faiths, and especially where such

faiths are unwilling to tolerate conversions or the existence of minority Christian communities.

We, therefore, appeal to the leadership of the Church of England to oppose and, where possible, prevent such gatherings for interfaith worship and prayer in the Church of England and to seek to discourage them elsewhere. We also call upon Christian people to pray that this will be done.

Our objections to interfaith worship are theological, spiritual and, indeed, constitutional. Recognizing that the Christian faith belongs to all races and nations, we deplore objections to such worship arising from racism or nationalism.

To avoid all misunderstanding, we wish to make it clear that we seek the good of all, of whatever faith, and obedience to our Lord Jesus Christ obliges us to proclaim him as uniquely Lord and Saviour for all.

Two questions are of interest by way of reflection on the events and the accompanying controversy. The first is to ask what cathedrals and other churches should in fact do when faced with choices concerning relations with other faiths. In answering this question the Open Letter is of little help. It has the feel of a group of people 'beating the bounds' in a manner which is far from the hospitable Anglican tradition. It does not define what it means by 'interfaith worship and prayer' and appears to be against them whatever form they take. There is no attempt to reconcile the wideness of God's mercy with the specificity of his revelation. Members of other faiths are left in the position only of being the objects of evangelism, for all the truth is with the Christians. There is then no possibility for exploration and growth, except perhaps in the social areas to which the Open Letter refers.

To restrict exploration to such areas is, however, too narrow. It is probably also fruitless as the various dimensions of human life and of religion cannot be so easily separated. The crucial question is to ask in what sense Christian claims should be understood. If human beings can respond to God only as he is in Jesus, then there is no more to be said. Many Christians have, however, held that God is to be discovered in all his creation; he reveals himself in many ways. Yet to believe that does not imply relativism. The Christian belief that God has revealed himself supremely in Jesus Christ can be understood in a non-exclusive sense. In other words it does not imply that denial of all other truths but, rather, that other responses to God find their ultimate fulfilment in Christ.

It follows that this non-exclusivism should be pursued in practice. The amount of co-operation, as in other spheres of life, will depend on the degree of trust and a discernment of how much is genuinely shared. As in Christian ecumenism, so in wider relations, there will be line-drawing. Discrimination is likely, for example, to exclude the Unification Church and Scientology and to include great world faiths when considering welcome and dialogue.[3] How far people go beyond dialogue into more liturgical occasions of scripture-reading, meditation or prayer will depend on the degree of unity shared. On those occasions, a balance of sensitivity and honesty will enable events to be welcoming while at the same time preventing them from being bland and painless. All division in the human family is painful, especially when that family is faced with such massive challenges.

In being open to those of other faiths, cathedrals have an important role because they have the particular character of a meeting place, a piece of common ground, on which very different groups of people may interact in safety. One of their greatest strengths is in being accessible, an accessibility protected by their dedication to God. Here are places where meaning can be discovered and threats can be handled: spaces in which many people feel that they have a stake and that they can expect a welcome. So cathedrals can probe areas of potential conflict and confusion in a way which other institutions and organizations may find more difficult.

This role as common ground stands alongside the cathedral's specifically Christian task. In the language of evangelism it means that cathedrals are often best at what is called 'pre-evangelism', in other words at opening people to the possibilities of faith within the Christian tradition and latent within themselves. Yet for some purposes the language of evangelism may not be the best language to use, for it immediately puts the visitor in the position of the object of evangelistic attention, rather than being first and foremost someone to be treated with respect and sensitivity.

The second question which is of interest is a more sociological one, namely: 'What is going on here in the controversy over relations between faiths?' Two forces at least appear to be at work. There is a sense in which the world is shrinking and becoming 'one world', faced with common problems and challenges. There is a watershed brought on by growing global consciousness. The ecological crisis in particular brings the fragility of the creation to our attention. Relations with other faiths thus take on a new urgency and demand a rethinking of the context and language in which Christian theology has been done. In particular there is the realization by more and more Christians that the other great world religions are mature responses to God which are not mistakes and are not going to vanish away.

And yet at the same time, English society is becoming in many respects more fragmented and more secular. As different and increasingly dissimilar social groups attempt to express what they believe to be true about the world, so there is increasing ideological competition. The Church of England is also at a watershed; can it be in some sense the Church of and for the nation, attempting to minister to all? Or is it a gathered group made up only of the obviously converted and stating Christ's claims in an exclusivist manner?

It is tempting to analyse many of the current issues in the Church of England in terms of such a choice: the ordination of women, issues of sexual morality and relations with other faiths. The argument would then run that here is a struggle between inclusivists and exclusivists which surfaces now in one issue now in another. Observers of the General Synod of the Church of England might incline to such a view.

Yet that would be too grand a theory. The issue of relations with other faiths is the most crucial now facing the churches and it is of a different order. In particular the question facing the Church of England is: has it an open or a closed mind?

CHRISTOPHER LEWIS
Canterbury Cathedral

Part I
CHRISTIANITY AND OTHER FAITHS

1 TOLERATION
George Carey

When I told a close friend that I was to give this lecture on toleration he was amazed. He offered two viewpoints. The first was unsurprising: 'It isn't very interesting, is it?' How wrong he is. But the second comment did surprise me. He said: 'They could have given you a more relevant subject to speak about. Surely there are more pressing matters to discuss these days!' I thought of Northern Ireland, of Serbs and Croats in Yugoslavia, of Israel, of the Shias and Kurds in Iraq, of the black majority in South Africa, of the Orthodox/Catholic tension in the Ukraine and of Sikh/Hindu strife of India. But then I thought too of minority groups in our own country seeking acceptance, authority, even power. I have in mind groups at loggerheads over abortion or homosexuality or animal rights, just three of many issues in which many people have limits to their tolerance. And then I began to see why my urbane and civilized friend was so puzzled: he was not personally involved in these issues or in the troubles elsewhere in the world. For him they were matters which affected other people. He did not know much about them and did not care about these things.

The title of this address is deliberately double-edged. How can religion itself be tolerated? No serious commentator on world events today can discount the significance of religion – whether in Eastern Europe, Southern Africa, Latin America or the Middle East. So we have to learn how to come to terms with, how to tolerate religion. This lecture is also about how, with integrity, religion itself might be tolerat*ing*, accommodating, of that over against which it stands.

Religion will not disappear. It may well be that those who say we should expect a resurgence of religion in the West are right. But conjectures aside, what is undeniably the case is that many societies are now becoming increasingly pluralistic. Different faiths exist side by side in many more places in the world than a century ago. Britain, which once knew only Judaism as a minority faith, is no longer as predominantly Christian as it was; Islam, Hinduism, Jainism and other Eastern faiths are present in growing numbers. It is perplexing to many so it is timely to ask: What is the nature of a tolerating religion? Can it get on with others and on what basis? And there are questions too for the secular citizen who has no faith at all or, at best, is only a nominal Christian adherent. To this person the question is addressed: What place do any faith communities have in our secular world? On what basis do we tolerate them?

But the concept of tolerance itself needs to be defined. The dictionaries do not take us very far. 'To put up with', or 'to permit', each suggests a deprecating attitude towards something which is not wholly approved. Perhaps we cannot both 'like' and 'tolerate' something at the same time. The terms are mutually exclusive. A domestic analogy might fill in the picture at one level. I have a teenage daughter who loves pop music. You know she is at home when the house erupts with noise. The nearer you get to her room the greater the danger to your ear-drums and the lower your tolerance level of the music. But that doesn't mean I don't love my daughter. Such an issue does not defeat the lasting quality of the relationship simply because what is bonding us is so much greater than this minor irritation.

But what domestic illustrations do not help us to see very easily is that passions can be held so deeply that people have become prone to persecute rather than tolerate and are willing themselves to suffer for their beliefs. Here another modern analogy might help us. We talk often of pain tolerance, we may pride ourselves on being able to have our teeth filled without an injection if our pain threshold is high. Or to quote Bacon's splendid *Apothegm* 138 (1621) on Tolerance, with its double meaning: 'Diogenes, one terrible frosty morning, came into the Market-Place, and stood Naked, shaking, to show his Tolerance.'

Perhaps this helps us towards a better definition. 'Tolerance' has something to do with intensity of commitment: it is the 'obverse' of commitment's 'reverse'. There are those whose commitment to their goals, God or values are such that no cost is too great for them to bear in order to achieve them. Pain and sacrifice are gladly borne by them.

This link between tolerance and pain is important. Tolerant people do not attempt to impose their opinions on others by external pressure or enforce them by any means except thoughtful persuasion. But this holds true only if you or I hold opinions. People with no convictions are not being tolerant if they allow others their way or acquiesce with their opinions. They are simply 'indifferent'. The very word 'apathetic' expresses this. It refers to someone who does not 'feel the pain'. And for our society this needs to be emphasized. *Indifference is not toleration.* People steeped in the laziness of mental or moral indifference sometimes pride themselves on their tolerance. They are not tolerant. Indifference is never a virtue. The indifferent exercise no self-restraint. They don't have to cultivate humility when faced with a clash of values. They don't have to balance the demands of their integrity against respect for the convictions of others. There is no moral struggle. Ogden Nash put it so well:

> Sometimes with secret pride I sigh
> To think how tolerant am I;
> Then wonder which is really mine:
> Tolerance or a rubber spine?

Baroness Wootton observed similarly: 'People are tolerant only about things they don't really care about.' But true tolerance implies convictions and deeply-held values.

The history of tolerance has sometimes been dismissed as a terrible story of religious people tearing one another apart in the service and love of God. I am often asked how do I justify that? The simple answer is, of course, that I do not and have no wish to try. The story may be told, but I would never want to justify those who believe it right to persecute and kill others whose convictions are just as honourably held. But before we take the high moral ground let us remember that in this century alone more people have been persecuted and killed for their beliefs and differences than perhaps in all other centuries put together. And most of these deaths have not come from religious conflicts. Atheistic ideologies have proved astonishingly capable of sending millions to their deaths. We moderns have very little to boast about.

In the history of religious toleration, I believe there are three phases. These I describe as the emergence of Individualism, the attempt at Establishment and the development of Co-existence.

First, the emergence of individualism. Lambeth Palace, my London home and office, echoes with reminders of intolerance. I am surrounded by portraits which recall how many brave people have been willing to lay down their lives for what they believed to be God's truth. Archbishop Cranmer, who died at the stake in the time of Queen Mary; Archbishop William Laud whose cause was too tightly tied to Charles I, and who was taken from his prayers to the Tower of London and his eventual execution. Then there is Cardinal Pole, the last Roman Catholic Archbishop who died but a few days after Mary Tudor, perhaps just missing a martyr's crown. Then in the Lollards Tower at Lambeth Palace there is one of the saddest rooms in London. Eight iron chains testify to people once held in the Lollards prison because they followed the teachings of John Wycliff: their fourteenth-century names are carved into the woodwork. Yet the martyrs and the persecutors – and Lambeth's art and architecture reminds us how often the sides change – would not have used the word 'intolerance'. All were convinced that God's truth could be found, that they had found it and that it was so important for the life of the nation that it should be held, embraced and believed, just as *they* held, embraced and believed it. There were no half measures, no time for qualifications. Passion led them forwards and they were willing to bear the pain. Such was the indivisibility of State and religion that the persecution of the heretic was considered a necessary and inevitable consequence of such religious individualism. If individuals could believe what they liked, and proclaim what they believed, society would collapse. Religious freedom and anarchy were identified. Heresy had to be eliminated from the State just as much as from the Church. The soul of the heretic could be saved only by persuasion, torture to correct beliefs, perhaps death. The medieval mind sometimes even understood the burning of heretics to be the loving thing to do. Purified by a few moments of earthly fire, the heretic might thus avoid a greater conflagration! It does not seem a convincing argument to the modern mind.

Although it is sometimes said and believed that it was a gradual religious indifference which led to genuine toleration, the seeds were already present in the very conflict. The Reformation was a witness to the emergence of the *individual*. Personal response to the love of God was decisive. Justification depended on faith, not the faith of the Church as a whole, but the faith of each of its members. As John McManners notes: 'Religion was on its way to becoming a matter of intense personal decision; if there was a single message and driving force behind Reformation and Counter-Reformation, it was this. Secularization was the inevitable counterpart, the opposite side of the coin, the reaction of human nature to a demand almost too intense to bear.'[1]

The aftermath of the Reformation with its unhappy history of religious wars led not to religious liberty but to an uneasy peace. The attempt at *establishment* meant the creation of separate religious states each with its distinctive religious ethos as the bond of the tribe. The principle was *'cujus regio ejus religio'*, to each region its own religion. This of course was tolerance for governments rather than the individual who still had to conform to the dominant faith where she or he lived. The most liberal thing you can do in such circumstances is to make your single church as wide and as comprehensive as possible. But even in England where the established church did make such an attempt – and still claims to be comprehensive – unreconciled parties were left on the wings unable in all conscience to accept the *modus vivendi*. Such a situation could not last very long because individual conscience could no longer be suppressed once the Reformation had liberated it. Seventeenth-century England shows the policy collapsing through the pressure brought to bear by two religious systems. Episcopalian and Presbyterian, each claiming to be the right faith for English society. They were fighting to decide the character of the English nation in its capacity as an organized religious society.[2] Contrary to the way Oliver Cromwell has been depicted, it was he who established a tolerance that was in fact wider than he dared openly to avow. He adopted a tolerant attitude to Jews who were already living in the country and gave private assurances to them that the recusancy laws would not be put into operation against them, even though he judged the time was not ripe to remove such laws. This *genuine* toleration (as distinct from eighteenth-century indifferentism to which I shall refer later) was endorsed powerfully at the end of the century by Locke. In his Letter on Toleration (1689) he wrote, 'Since you are pleased to enquire what are my thoughts about the mutual Toleration of Christians in their different Professions of Religion, I must needs answer you freely, that I esteem that toleration to be the chief Characteristical Mark of the True Church.'

Thus we see heralded the development of co-existence. The territorial idea of religion simply gave way under the force of those whose commitment and pain prevented them accepting an enforced religion. Precisely because religion was so supremely important it came to be held that one man could not impose it upon another and even a whole society could not impose it upon an individual. So William Penn, one of the great founding fathers in the New World wrote in 1685:

> All forms of persons are for liberty of conscience for themselves, even those that are most imposing upon others. As a variety of flowers may grow on the same bank, so may Protestants and Papists live in England. Union in affection is not inconsistent with disagreement of opinion. We cannot come together in the same church but may live in the same land and as we are under the same gracious King, he may protect both and suffer no party to persecute one another.

It was much weariness with controversy about tolerance and real acts of intolerance that led persecuted groups to seek asylum in the New World to create their own societies in which people might be free to worship and live as they please. Thus from passionate commitment to worship God freely there arose in possibly the most religious society in the world, the separation of State and religion.

But we must not fall into the trap of thinking that toleration was achieved with the emigration of the Pilgrim Fathers. The eighteenth and nineteenth centuries were times of *co-existence*, not genuine tolerance. Even up to very recent times in western Christianity we have examples of attitudes where little has changed. It is worth tracing the more recent history of this in the Roman Catholic Church, for instance, to see how lately 'toleration' has been understood as a necessity of, not a threat to, faith. We may begin with Monsignor Ronald Knox, the famous Roman Catholic intellectual who in his *The Belief of Catholics* trenchantly argued that the very truth of the Catholic faith meant that in a country with a strong Catholic majority the Church must insist on Catholic education being universal and would proscribe those who come with deviant teachings. He stated: 'A body of Catholic patriots entrusted with the government of a Catholic State, will not shrink even from repressive measures in order to perpetuate the secure domination of Catholic principles among their fellow-countrymen.' Against the view that this is intolerant, Knox continued in swashbuckling fashion:

> When we demand liberty in the modern state we are appealing to its own principles not to ours. The theory of the modern state is that all religions should be tolerated, as long as they do not disturb the peace or otherwise infringe the secular laws of the country; we only claim to share that right amongst the rest.[3]

We must allow for the fact that Knox was well known for his over-statements but even so the claim reveals that 'genuine toleration' was far from his mind.

However, the double standard inherent in Knox's response was a classical Roman Catholic argument prior to the Second Vatican Council, stemming from the views of Bishop Felix Dupanloup of Orléans and distinguishing between 'thesis' and 'hypothesis'. The 'thesis' was that when Catholicism was in power, error should be repressed. Only when Catholicism was not dominant should error be tolerated as a lesser evil – that was the 'hypothesis'. Before we condemn and criticize this argument as peculiarly Roman Catholic, we have to recognize that such a view has *never* been exclusively Catholic or even religious. Many ideological movements as well as religious groups have claimed a freedom when in a minority which they have not been prepared to concede to others when in power. (Milton, faced with the behaviour of the very Presbyterians he had helped to put in power in England, wrote bitterly: 'New presbyter is but old priest writ large.')

But this view was already changing before the Second Vatican Council pronounced firmly against it which, let no one doubt, it *firmly* did. It was the great Jesuit thinker John Courtney Murray who argued that religious freedom, far from being a necessary evil, is a personal and political *good*. The Second Vatican Council's landmark document *Dignitatis Humanae* (Declaration of Religious Freedom) codified Murray's philosophical ideals and explicitly acknowledged the fact of the religiously plural society.[4]

This necessarily brief survey suggests that, at best, genuine tolerance is only a recent reality. The thesis of this paper is that it is still not securely founded, and we have a long way to go before it can be considered a genuine fact in modern society and in personal life. To get to the heart of the matter, therefore, we must consider the dynamics of tolerance.

Tolerance involves commitment not indifferentism

I return to a thought that was expressed earlier. It is simplistic to think that tolerance is achieved merely by a shoulder-shrugging indifference to people who believe and act differently. 'As long as they do not trouble me, I'll tolerate them.' That attitude is not tolerance: it is apathy. Genuine religious toleration is achieved when people hold their religion as so important, so absolute that to part from it is to die, and at the same time realize from their absolute centre of being that *another* person's values and beliefs are just as important and as real. That is the moment of genuine tolerance, because there is a *cost involved* in the act of tolerating another person's way of living and believing. The pain involved is not only in preserving inviolate one's own convictions but enduring the reality of the other person's, and, while deeply disagreeing, respecting them – with a consequent sharing of *their* pain as well as their own. In my Enthronement sermon the word I used was 'integrity' – the act of recognizing that a strong and robust faith does not necessary flow into tolerance and hostility but can mean respecting another whose commitment is just as deep but is different.

Let me quote Elizabeth Templeton, that fine Presbyterian theologian, on the issue that currently most seems to engender intolerance in the Church of England – the ordination of women.

> I have been constantly struck [she said at the Lambeth Conference of 1988] by the best generosity of your Anglican recurrent insistence that across parties, camps, styles and dogmas, you have need of one another... I am sad you feel you are under some pressure to renounce this remarkable openness of being... My hope is that you can see the issue of women's ordination as a gift... not just because it opens up deep and wide theological questions, but because it also touches the levels of pain and passion which test what it means that we love our enemies. The world is used to unity of all sorts, to solidarity in campaigns... communities of party, creed, interest. But it is *not* used to such possibilities as this: that, for example, those who find the exclusion of women from the priesthood an intolerable apartheid, and who find their inclusion a violation of God's will *should enter one another's suffering*. Somewhere in there authority lies.

'Somewhere in there authority lies': in there, where we tolerate *pain* – each other's and our *own*. That is the dynamic and new understanding of toleration I seek to share with you, because it is what as a society as well as as a church we need to learn. It is in that dynamic and suffering *tolerating* that we gain in 'authority' as a nation – not a *loss* of authority, but a gain.

Tolerance involves entering into the 'strangeness' of others and feeling their pain

Let us put this on a less lofty level, applying it to daily life. Minorities always feel persecuted, alone, outnumbered and misunderstood. Majorities usually regard minorities as prickly and oversensitive, introverted and always on about their rights. Both views are accurate to a degree and both are due to the element of 'strangeness' which forms a barrier to understanding and friendship, creates fear and ultimately hostility. We can of course put up with 'strangeness' when we are tourists and visiting a foreign country – that, after all, is one of the reasons we go. My official visit to Papua New Guinea gave me a fresh nuance on 'strangeness' when I noticed that the very savage-looking people with their painted faces and naked bodies were taking photos of me in my cope and mitre with expensive Japanese cameras! The boot was on the other foot. My wife, similarly, reported that when we visited a remote part of the Highlands of Papua New Guinea many of the older women crowded around her to touch her skin, her clothing, her hair because she was strange to them. Strangeness moves both ways.

But 'strangeness', of course, can lead to 'alienation', something very dangerous, especially if the stranger becomes our neighbour bringing different smells, clothes, speech and behaviour into close proximity. That alienation may be deepened when the stranger takes over shops and jobs and becomes a competitor. The scene is then set for conflict. The strange minority may become the focus of pent-up frustrations and bitternesses which have little to do with them.

Differences can be overcome only when they are recognized as potential enrichments to our society and lives, even when there is a high price to pay. It may start with a genuine liking for Indian cooking. That may lead to an inquiry about why people dress as they do; about what goes on in a Hindu temple; about the lifestyle of these people whose strangeness is both fascinating and disturbing. People who live in a monochrome culture need to be made aware of the exciting possibilities, as well as the disturbances to their settled lifestyle, of a multi-cultural society. And that can only come about as we discover that 'strangeness' does not necessarily mean bad but a different expression of good.

Tolerance involves understanding and education

Charles Raven records an episode during the Second World War which started out well and nearly became a tragedy. In the autumn of 1940 a Fenland village near Ely had arranged to put up a number of children from Bethnal Green. The families sent to them happened to come from a Jewish club. The economics and diet of the villagers centred, as it used to in the older rural areas, upon the household pig. In welcoming their honoured guests the treasured rashers were generously offered in complete ignorance of Jewish food rules. To the older children and to the supervisor who escorted them such an offering seemed a calculated insult. They were outraged. All sorts of authorities became involved. Both sides were deeply offended. What should have been a memorable yet happy day ended in near riot. The Jewish group, so oppressed by the terrible events happening to their people elsewhere in Europe saw this as yet another element of persecution. The villagers were bruised that their great act of charity was flung in their face by what seemed to be a trivial matter of eating. It is an example of how ignorance and misunderstanding can produce situations which poison human relationships.

Ignorance exacerbates the problem of strangeness. We might reflect on the misunderstanding of the passionate reaction of the Muslim community to Salman Rushdie's *Satanic Verses*. Many non-Muslims who read the book could not understand what lay behind such passion because *our* tendency is to view a novel as a 'fictitious exploration of reality'. So 'fictionalized blasphemy' is not, and in the opinion of many secular people, cannot be, 'blasphemy' at all. To that we have to add that to many people whose values are wholly secular there can be no such thing as 'blasphemy' since you cannot insult a God who does not exist.

But the devout Muslim does not see it this way. The book contained an outrageous slur on the Prophet and so was damaging to the reputation of the faith. I well understand the devout Muslim's reaction, wounded by what they hold most dear and would themselves die for. Because we are strangers to Islam, and many of us to any concept of holiness at all, *we* do not *feel* the offence, the pain – and there we are, back with the image of pain, with *our* reaction, one of indifference. But Christians, like Muslims, living in an increasingly secular world, are likely themselves to encounter this pain more and more. The film *The Last Temptation of Christ*, for instance, contains scenes that would shock and outrage many Christians. I am glad that the BBC, recognizing this, is not now going to show it. But that its showing could be contemplated, and that there could be real inability to understand or *tolerate* the distress of Christians, ought to help us better to enter the distress of the Muslim community.

Only sensitive understanding of the value structures of others on everyone's part will lead us into the tolerant society we seek for ourselves and our children. The same kindness and forbearance we want for our own integrity and life-style, we should offer to others. It is our ignorance and prejudice which so often gets in the way: and our unwillingness to bear the pain of the cost.

Tolerance involves freedom for religion and from religion

Linked with tolerance is freedom. To tolerate another means to make him free to follow his conscience and exercise his freedom in whatever way suits him within the boundaries of the law. It follows that when we talk of the 'free world' we must make sure we know what we mean, to be warned of dangers to our freedom, and to note ways in which our freedom may be deepened. But freedom is a trans-cultural, universal idea. We want all people to enjoy it. We are glad that the forms of mental, moral and philosophical servitudes which existed behind the 'Iron Curtain' are no more. But freedom is surely much more than simply the individual's right to think and be. Freedom and toleration combined offer us several challenges.

First, that the free person cannot tolerate injustices and evils in the world. For example, we ought not to be complacent about our nation's 'freedom' when so many people are homeless. Although efforts are being made to address the causes which create homelessness, for those reduced to such circumstances 'freedom' is curtailed. Or to give another example, how can we talk easily about freedom when, even more terribly, so many people in our world are starving and are the victims of war, natural disasters and economic systems not of their making? This involves countries like ours in the spreading of freedom, including *economic* freedom. *Freedom is never defended by building walls around a state but it is defended by being exported to those who lack it.* It is exported when richer countries share the fruits of freedom with countries where there is great poverty and hunger. For Russia and the Eastern Bloc political freedom will be secure only if their economies improve and grow secure. The West has a duty to help them at this moment; lest their desperation produces another tyranny if they sense we abandon them.

Second, in the religious domain, freedom is the fruit of toleration. John Courtney Murray isolated three aspects of human dignity and freedom and he distinguished between the 'common good' and 'public order'. The 'common good' includes all the social, spiritual and moral goods which people need to live and which together we must strive to achieve. Public order, on the other hand, includes three goods which the State must supply: public peace, public morality and public *justice*. And, comments Murray, the first thing due to people in *justice* is their freedom, the proper enjoyment of their personal and social rights. The truly tolerant religious person therefore is led to embrace not grudgingly but gladly the view that those who differ from him or her have every right to worship as they choose. This in turn poses a challenge to which we shall turn later: Does this not commit us to a recognition of a universality of faiths?

The Distinctive Contribution of Christianity

We turn now to consider what is the nature of Christianity's contribution to the search for a genuinely tolerant society. We have seen that although it was itself a persecuted minority for the first three hundred years or so, the freedom it sought for itself it has not always desired to give to others. Its own search for tolerance has dark shadows and even today some fundamentalist groups repel thoughtful people by their language of intolerance.

The distinctive contribution of Christianity to the discovery of a dynamic tolerance of the kind I envisaged as a hope for our age, arises from the very nature of God himself as Christians understand him. The words 'tolerating' and 'tolerant', when used of the nature of God, are more frequently translated in modern versions of the Bible as 'forbearing', 'long suffering', 'patient', 'enduring'. It is that aspect of God which, complementing the absoluteness of his power, exercises gentleness and long suffering even with those who abuse him or confront him. It is what the writer of Peter describes as 'forbearing, not wishing that any should perish'; or the writer of Numbers or Exodus describes as 'long suffering' – the 'Lord God Incarnate, we find an expression of it in Christ's reported words in Mark 9.19 when the crowd were being more than usually unperceiving; 'unbelieving generation', he says, 'How long shall I stay with you? *How long shall I put up with you?'* (i.e. 'tolerate' you). As one very perceptive commentator remarked, *his being with men involved him in 'putting up with them'*. It is the complement of the heavenly majesty that Christians claim as rightly Christ's.

This glimpse of the Christian understanding of the nature of God and its implications for the distinctive contribution that mainstream churches *could* make today to the life of our world, leads me to identify three main qualities we ought to look for, which should inform the dynamic of toleration of which I speak.

The first lies in value of *magnanimity*. Paul in Philippians 4.5 writes: 'Let your magnanimity [*epieikeia*] be known to all people.' The word expresses breadth; the quality of taking in as much as possible. Aristotle describes the meaning of '*epieikeia*': 'it is *epieikeia* to pardon human feelings and look to the law-giver not to the law, to the spirit not to the letter, to the intention not to the action, to the whole and not to the part... to remember good rather than evil' (Rhetoric, 1.13). Christians should be able to find the pattern of magnanimity in the Lord they follow because in his pattern of teaching and living the way of tolerance is observable in his delight in people, in his protection of the defenceless and in his refusal to take up arms against those who differed from him.

The second is the nature of love or '*charity*'. Mainstream Christianity emphasizes the personal because of the Christocentric nature of its mission. Central to Christianity is the conviction that God has taken human existence into his life because the divine took human form and suffered for us. William Temple's quip that 'Christianity is the most materialistic of all religions' has its roots in that theology. God's love for all people finds its origin here and it may possibly be the case that Paul's glorious paean of praise to 'Charity' in 1 Cor. 13 is derived from a meditation on the person of Christ himself: 'Charity suffers long and is kind; charity envies not; charity vaunts not itself, does not behave itself unseemly, is not easily provoked, thinks no evil, rejoices not in iniquity but rejoices in the truth; charity bears all things, believes all things, hopes all things, endures all things.' Paul's beautiful words express a deep conviction about the worth of all people – that we are valued by God because we are loved by him. *The principle of charity will stop any group which has a high doctrine of exclusivity from becoming narrow-minded and intolerant.*

The third idea is the nature of *community* as '*koinonia*'. For genuine Christianity belonging to the body of Christ takes the form of personal choice as well as God's call. The individual is not coerced but joins gladly. Yet by belonging we take upon ourselves obligations to share the Christian faith with others and to live out its moral obligations in society. I concede readily that there have been repressive Christian communities in the past and there are possibly some around even today. *But the notion of a tolerant body of people who join together in mutual bonds of affection and service can be and is an inspiring model of community today.* Such a body will recognize the rights of others and will be eager to learn, share in dialogue and debate and be willing to embrace new insights and new learning. And such a body will be open to the society in which it is earthed and so resistant to narrow-mindedness.

However, such a vision of Christianity faces two major challenges from a multi-cultural situation. The first is in relation to that 'exclusivity' which seems to deny the value of other faith communities. Recently, the press has carried stories of an Open Letter to the leadership of the Church of England. It comes from a group who fear that the Christian message is being vitiated by interfaith worship. They fear an *in*clusivity which rejects the uniqueness of Christ. They are worried that evangelism might be abandoned. Can one believe with integrity that Jesus Christ is the Way, the Truth and the Life and *still* believe that other faiths are not simply of value, but that they matter to God, or are in some way vehicles of salvation? There are many different levels at which we have to respond to that question and we cannot explore them all here. What we have to recognize is that because God is the kind of God he is, our integrity as believers in Him *compels* us to behave in such a way that *tolerance*, and not *intolerance* is our instinctive reaction: and that honest engagement with each other as valued by God becomes the context in which our differences are *faced: strenuously* faced.

But it would be exceedingly disingenuous of all parties to throw up hands of horror at the thought of preaching an exclusive creed. Islam and Christianity have from the very beginning been quite open and explicit about the nature of their faith. Both claim to be universal faiths and both are missionary. What has changed is that no longer are these separated for the British by thousands of miles, but we are now in one another's backyards – and we rightly feel the pain which is the other side of tolerance. (As converts in the past, in other lands, have always felt the pain.) Both religions, and other faiths too, must to be true to that justice which is of the nature of the God both faiths celebrate, and concede to each other the toleration our nation needs.

A second challenge relates to *missionary tactics*. A fresh humility is required by which the integrity of other faiths is recognized and their genuine contribution to the well-being of human kind honoured. One can, I believe, be a Christian wholly convinced of the uniqueness of Christ and his abiding relevance to humankind, and still affirm that other faiths possess value, significance and integrity. The Bossey Consultation of 1956 stated that 'all mission has the nature of dialogue'. Dialogue can only take place between those who value each other. Christians engaged in dialogue may thus approach their own faith in a new way. It opens up new and exciting opportunities – to engage with the living faith of another and to have one's own faith enlarged and deepened by it. And that happens properly at the same time as we are sharing how our life is charged and sustained by our own faith in the God and Father of our Lord Jesus Christ.

But a pressing issue for a missionary faith such as Christianity remains. *Evangelism is still a binding obligation* on the Christian believer. How does that relate to a pluralism of many faiths in which mutual respect and tolerance is prized? How does one avoid the pitfall of proselytizing on the one hand and the negation of the task on the other? The answer must lie in acknowledging that although the task remains the same, the method of sharing faith will be different in our new context. As neighbours now, the cultural implications require the greatest sensitivity to those who are our fellow citizens: that dynamic tolerance which enters into the 'faith sufferings' of those whose faith is not ours, and yet retains integrity, true to its own convictions.

The implications of what I have said are of consequence for us all. I have painted a picture of an emerging world order in which religions are not a declining factor, but growing no longer in total separation from each other but side by side. We have to recognize the fear that our 'strangeness' can cause each other. Just a few weeks ago when I was answering questions on BBC World Service a listener asked me my reaction to the coming catastrophe of the clash between Christianity and Islam. He went on to focus attention on the intolerance of fundamentalists in both faiths and suggested their existence was a threat to humankind. Although I questioned his gloomy foreboding I went on to agree that the task of mutual understanding and accepting is urgent. 'Fanaticism' may be as Shabbir Akhtar puts it *'other people's* passions' (and by implication our own passion is 'faith'). But if adherence to religious principle threatens whole communities by the intensity of commitment, civilized society cannot and must not tolerate such an invasion of public order. Not, finally, because of liberal humanism, but because the profoundest toleration is rooted in the nature of God. Shabbir Akhtar's excellent book *A Faith for All Seasons* shows that different though Judaism, Christianity and Islam may be, they do possess common values and beliefs. That should be the starting point of our common task to share our humanity together.

There are implications here for our secular world which, bewildered by the profusion of religious belief, is tempted to throw up its hands in horror, cry 'A plague on both your houses', and get on with its task of living, without benefit of any religious faith at all. But the pluriformity of life which the secular State has to recognize forces it not only to observe the fact of minorities and to cater for them in its laws and in its life but to respect and value them. All religions are not the same, as law-makers and the media have found out to their cost and their value-systems should not, and, thankfully, cannot, be easily dismissed.

But ultimately the chief implication challenges all religious leaders who, passionate for the truth, are called not simply to an affable co-existence – a *denial* of true toleration – but an active partnership and deeper co-operation which means entering into and sharing each other's 'pains'. Jonathan Sacks in *The Persistence of Faith* says strikingly: 'That is counter-fundamentalism, the belief that God has given us many universes of faith but only one world in which to live together.' And in this overcrowded and rapidly exhausting little planet the need for co-operation and sharing is an urgent and necessary task. Resurgent faiths can no longer afford to exhaust their total strength simply on enlarging their frontiers but must be challenged to expend the same energy on the social face of faith – the enormous and growing numbers of the poor and starving and the ecological desert we are creating through misuse and exploitation. The Heavenly Father Christ describes is not one who, if asked for bread, would merely give a stone – even a Tablet of Stone.

My dominant image in this paper has been that of pain; pain of believers who learn in real situations that 'to tolerate' is not just the 'right thing to do' but the moral and just way to be. The genuinely tolerant are not those indifferent to others who believe different things. They are the ones who, themselves of passionate beliefs, endure the pain of that and enter into the pain others feel in their conflicting passionate beliefs. Only out of such mutuality of toleration will the dynamic come that gives freedom and space to all. It is my passionate conviction that when we are prepared to die for another's right to belief, in just the way we might be prepared to die for the right to our own, we might then have begun to explore the toleration of God. For it is his tolerating us which will make us all ultimately free as citizens of this world and of the world to come.

2 CHRISTIANITY AND WORLD RELIGIONS
Robert Runcie

Let me say first what a pleasure and privilege it is for me to give the Sir Francis Younghusband Memorial Lecture during this fiftieth anniversary year of the World Congress of Faiths. I am grateful for the opportunity this gives me to share with you some of my own reflections on the encounter of Christianity with other religions, and to raise a number of questions which spring from what is a relatively new dimension for Christian experience, thought and identity.

Our present age is characterized by the resurgence and renewal of religions in many parts of the globe, as well as by attempts to translate their original message into the terms of a world transformed by science and technology. Behind this lies a widespread pessimism about the future of humankind, an unsatisfied longing for alternative paths to salvation, and a search for some 'golden core' of religion independent of any specific tradition.

Increased travel and improved communication have provided many more opportunities for meeting people of other faiths and cultures. In turn, interreligious encounter and dialogue have generated hope for greater global unity and for wider global ecumenism. Historically speaking, this is a very recent development. Religious diversity has often been disruptive of community, and it remains the root cause of tensions and deep divisions between different human groups. It is premature to presume that the age of holy wars is long past. The twentieth century has seen much bloodshed where religious differences have been a fundamental factor. But today a number of interfaith movements exist with the explicit purpose of fostering a better understanding of religious differences and similarities. Through nurturing a spirit of friendship and reconciliation, true dialogue can help us to overcome religious divisiveness and create new conditions for greater fellowship and deeper communion. It can help us to recognize that other faiths than our own are genuine mansions of the Spirit with many rooms to be discovered, rather than solitary fortresses to be attacked.

All of us have a part to play in this development, but some individuals have been outstanding in carrying the torch. Such a personality was Sir Francis Younghusband (1863–1942). In his book *A Venture of Faith* (1937), he movingly describes how he first had the idea of holding a World Congress of Faiths. He came from a Christian background and, in his own words, inherited a religious disposition and was encouraged in religious practice in his youth. But his experience of scientific thought, of government service and politics, of wide travelling and reading, made him see religion in a new perspective. Through numerous expeditions in India, China and Tibet, he encountered many expressions of Hinduism, Buddhism and Islam and developed a deep interest in eastern religions and philosophies. Profound personal experiences and the inspiration of earlier examples made him perceive the need to replace the spirit of rivalry among members of different faiths with a spirit of fellowship and a search for greater unity. He also developed a global vision of the role of religions in the development of society, and saw the need for a shared spirituality to give direction to mankind. Sir Francis Younghusband has been described as a mystic who pondered the mysteries of life, and answered the call of the spirit while remaining a devout Christian throughout his life.

'World fellowship through religion' – that was the keynote of the first Congress held in London in 1936. Younghusband expressed the hope that 'efforts will be made to take a world-view, to develop a world-consciousness, and to create a sense of world-fellowship'. He was not a dreamer but a practical man who knew well enough the obstacles which stand in the way of human harmony. The human spirit in each of us is as contentious as it is creative.

Yet despite opposition and criticism, the religious and cultural diversity represented at the Congress was considerable. It also included representatives of different philosophical, scientific and humanist world-views. Out of the experience of so many different people meeting together, sharing their thoughts, insights and even worship, there came a sense of exaltation and vision of the enriching possibilities of closer contact between peoples of different faiths. There was a clear rejection of any idea that the Congress intended to evolve some overall synthesis or new kind of eclectic religion. Instead, there was the recognition that, in Sir Francis's words:

> Religion, taken as a whole, benefited much from the variety in its different forms. All the centuries that the spirit of God had been working in Christians, He must also have been working in Hindus, Budd-hists, Muslims and others... And recognizing this all-important fact, members of the Congress showed no disposition to try to form any new religion: rather were they inclined to draw inspiration from others for the development of their own.

In his personal conclusions Younghusband affirmed that 'we shall have to make our lives conform to the greater conception of the world which is now emerging'. He also admitted that his continuing loyalty to Christianity was sometimes strained to breaking point by the air of superiority and indifference so often adopted by Christians to those of other faiths. But the main impression left by the Congress was

> that it deepened each man in his own faith... the Hindu was made all the better a Hindu, the Muslim all the better a Muslim, and the Christian all the better a Christian. Each was driven down to his foundations – down to where he had perhaps never reached before. Each sought the permanent and abiding amid the great diversity of gifts.

A Visit to India

The experience of that first conference of the World Congress of Faiths shows what many more of us have experienced since; namely that interreligious encounter and dialogue do not occur at an abstract, but at a personal level. They are at their liveliest when people meet with each other to share the sustaining insights and transforming treasures of their faith and to recognize an affinity of the human heart in the fellowship of the spirit. Such encounter nourishes new life and vision, and from it arises the need for fresh reflection on the unprecedented religious, cultural and ethic pluralism which most human groups experience today.

Speaking personally, my recent visit to India proved just such an experience, and I returned to this country with a fresh awareness of the need for reflection on the deep questions which arise for any Christian who takes the religions of India seriously. I went with a genuine but somewhat notional commitment to the need for dialogue between the great faiths. I returned with a deep sense of urgency of our need to listen, revere and reflect.

India can be a stunning experience – not in any Hollywood sense – but rather as an experience which leaves one dazed and uncertain of one's bearing. Before, there were the certainties of an encapsulated western Christianity. After, there are new ways of thinking about God, Christ and the world. A number of vivid and haunting images remain and continue to pose disturbing questions.

There was a conversation with a Parsee in Bombay. To meet a living Zoroastrian is to be reminded that even the most ancient faiths are still alive. Here was someone for whom the utter *holiness* of God was indeed as fire. God's holiness is such that only the faithful may worship in the Temple of Fire. And I wondered whether contemporary Christianity had not something to rediscover about the awesome 'otherness' of a God we have at times neutered and domesticated.

Then there were the marvellous early Hindu sculptures at Mahabalipuram, near Madras, where gods and goddesses take hundreds of different forms and images. The sheer diversity of the divine was disconcerting. God seemed somehow greater than western monism. In the same place there was a moving carving of Vishnu resting on the waters of creation. Serenity and creativity do not normally go together in western thought. Again we have lost something which other faiths may restore to us. Though I did not have the opportunity of seeing a Buddhist shrine, the serenity of that early Hindu carving gave some intimation of the Buddhist gift of tranquillity and recollection.

In the north were the great Islamic monuments of the Moghul Empire. They speak again of the transcendence of God which is so prominent a feature of Islam. Symmetry and mathematical perfection in the architecture of a mosque or palace are a reminder to the Christian of the source and goal of the human search for the perfect beyond this mutable world, for the changeless behind the transitory state of human life.

But I not only saw great temples and mosques. There were also the little street corner shrines of the cities with their garish painted idols and loud canned music. There was the simple rural mosque with no walls and with two stumps for minarets. In the countryside I saw the painted rocks and hill shrines which told of the piety of the animist – India's earliest aboriginal faith, continuing still alongside both the great religions and godless secularism of modern India. All this suggests the intimacy and holiness of faiths incarnated in the everyday life and culture of ordinary people.

Encounter with Other Religions

Encounter is the proper word for such experience. And it calls for rigorous reflection on matters Christians often take for granted: the uniqueness of God's revelation in Christ, or the universal significance of his incarnation and redemption. I do not question these basic Christian affirmations, but an experience of other faiths insists that we reflect upon them more deeply.

Over the last few decades many have written of the encounter of Christianity with other religions. They have done so largely in a spirit of openness, of inquiry and search for greater truth and understanding. But they are not the first to adopt this more enlightened approach. That search is a long-standing one. In the fifteenth century, Nicolas of Cusa, a Roman cardinal, set out in his *De Pace Fidei* the formal proposition that behind all the differences of religious practice there is one universal religion on which Jews, Christians and Muslims can agree. It turned out, however, that this one true religion involves the doctrines of the Trinity, the Incarnation and the Mass. But the *idea* of the harmony of all religions beyond the diversity of practice is a prophetic vision which we find again and again in Christian thought.

F.D. Maurice

An impressive example of an early Anglican involvement with these concerns is to be found in the writings of Frederick Denison Maurice (1805–1872), and particularly in his Boyle Lectures of 1845 on *The Religions of the World and Their Relations to Christianity*. Maurice was a seminal nineteenth-century theologian who is perhaps as difficult to read as he is to classify. He is, I suppose, best remembered for his central work *The Kingdom of Christ*, and for his part in the foundation, with Ludlow and Kingsley, of the Christian Socialist Movement. By contrast, his lectures on *The Religions of the World* are much neglected and today overlooked, although they have been described as Maurice's 'most popular work during his lifetime'.

While *The Kingdom of Christ* augured ideas which proved important for the ecumenical movement among Christians, Maurice's thoughts on world religions in relation to Christianity foreshadowed some current and prevalent ideas in global ecumenism and interreligious dialogue. He delivered his lectures in two series: the first described some major religions of the world, and the second dealt with the relation of Christianity to them. The examples used were drawn from Judaism, Islam, Hinduism and Buddhism. While Maurice may have ventured beyond his depth in dealing with such a wide range of subjects, and while he did not always make the best use of the historical information available to him, he none the less spoke and wrote with considerable sympathy, understanding and insight about people of other faiths. He produced a pioneer work which in its own way helped Christians to develop a new attitude to world religions.

Maurice considered faith an essential constituent of being human, and recognized that all religions bear witness to man as a spiritual being. He insisted that some truth, but not necessarily the same truth, exists in all religions, and whatever this may be, it must stem ultimately from the Source of all truth. While he approached other religions from the perspective of Christianity, and interpreted them by taking his own religion as the norm in a way more characteristic of the nineteenth century than our own, Maurice was also prepared to admit that Christianity might need the corrective contained in the insights of other faiths.

Maurice's insights went further than most other Christian writers of his period. He not only affirmed the truth of his own religion, but insisted on the possibility of learning from the truths present in others. Maurice believed in a divinely implanted religious aspiration in all human beings, at all times and in all places, even though he had yet to develop a realistic appreciation of the sheer pluralism of world religions. However, he readily recognized the pluralism to be found within Christianity itself, and perceived the need for a closer integration of all human kind through the forces of both religion and science. He saw the unity of all human beings grounded and crowned in the ultimate unity of God.

The Religious Meaning of Pluralism

These thoughts can still be relevant and inspiring, in spite of the fact that our contemporary religious pluralism has become far more complex and implies many new challenges. Several twentieth-century thinkers with a sensitive ear for the needs of our times have indicated that we have reached a new historical moment when a global consciousness is emerging, with a new awareness of the religious diversity and spiritual heritage of mankind. Instead of simply acknowledging such diversity as mere plurality, we need today to reflect critically and theologically on the religious *meaning* of pluralism. Such reflection is an urgent task for all faith communities.

I cannot speak here about the impact of interreligious dialogue on other religions, but must restrict my remarks to reflections made from a Christian perspective. Certainly, given the experience and witness of Christian faith, encounter with other faiths can deepen and enrich us, and make us reflect anew on matters central to our own faith. It should not be forgotten that Christianity itself was formed in dialogue with Judaism. Jesus of Nazareth was himself a Jew, and always remained a Jew, regularly joining in the worship of the synagogue, regardless of how fiercely he may have criticized the establishment figures of the Judaism of his time. The Christian church too first gained self-consciousness through wrestling with the pressing issue of its relation to Judaism.

Freeing ourselves from isolation

First, interfaith encounter and dialogue helps us to avoid making crude choices between what is 'true' and what is 'false' in different religions. For whatever we say about religious experience it is clear that it is no respecter of credal differences. We have already begun, painfully, to emancipate ourselves from the isolation which limits religion to the insights and errors of one stream of tradition. I am reminded of a story told by Ninian Smart of the lady missionary who was driving him to a hospital not far from Benares. They passed a shrine, and she remarked: 'I'm always very sad to see the piety with which those Hindus worship at that shrine.' He asked why. 'Well,' she said with a sort of simple finality, 'there's no one there to hear them.' That 'simple finality' has no place today. Was it Max Muller who urged that in respect of religion 'He who knows one, knows none'?

Deepening our spirituality

Secondly at a deeper level, interfaith dialogue has important implications for the experience and practice of *spirituality*: for the life of faith, both in the individual human heart and in our respective communities. We must learn to recognize the work of the spirit at the centre of each of our faiths. 'Live Aid' and 'Sports Aid' are powerful signs that we are learning that the life and destiny of all human beings are closely interdependent, at the material and economic level, but we must also learn that we are globally interdependent in spiritual matters too.

Such an encounter of people from different faiths is a global event of great historical importance. We, as people of faith, owe it to the world to respond to the challenge of contemporary religious pluralism, not by weakening the intensity of our religious commitment, but through entering into dialogue at the deepest level by strengthening the depth of our own faith, by renewing the sincerity of our own worship, and by increasing the fervour of our own spirituality.

If we trust the life-giving power of the spirit within and among us, we can meet each other in openness and trust; we can learn to explore together the moments of revelation and the spiritual treasures which our respective faiths have handed down to us – a spark of divine life and a vision of holiness whereby the lives of countless people in past and present are nourished, sustained, transformed and sanctified.

Again, the Indian religious heritage contains a great variety of spiritual disciplines and knows many saints and sages who have lived and taught the path of meditation and inwardness. Indian spirituality invites Christians perhaps above all to the practice of contemplation, to a life of inner and outer simplicity. Many western Christians have gone to India to learn precisely this, to be schooled in the inner life. It is remarkable how many Christian ashrams have been founded all over India in recent years.

But while Christians may strive for greater inwardness, contemporary Indians are actively engaged in moving outwards, into areas of social and political action, in the affirmation of their distinct cultural and national identity, the building of nationhood, and in working for greater social and economic justice. This, of course, is part of the great Jewish tradition. It requires a certain kind of dialogue, too, so that harmony and balance are maintained between the different ethnic and religious groups.

We need both courage and humility to recognize this work of the spirit among us in other faiths. It takes courage to acknowledge religious diversity as a rich spiritual resource, rather than a cause for competition and tension. And it takes humility and sincerity to concede that there is a certain incompleteness in each of our traditions. However diverse in their development and message, they always remain in a process of becoming, so that there is always room for growth towards a fuller, richer vision of the truth. We must also recognize that ultimately all religions possess a provisional, interim character as ways and signs to help us in our pilgrimage to Ultimate Truth and Perfection.

Rethinking our theology

Thirdly, for the Christian the *theological* challenges of religious pluralism are compelling enough. In particular, they affect our understanding of God and his grace, of Christ and his mission, and also our perceptions of community and the nature of Christian love.

Theology is literally 'talk about God'. In a wider sense it represents the struggle of 'faith seeking understanding', and concerns every attempt to conceive of ultimate reality and divine transcendence as revealed to us. Any dialogue must wrestle with this task. But if we are honest, we must recognize that no words, no thoughts, no symbols can encompass the richness of this reality, nor the richness of its disclosure in different lives, communities and traditions. Signs of divine life and grace, of the outpouring of the spirit on earth can be seen in myriad forms in human history and consciousness. From the perspective of *faith*, different world religions can be seen as different gifts of the spirit to humanity. Without losing our respective identities and the precious heritage and roots of our own faith, we can learn to see in a new way the message and insights of our faith in the light of that of others. By relating our respective visions of the Divine to each other, we can discover a still greater splendour of divine life and grace.

Different religions have found many names and symbols for transcendence, many faces and forms as partial expressions of the Ultimate Mystery. Alternatively, they have followed the *via negativa* of the apophatic method, and have denied and emptied all concepts and categories to point to the *Cloud of Unknowing* beyond which we encounter the One who encompasses all realities and existence. To find the invisible behind the visible, the everlasting behind the everchanging turmoils of existence is the great longing and hope of the human heart. We yearn for peace, salvation, freedom and fulfilment, for the plenitude of the spirit promised to us, summed up in India in the one word *Brahman* which stands for pure Being, Consciousness and Joy. Although we may come from different religious backgrounds, we can all recognize a prayer of profound longing and hope in the well-known invocation of the *Upanishads*:

Lead me from the Unreal to the Real,
From Darkness to Light
From Death to Immortality.

Indian religious life presents us with an amazing variety of perspectives on the Divine Spirit as source of all life, whether this spirit is celebrated as utterly impersonal transcendence, worshipped as Lord of all beings, meditated upon as innermost centre of human person, or praised as a loving God of grace. When Thomas Merton visited India, he reflected on the spiritual significance of his pilgrimage in his *Asian Journal*, where he describes his encounter with Hindus and Buddhists. Merton felt that Hinduism was vibrating with a God-consciousness as presence – God not primarily understood as concept or image, but encountered in the fullness of experience as ultimate ground of reality and meaning from which flow all life and love. Some years ago John Robinson wrote a book about the encounter of Hinduism and Christianity which he entitled *Truth is Two-Eyed*. Given the richness and diversity of Indian religious perspectives, it might be rather more appropriate to say, drawing on a well-known Indian image, that 'Truth is a thousand-eyed'. For Hindus, the fullness of truth is reflected in myriads of facets and faces, all of which the unfathomable mystery of the Divine must encompass in ways which surpass our understanding.

The Universalism of Christ

For Christians, the person of Jesus Christ, his life and suffering, his death and resurrection, will always remain the primary source of knowledge and truth about God. The central message of the Christian gospel is a message of love, love poured out in the complete self-giving of God in his Son for the sake of all life and creation. For the Christian, this is firm and fundamental – it is not negotiable. None the less, Christians recognize that other faiths reveal other aspects of God which may enrich and enlarge our Christian understanding. I am reminded here of that eloquent passage in Ninian Smart's contribution to *Soundings*:

> Journeying into foreign lands and alien cultures can bring one to a better understanding of one's own faith. One can see certain general features of good religion which can be used as a yardstick for measuring the inessential accretions of one's own faith. And just as studying Tolstoy may throw indirect light upon Turgenev, Mozart upon Brahms, Goya upon Picasso, so the gentle wonders of Buddhism and the subtle theologies of Hinduism, the poetry of the Tao and the single-mindedness of Islam, will shed some illumination upon the heart of Christianity.

One of the greatest challenges of interfaith dialogue which Christian theology must face is the question of the universality of Christ and his mission: the question as to the meaning and significance of the incarnation within the context of religious pluralism. There exists no easy answer to these questions, and it would take time before Christians can accept that there may be a plurality of answers within Christian theology itself, even before one moves to the wider pluralism of interfaith experience.

What is at stake is our understanding of the finality and significance of Christ's life and work, of, to use F. D. Maurice's term, 'the universalism of the Kingdom of Christ' at the centre and heart of the Christian faith. For Christians the coming of Christ is the ultimate sign of the fullness of God's grace. But in an age of radical historical consciousness an understanding of the incarnation as the central Christian event must also be linked to an understanding of the historical circumstances in which this belief first took root and developed.

Theological reflection must take account also of contemporary circumstances to which this message must now relate. These are not only questions of theological import but of pastoral concern. An honest attempt to seek for answers would require an attitude of love and respect towards neighbours of other faiths. It would also open up new possibilities for mutual witness. If we want to find viable and helpful answers in a situation of great need, we will have to abandon any narrowly conceived Christian apologetic, based on a sense of superiority and an exclusive claim to truth.

Instead of triumphalism and rejection, Christians must practice reconciliation. We need to hear afresh the call of our Lord to follow his example of generous self-giving and loving service, his example of compassion amid suffering, of help and hope for the poor, of strength for the weak. There is a call to universalism here, to the universal power of love and forgiveness which can transform the world.

I glimpsed something of the universalism of Christ's love in Calcutta when I visited Mother Teresa's Home for the Dying. I had not realized before that her hospice is build on temple property – dedicated appropriately enough to the Goddess Kali. But there was more to it than that. Here was the love of Christ given and received by men and women of all faiths and of none alongside the goddess who symbolizes a mixture of destruction and fertility. At work was a saintly woman dedicated to the ministry of the mystery of dying and rising. That juxtaposition speaks powerfully of the universal power and significance of the love of Christ.

But most current models of theology do not yet proceed from a situation of dialogue. They are still mostly monologues internal to each of our faith communities. Yet things are changing. While in the past the goal of Christian mission has mainly been the awakening of faith, the founding of churches, the growth and maintenance of Christ life we now perceive more clearly – as I perceived in Calcutta – another goal as that of giving witness to the spirit of love and hope, of promoting justice and peace, of sharing responsibility with others for the development of a caring society, especially where people are in need. Interfaith dialogue can help to remove barriers between us by creating conditions for greater community and fellowship. This will mean that some claims about the exclusiveness of the Church have to be renounced, but also that past and present prejudices about other religions have to be overcome, and ignorance and contempt actively resisted.

The Cambridge Divine, Brooke Foss Westcott, used to prophesy that new life for the Christian Church would come out of India. Devoting his intellectual life to resisting the German thesis that primitive Christianity had been corrupted by the influence of Greek philosophy and culture, he believed on the contrary that Christianity reached out to other cultures and dominated them, but in dominating them received new life for itself. And so he saw the Church as reaching out to India, and appropriating all that was best in the indigenous Hindu tradition.

What would emerge was doubtful: he prophesied that we might receive a new insight into St. John's Gospel, a new light upon Christian mysticism. That still remains to be seen.

We thought there was peril in the Indian Church if they so

undervalued the need for truth transmissible in proposition that they might fail to see the dangers of eclecticism. But there has been strength in the fact that they have found it impossible to think in old and rigid categories about schism, sects, bell, book and candle. It is not an accident that some of the most significant strides towards unity have been Indian – and never at the cost of the vitality of Christian discipleship.

Partners and Fellow Pilgrims

I am not advocating a single-minded, and synthetic model of world religion. Nor was Sir Francis Younghusband. What I want is for each tradition, and especially my own, 'to break through its own particularity', as Paul Tillich put it. Indeed Tillich is worth listening to here. The way to achieve this, he says,

> is not to relinquish one's religious tradition for the sake of a universal concept which would be nothing but a concept. The way is to penetrate into the depths of one's own religion, in devotion, thought and action. In the depth of every living religion there is a point at which religion itself loses its importance, and that to which it points breaks through its particularity, elevating it to spiritual freedom and to a vision of the spiritual presence in other expressions of the ultimate meaning of man's existence. That is what Christianity must grasp in its encounter with the world's religions.

Our world is in desperate need of a new and larger vision of unity which transcends our differences. All people of faith possess potential for seeking greater unity through dialogue, through bonds of fellowship, and through shared service of the wider community. It is not the communion experienced in interfaith dialogue ultimately about a new way of life, a new mode of being, where we no longer see each other as competitors but as partners and fellow pilgrims called to bear witness to the same spirit among all people?

'Faiths and Fellowship' was the theme of the first World Congress of Faiths Conference in 1936. Later, Sir Francis Younghusband prefaced its published *Proceedings* with the words: 'To promote the spirit of fellowship was the one aim of the Congress.' And the final impression of the Congress was that: 'Members, through meeting and working together to achieve one high object, had experienced something of that deep soul-satisfying joy such as only spiritual communion can give. There was a great gladness that such a thing was possible – and, if possible once, then possible again.'

This is a word of hope and encouragement which fifty years later should inspire and strengthen us to go forward in the same direction. Arnold Toynbee, in a remarkable prophecy, suggested that the present century would be chiefly celebrated by historians hundreds of years hence as the time when the first sign became visible of that great interpenetration of eastern religions and Christianity which gave rise to the great universal religion of the third millennium AD. That is further than we can see, and certainly further than many would like to see happening – now or at any time. A rich diversity of religious experiences and forms is one of God's greatest gifts to his world. But it requires from us the virtues of understanding and sympathy, humility and readiness to listen and to learn. Only then can we build a greater global unity in the spirit of faith, hope and love.

3 CHRISTIANITY AND OTHER RELIGIONS
Gavin D'Costa

In Henry Fielding's novel *Tom Jones*, the strident Parson Thwackum pronounces, 'When I mention religion, I mean the Christian religion, and not only the Christian religion, but the Protestant religion; and not only the Protestant religion, but the Church of England.' Such was the state of inter-*Christian* ecumenism not so long ago. Proportionately, inter-*religious* relations were relegated even further down the agenda. The situation has changed today. Thwackum's England is now far more cosmopolitan and multi-religious: *The Jewel in the Crown* and *Far Pavilions* are ambivalent reminders of a colonial past; so called 'race riots' and National Front stickers signify that with change comes turbulence; and the Buddhist Peace Pagoda and Hindu Yoga/Meditation Centre embody a glimpse of a rich, rewarding and harmonious multi-religious, multi-cultural future. If 'Thwackum was for doing justice, and leaving mercy to heaven', let us hope that both justice and charity may prevail in our future society.

Thwackum's views, and no doubt behaviour, were affected and partially formed by his theological outlook. In this paper I want to examine, as a Christian, some Christian attitudes to other religions. I also want to develop and defend a particular approach to this issue which for me remains faithful to the gospel as well as my experience (both practical and theoretical) of other religions – and non-religious movements. Whether 'other religions' and 'non-religions' can be lumped together like this remains to be justified.

In the first part of my paper I will outline and comment upon three types of Christian responses to other religions. These responses are to be found in varying degrees through most of Christian history. There are nuances and differences within theologians belonging to the same 'camp', but the validity of distinguishing three, rather than thirteen or thirty, camps is justified for the purpose of an introductory guide such as this. I shall call these three approaches: *exclusivism* (only those who confess Christ and surrender their lives to him are saved), *pluralism* (all religions are equal and valid paths to the one divine reality), and *inclusivism* (Christ remains the normative revelation of God, although salvation is possible through religions other than Christianity). In the second part of my paper, I shall develop my own reflections as an extension of one of the positions outlined above.

Three Types of Christian Responses to Other Religions

The exclusivist position is most dramatically exemplified by a Portuguese Roman Catholic explorer by the name of Martin de Encisco. He travelled widely in South America. He also composed what is called the *Regnerimento*. This was a manifesto read to the native Indians whom he wanted to convert. It was written in Spanish or Latin and set forth a brief history of the world since creation, the coming of Christ, followed by an account of the institution of the papacy. The so-called preaching of the gospel concluded with a grant, by Pope Alexander VI to the King of Spain, of certain islands and territories. The Indians were also required to recognize the Church's and Pope's sovereign authority over the world, and, in the Pope's place, the King of Spain. The result of rejecting the gospel led to the enslavement of the Indians as they could now be considered wilful idolators.[1]

The example is real, but somewhat extreme. However, it does highlight a form of racism and colonial imperialism that has too often motivated and informed Christian mission. The rape of cultures and civilizations has often been justified in the name of the Christian religion. And if both justice and mercy are missing from this enterprise, Swift's comment that 'We have just enough religion to make us hate, but not enough to make us love one another' is often sadly the case.

What is astounding about de Encisco is not his following of Christ's injunction to preach the gospel to all nations, but his total disregard for the proper conditions of preaching the gospel. Here the comments of Rammohun Roy, the erudite Bengali Hindu reformer, concerning Christian mission in British India are appropriate:

> It is true that the apostles of Jesus Christ used to preach the superiority of the Christian religion to the natives of different countries. But we must recollect that they were not the rulers of those countries where they preached. [He goes on to commend the true preaching of Christianity 'in countries not conquered by the English'.] In Bengal, where the English are the sole rulers, and where the mere name of Englishman is sufficient to frighten people, encroachment upon the rights of her poor, timid and humble inhabitants and upon their religion cannot be viewed in the eyes of God or the public as a justifiable act.[2]

Another criticism of de Encisco concerns his total disregard and lack of interest in what religion or way of life was practised by the native Indians. Last but not least was his exploitative intention in preaching the gospel. Territory and capital were undoubtedly his main interest.

Needless to say, the attitude of exclusivism is far more complicated. I started by highlighting these issues to keep our attention on the ways in which theological attitudes have often been translated into practice. There should be, among Christians, a constant self-critical reflection, so that theology does not become a form of idolatry which is then translated into ideologies of oppression.[3] Nevertheless, there are serious theological issues underlying the exclusivist position. The early work of the great German Protestant theologian Karl Barth can be used to examine some of the theological issues.

Barth's theology was propounded in the light of two basic theological convictions. The first, common to a number of Christian denominations (although stressed in different degrees) concerned the fallen state of men and women. Because human beings live in a sinful state, all religion, including the Christian religion in certain circumstances, is *idolatrous*. All human formulations concerning God are precisely that – *human formulations*, inevitably falling short of the real God and thereby inevitably idolizing a false human-made God. Such was the import of Barth's classic essay, 'The Revelation of God as the Abolition of Religion'.[4] You will notice that the title also reflects Barth's second premise, concerning the revelation of God. For Barth, one premise rests upon the other. The other being that God uniquely discloses himself in Christ. Consequently, all 'religion' and all human culture is judged in the light of Christ. By the standard of Christ, human history is judged as idolatrous. Barth's theology is profoundly *Christocentric*.

Barth's attitude to a different set of Indians from de Encisco is somewhat analogous. D.T. Niles, the Indian Christian theologian, recalls a meeting with Barth in 1935. Barth asserted that 'other religions are just unbelief'. Niles replied, asking 'How many Hindus, Dr Barth, have you met?' Barth's unhesitating reply was 'Not one.' To this, Niles pressed the issue a little further: 'How then do you know that Hinduism is unbelief?' Barth's answer, which took Niles by surprise, was quite simply *A Priori!*'[5] Barth was simply expressing the working out of the logical implications of his exclusivist Christocentric theology. As a human being he was warm and gracious and resisted Nazism because of its imperialist ideology.[6] I say this to emphasize that Barth's exclusivism derived from purely theological motives, unlike that of de Encisco.

I have taken Barth as a representative figure and do not want to discuss *his* views in detail because I only wish to highlight some of the theological issues at stake.[7] Some of Barth's followers have developed his suggestions in various ways that remain exclusivist in as much as for those who do not encounter Christ, there is no salvation.[8] Hence, the proclamation of the Congress on World Mission: 'In the years since the war, more than one billion souls have passed into eternity and more than half of these went to the torment of hell fire without even hearing of Jesus Christ, who He was, or why He died on the cross of Calvary.'[9]

This type of exclusivism faces a number of theological objections which have caused me to reject it while also acknowledging its limited value. First, while valuing its Christocentric emphasis I would criticize its *use* of this Christocentric emphasis. As a Christian I believe that God has unreservedly disclosed himself in Christ.[10] *But* the God disclosed in Christ is a God of *universal love, mercy and judgement*. Central to the Christian tradition's emphasis on Christ, has also been an emphasis on God's loving nature and desire to save all men and women.[11] A God of infinite love, mercy and justice surely could not condemn the majority of humankind to perdition, most of whom have never even heard the gospel, let alone rejected it. Such a God could only be deemed an unjust tyrant. I think that the simple historical fact that most of humankind has never encountered the gospel, coupled with the theological doctrine of a God of universal love, begins to undermine a rigorous exclusivist position.

Another objection to such a view lies in the notion of *grace* often implicit within such exclusivist positions. While wishing to retain the conviction that God discloses himself unreservedly in Christ, it is theologically and historically untenable to maintain that saving grace is limited only to those who submit to Christ. This contention is based on a number of arguments. In traditional Christian theology, Judaism, up to the time of Christ, was certainly accorded revelatory and salvific status. That is, it was believed that God both revealed himself and thereby acted salvifically within Judaism. (The related issue of the Christian history of anti-Semitism is beyond the scope of this essay.)[12] Hence, a Christian exclusivist who denied any revelation outside Christ would be hard-pressed to explain the use of the Old Testament as part of Christian scripture. In fact, Marcion (second century) was deemed heretical for just such an exclusion of the Old Testament. If my point is accepted, in principle it may also be true that God has acted salvifically in various ways and in different degrees throughout human history. And given the doctrine of a God who desires the salvation of all men and women such a possibility is likely to be the case.

Besides the history of Israel testifying to salvific grace outside the particular event of the historical Jesus, there are also a number of passages within the New Testament that highlight the importance of *right living*. If for instance, a person's courageous self-sacrificing love is due to certain demands within their religion, can these acts of responding to grace be divorced from the mediators of such grace? Or, can the humanist's self-sacrificial love for another, so powerfully portrayed in Camus's *The Plague*, have nothing to do with Jesus's implied teaching that 'as you did it to one of the least of my brethren, you did it to me' (Matt. 25:40)? I do not want to conflate religious truth with practice and action alone, but I would question whether the two can be completely separated. Accordingly, a person's way of life, and not simply their assent to a set of beliefs (concerning Christ), is of great importance.[13]

My case is cumulative. There are a number of considerations that leave me dissatisfied with exclusivism. They centre upon the restricting of saving grace to those who submit to Christ. While Christ, for the Christian, is the *definitive* revelation of the shape of grace, Christ is not, I have argued, the *exclusive* revelation. The exclusivist stance runs counter to the heart of the Christian revelation of a God of love.[14]

On the other end of the spectrum we have *pluralism*. In the symphony of Christian history this stance has been a very minor melody, whereas exclusivism has often been the dominant key. The pluralist position is nicely exemplified in a Buddhist parable, turned into a poem by John Saxe. The poem highlights the convictions that the different religions are equal paths to the one divine reality and exclusivist claims can only lead to gross distortion. It is the parable of *The Blind Men and the Elephant*:

> It was six men of Hindostan,
> To Learning much inclined,
> Who went to see the Elephant,
> (Though all of them were blind):
> That each by observation
> Might satisfy his mind.
>
> The first approached the Elephant
> And happening to fall
> Against his broad and sturdy side,
> At once began to brawl:
> 'Bless me, it seems the Elephant
> Is very like a wall.'
>
> The second, feeling of his tusk,
> Cried, 'Ho! what have we here
> So very round and smooth and sharp?
> This wonder of an Elephant
> Is very like a spear.'
>
> The third approached the animal,

And happening to take
The squirming trunk within his hands,
Then boldly up and spake:
'I see,' quoth he, 'The Elephant
Is very like a snake.'

And so these men of Hindostan
Disputed loud and long,
Each in his own opinion
Exceeding stiff and strong,
Though each was partly in the right
And all were in the wrong.

When religions claim exclusive rights to the truth, they are analogously like the blind men.

The English philosopher-theologian John Hick is a leading proponent of pluralism.[15] If Barth was *Christocentric*, Hick is avowedly *theocentric*. He asks: 'Can we... accept the conclusion that the God of love who seeks to save all mankind has nevertheless ordained that men must be saved in such a way that only a small minority can in fact receive this salvation.'[16]

Hick's answer is 'no'. He also argues that Christians should view Christ as just one window looking in on the divine reality. He suggests: 'May it not be that the different concepts of God, as Jahweh, Allah, Krishna, Param Atma, Holy Trinity, and so on... are all images of the divine, each expressing some aspect or range of aspects and yet none by itself fully and exhaustively corresponding to the infinite nature of ultimate reality?'[17]

In his more recent work, Hick has had to move away from his theocentric basis to accommodate non-theistic religions and non-religions.

As with the position of exclusivism, there are a number of points that cause me fundamentally to disagree with this stance while greatly valuing some of its concerns. As with Barth, I have chosen Hick as a representative figure and do not wish to discuss his views in any detail.[18]

What I value in the pluralist stance is its openness to the fact of the universality of God's grace and love; that God is salvifically present in other religions and non-religions. What I object to is its attempt to establish a theocentric solution by bypassing Christocentricism. That is, the attempt to speak to God, while being a Christian, without reference to Christ as the basis and norm for the revelation of God.

If we return to the parable of the elephant and the blind men my point can be illustrated more clearly. Saxe's poem omits reference to the prince who conducts this experiment; and if it were not for his particular vantage point from which he is able to say that 'each was partly in the right', how could we know that the 'elephant' was not in fact a wall rather than a spear or snake? Or how could we know that the blind men were in fact touching the same object? If we are to say that God (or the divine) is present in all religions and non-religions, how are we to identify, recognize and justify this claim? Why, for instance, should Nazism be denied the self-claimed status (supported by many of the German churches at the time) of being part of God's unfolding revelation? If we do not have some criteria by which to identify and recognize the action of God, the valuable openness of the pluralist position collapses into a self-destructive and theologically uncritical stance.

Barth's *Christocentrism* tended towards exclusively restricting God to Christ. Hick's theocentrism moves towards the opposite extreme. He denies any normativity to the revelation of God in Christ, in his attempt to break away from Barth's exclusive coupling of God and Christ. In following this strategy, pluralists tend either to utilize an abstract and non-revelatory notion of God, or to operate with hidden assumptions that really run counter to their pluralist position. For example Hick claims that both personal and non-personal images of the divine are equally valid and authentic. However, because of his hidden theistic assumptions, he argues in a work on life after death that ultimately there will be a loving communion of souls with the divine. This view seems to run counter to certain Hindu and Buddhist schools as Hick acknowledges in an aside: 'This [position] implicitly rejects the *advaitist* view that Atman *is* Brahman, the collective human self being ultimately identical with God.'[19] However, such an acknowledgement runs counter to the pluralist thesis and also raises a further objection.

Most religious and non-religious believers hold the conviction that what they are talking about is *true*; that their convictions actually relate to reality, the state of things as they are. The problem with the pluralist stance is that it too easily bypasses the very genuine problem of conflicting truth claims. None of the examples I give is necessarily intractable, but the examples *do* pose genuine problems that must be faced fairly and squarely, and also peacefully and charitably. These examples are random and I select them from recent debate: did Jesus die on the cross as Christians claim or is the Qur'àn correct in saying that he did not die on the cross? For Christians this issue is paramount. Or, is the theistic God of Semitic religions only a provisional and inadequate representation of the divine which is, as Radhakrishnan claims, ultimately non-dual and identical to the soul: i.e. Atman is Brahman.[20] Examples can be multiplied.[21] Does pluralism arrive at its solution far too quickly and far too easily? I think that it does.

It will be clear by now that I have only one option left of the three stances mentioned at the outset. What I now wish to do is briefly outline inclusivism and then go on to defend and develop this position in the light of questions that are raised – both by my paper and I hope, in the mind of the reader.

The German Jesuit Karl Rahner was a leading exponent of inclusivism.[22] Rahner's inclusivism is determined by holding together in creative tension the strengths of both exclusivism and pluralism, while rejecting their shortcomings. He affirms the following two axioms: 'God desires the salvation of everyone. And this salvation willed by God is the salvation won by Christ.'[23] While retaining the centrality of Christ as the definitive disclosure of God, Rahner argues that God's grace is nevertheless operative throughout history and begins in creation. Rahner coined the controversial term 'anonymous Christian'. He uses this term to denote the fact that for Christians, God's grace cannot be separated from Christ's disclosure of God. So, whenever God's grace is spoken of, it is, by virtue of the Trinitarian nature of God, also Christ that is spoken of and present – even if this is not acknowledged or understood as such. Hence the technical term 'anonymous Christian'.

Rahner's thesis is far more complex, but, as with Hick and Barth, I have simply chosen him as a representative of a position. I am not primarily concerned with discussing his thought in any detail.[24] He represents what I consider to be the most viable Christian approach to other religions. Inclusivism may be characterized as positively affirming God's salvific grace in the religions and non-religions of the world, while nevertheless retaining what I take to be the central Christian claim that God's grace is revealed most normatively and definitively in Christ. As a consequence, Christians cannot positively affirm God's universal desire to save all men and women without anchoring this concept of God – which is anchored in Christ.

Inclusivism

In the remainder of this paper I want to develop some reflections in the light of my outline above, opting for what I call an inclusivist approach. Perhaps presumptuously, I want to anticipate some of the questions that may arise from Christians and others regarding my position. This process will allow me to clarify the sort of inclusivism that I wish to defend.

The first and perhaps the most obvious question may arise from those within religious or non-religious movements who do not believe in a personal God. From a Humanist the following question may arise: 'I respect the fact that you see the world differently, although I cannot, in good faith, share your belief in God. In fact, my sincere conviction leads me in an altogether different direction. However, I do find it offensive, if not a little absurd, that you nevertheless insist that I am "saved" by a God that I do not believe in – despite myself. If Barth's position had the weakness of forcing people out of the arena of salvation, your position has the weakness of forcing them in – and if they do not like it, you call them "anonymous Christians".' In not so many words, and sometimes less politely, this question has been put to me on a number of occasions.

I *try* to answer this objection in the following way. If our beliefs have cognitive sense (if they concern 'reality' rather than only our own attitudes), then inevitably there is a certain 'arrogance' in holding any belief whatsoever. For instance, the humanist must by implication think that my belief in God is either a psychological projection (Freud and Feuerbach), an infantile rejection of true autonomy (Neitzsche and Cupitt), a false way of coping with the abyss of nothing (Camus), and so on. Assuming the questioner is an atheist humanist, his or her belief in the nature of reality must necessarily interpret and make sense of other beliefs that are in direct contradiction to their own. Unless one could intelligibly entertain the notion that 'there is and there is not a God', such a situation is inevitable. They will interpret me and I will interpret them.

However, the situation is not so desperate as to be analogous to two entrenched armies sniping away endlessly at each other, never losing or gaining ground. If we dialogue with theoretical positions rather than people, then we may end up with a fruitless exercise. But my experience has been that if two genuinely open people meet without discarding their convictions, more often than not there is a growing realization of the lack of understanding between them. A brief example will suffice. When in conversation with an atheist friend recently, I asked her to tell me what she rejected as 'God' and whether the 'God' she rejected was the one she thought I believed in. There was certainly very little in common between what we understood as 'God', which made it difficult for me to regard her as an atheist as I used to, and her to regard me as a Christian as she used to. The real difficulties in understanding the 'other' person as genuinely 'another' are paramount.

Nevertheless, to get back to my humanist friend's objection, I would argue that all of us, whatever our beliefs, cannot help viewing the world through a set of lenses. The important thing is to be open to questioning and clarification – to keep up the metaphor, to constantly have eye tests. And every now and then we may eventually come to change our spectacles altogether – dramatically, as was the case with St Paul on the Road to Damascus, or more gently and over a period of time.

My point is this. As a Christian who believes that self-sacrificial love partakes in grace, for self-sacrificial love is of the nature of the triune God, then I cannot help saying that where there is love there is God.[25] This is not an imperialistic attempt to inflate the number of church members (even if they are only anonymous members!), but the recognition that salvation is not exclusively related to the acceptance of a certain set of propositional beliefs.

However, I do need to qualify what I have said to avoid misunderstanding. Quite simply, only God can read hearts. It is impossible and absurd to say that this or that person is saved or lost. It is also extremely difficult to say this or that person is living a grace-filled life. Even the most apparently charitable and devout person may be masking a spiritual and moral egoism – as was the case in the parable of the Pharisee and the tax collector in Luke (18:9–14).

My next qualification also applies to the Christian as well as my humanist questioner. The type of inclusivism I am defending does not affirm indiscriminately that grace is at work universally, regardless of men and women's responses. If human freedom is taken seriously, then people cannot be bulldozed into salvation! A life lived in fearful self-centredness is what is called sin. Christians, like the Pharisees in Luke's story, can profess correct beliefs and pay their money to charities, but this does not in itself guarantee salvation. Similarly, to my humanist friend's charge that 'If Barth's position had the weakness of forcing people out of the arena of salvation, your position has the weakness of forcing them in', I can only plead 'ignorance' in as much as I (hopefully) force no one in or out, but am only arguing a theological case for the possibility of God's salvific activity throughout humankind. The implications of this case mean that theologically, a humanist who professes disbelief in God may be saved. Whether and where this happens is ultimately impossible to locate. That it can happen is all important.

What I have been arguing above is relevant to humanist and religious non-theists. Clearly, I am not asking that they be Christians to accept my defence, but rather that they inspect its coherence and plausibility.

Another criticism of the type of inclusivism that I have been exploring may be put thus: 'You argue that you've steered a midpoint between Barth and Hick, but you still keep claiming that Christ is the so called "definitive" and "normative" revelation of God. Surely this claim is as *a priori* as Barth's dismissal of Hinduism? If you have not confronted every religion, how can such a claim be historically, let alone theologically, credible? Furthermore, doesn't your form of inclusivism end up with the same superior attitude found in Barth's theology?' This criticism has been levelled at me by certain Christian friends, but could equally come from any other person.[26]

I *try* to answer this criticism in the following way. As a Christian my commitment is founded on faith. I do not mean this in a fideistic sense so as to imply a total invulnerability to questioning, evidence and reason. My adherence to Christianity comes from a subjective conviction that I have been objectively confronted by God through Christ. And if God is God, then I am speaking not only about absolute commitment (faith), but also about an absolute reality (God). If my Christian conviction has any cognitive status, which I believe it does, then it is difficult to use terms other than 'normative' and 'definitive' when speaking of God's disclosure in Christ. If I am to believe that this revelation is true, then the 'object' of belief dictates that it is not only true for me but also 'objectively' true.

Where I differ from Barth, in reply to the criticism put forward against me, is that because of my convictions outlined above I do not believe *a priori* that all other religions and non-religions are false and invalid. The form of inclusivism that I wish to defend stands in *committed openness* to all of humankind's history – past, present and future. It stands open to being interrogated, clarified and deepened – and this is all important – to being so corrected, that I cannot preclude the possibility of losing my faith altogether. Real openness cannot but be vulnerable and precarious. But in that very openness, it can also be receptive to richness and wealth from other religious and non-religious traditions. In fact, most of Christianity's history has been precisely this: an inculturation and incorporation of all that is worthwhile, true and good from the cultures and religious traditions within which it has developed. This is, of course, most evident in relation to Judaism. I say this with tentativeness in relation to the ugly underbelly of anti-Semitism that has characterized much of Christian history. But I do not think that one is a necessary concommitant with the other. Cardinal Newman outlines this inculturation process in regard to doctrine and liturgical practice when he writes: 'The use of temples, and these dedicated to particular saints, and ornamented on occasions with branches of trees; incense, lamps and candles; votive offerings on recovery from illness; holy water; holydays and seasons... perhaps the ecclesiastical chant, and the Kyrie Eleison, are all of pagan origin, and sanctified by their adoption into the Church.'[27]

Newman correctly notes a process that in fact characterizes the historical development of most religions, although I would qualify his comment in as much as many of these rites and doctrines were already 'sanctified' before their adoption into the Church.

Therefore, in response to this second criticism, I argue that my form of inclusivism does not entail an *a priori* superiority or judgement over other religions and non-religions. Rather, this form of Christian inclusivism in its committed openness is able and desirous of sharing with and learning from other ways of life and belief. It is open to the point where 'conversion' cannot be precluded – hopefully on both sides. It is committed to the point of necessarily declaring the Christian conviction that in Christ, the definitive revelation of God has occurred.

Allied to this issue, there is a third criticism which I would like to mention. Pluralist friends, both Christian and otherwise, have suggested that *interreligious co-operation* can proceed only when the partner's religion is accepted as equally valid and authentic. Otherwise co-operation is always paternalistic and like the 'Marshall Plan,' a strategy from a position of superiority.[28]

Historically and theologically such a claim is dubious. Historically, there have been many instances where even those who share many of the 'same beliefs' have clashed with each other – politically and militarily. The German Christians during Hitler's time are a prime example. There have also been many instances where interreligious co-operation has been successful while theological differences have remained.[29] It is, I would suggest, somewhat utopian to insist that before we can live in peaceful harmony, we all have to accept that every person's belief is true and equally valid. The institution of democracy is an attempt to safeguard plurality in unity. The right of each person to practise his or her religion, and have freedom of thought and speech is surely what is required. The inclusivist position is in keeping with this requirement. And in speaking as a Christian, aware of Christianity's checkered history, I would nevertheless argue that the fundamental right to religious and moral freedom is encoded in the gospel. As a Roman Catholic I may be permitted to quote from the document on *Religious Liberty* issued by Vatican II:

> The Vatican Council declares that the human person has a right to religious freedom. Freedom of this kind means that all men should be immune from coercion on the part of individuals, social groups, and every human power so that, within due limits, nobody is forced to act against his conviction in religious matters in private or public... The Council further declares that the right to religious freedom is based on the very dignity of the human person as known through the revealed word of God and by reason itself.[30]

In response then to the third criticism against my position, I argue that the inclusivism I am defending facilitates, perhaps more realistically, mutual co-operation between religions towards building a peaceful and harmonious future. No doubt, the differences in belief may differently inform and shape notions of 'justice', 'peace' and 'sisterhood' – and sometimes these differences may be intractable. But this apparent intractability should itself be a cause for, rather than an obstacle to, dialogue and eventual co-operation.[31]

Conclusion

There are many more issues that require clarification if my position is to be accepted by other Christians and made comprehensible to non-Christians. I have only touched on some of the difficulties that this particular Christian approach to other religions and non-religions raises.[32]

I also need to comment about the excessively theological and theoretical slant to my paper. I have concentrated on theological questions for two reasons. Two explore Christian attitudes to other religions, one cannot ignore the theological *raison d'être* of Christians, although, admittedly, the situation regarding attitudes in practice is far more complex. If, as a responsible human being, I am to account for my beliefs and attitudes to the community at large, I can do so only in theological terms. Admittedly, not everyone will share these terms, let alone beliefs, but I hope that my account is intelligible enough to Christians and others.

In summary: I have attempted to outline and criticize the positions of exclusivism and pluralism. I have tried to argue that the inclusivist Christian attitude to other religions is one which remains religiously committed and theologically humane. It remains committed to the truth that it is bound by; and is humane in the recognition that this truth does not *per se* invalidate the 'truths' that bind other men and women to their religions and non-religions. By its nature, inclusivism rejects the total 'systems' of extreme exclusivism, where *a priori* all are lost, or extreme pluralism, where *a priori* all are saved.

4 CHRIST AND INTERFAITH WORSHIP
Andrew Linzey

On 6 December 1991, an Open Letter signed by more than 2,000 clergy in the Church of England was published in the *Church Times*. The Letter appealed to the leadership of the Church of England to 'oppose, and where possible, prevent... gatherings for interfaith worship and prayer in the Church of England and to seek to discourage them elsewhere'. The critical paragraphs are as follows:

> Believing that Jesus Christ the incarnate Son of God, is both God and man, the unique revelation of God, the only Saviour and hope of mankind – we, the undersigned members of the Church of England, are concerned that his Gospel shall be clearly presented in this Decade of Evangelism... we believe it to be our Lord's command that his Gospel shall be clearly proclaimed, openly and sensitively, to all people (including those of other faiths) with the intention that they should come to faith in him for salvation.
>
> In this we affirm no more and no less than the Apostolic and Anglican tradition. Article XVIII says: 'For Holy Scripture doth set out unto us only the Name of Jesus Christ, whereby men must be saved.'
>
> In consequence we are deeply concerned about gatherings for interfaith worship and prayer involving Christian people... whether they refer to Jesus Christ or whether such references are minimal or excluded.
>
> We believe that these events, however motivated, conflict with the Christian duty to proclaim the Gospel. They imply that salvation is offered by God not only through Jesus Christ but by other means, and thus deny his uniqueness and finality as the only Saviour.[1]

From the ground staked out, the implication is clear that doctrinally orthodox Christians – those who believe that Jesus Christ is the unique Saviour of humankind – will oppose gatherings for interfaith worship 'whether they refer to Jesus Christ or whether such references are minimal or excluded'. But does Christian orthodoxy require such a position? It is this assumption or implication that I want to challenge.

We begin, of course, with Christology – the theology of the person and work of Jesus Christ. But we do well to remind ourselves of how the one Christological theologican *par excellence* – namely Karl Barth – viewed this matter in one of his last recorded utterances. After hearing a lecture by Hans Iwand in which he was accused of advocating a concentration of the whole of theology on Christology, Barth said: 'Sometimes I don't like the word christology very much. It's not a matter of christology, nor even of christocentricity and a christological orientation, but of *Christ himself.*'² Whatever we may think of the appropriateness or accuracy of Barth's remark in relation to his theology as a whole, he supplies a useful starting point.

For if we turn to the actual example of Jesus Christ as recorded in the Gospels certain familiar facts present themselves. Chief, and indisputable among these is that Jesus, brought up as a devout Jew, worshipped within the Jewish tradition. 'It is impossible to doubt that Jesus worshipped in the Temple,' argues C.F.D. Moule. There are allusions to this in all four Gospels:

> According to Luke, he is found in the Temple as an infant when his parents bring him to be presented as their first male child, in accordance with the Law; and again when he goes up to Jerusalem as a boy for his first Passover. According to the unanimous witness of all four Gospels, it was when he had come to Jerusalem for the Passover that he was arrested and put to death. The Fourth Gospel expressly mentions his presence in the Temple also for the 'feast of tabernacles' (John 7:2f.) and for the winter festival of Hannukkah or Dedication (John 10:22).³

Not only in the Temple did Jesus worship. Luke describes it as his custom to worship regularly in the synagogue on the Sabbath (9:16) as indeed was the custom of St Paul (Acts 17:2).

The significance of these simple facts should not be minimized. However imperfect he may have regarded such worship, Jesus as a child and as a man worshipped God in this context. Jesus identified *this* God in *this* context with the same God known to himself – and later Christians – as 'Abba, Father'. Jesus does not ask his disciples to worship other than at the Temple and the synagogue, indeed we know that for a considerable period of time after Jesus's death the early Christians continued to worship at these places and were thought more of as a sect within Judaism than a religious community outside it.⁴

Now it may be objected that to present the facts in this way obscures the point that Jesus was – to some degree – critical of Jewish worship. This is certainly true. There are some ambiguous references (to say the least) to the Temple in Jesus's recorded words (see especially Mark 14:57–59; cf. Matt. 27:40; Mark 13:2; and John 2:19). It is also significant that Jesus did not – as far as we can determine – sacrifice animals in the Temple. Moreover, there is the telling remark – recorded in John (9:21–23) that 'the time is coming when you will worship the Father neither on this mountain (in

Samaria), nor in Jerusalem... those who are real worshippers will worship the Father in spirit and in truth.'[5]

Nevertheless, even allowing for all this, the facts speak for themselves: Jesus prayed within the Jewish tradition. He used Jewish scriptures and regarded them as authoritative. Early Christian prayers were taken, borrowed or reshaped from Jewish prayers. However imperfect the Jewish doctrine of God or its worship, Jesus did not abandon this tradition or claim its God as unreal, untrue or idolatrous. Even though, as Moule puts it, Jesus 'refused to shut his eyes to the nemesis which was to overtake a Temple which had been made mercenary and exclusive' and even though 'he saw in his ministry and in his own self the focal point of the new Temple', it has also to be said – at the very least – that Jesus was 'satisfied with nothing but the absolute sincerity and spirituality of which the Temple was meant, but too often failed, to be the medium.'[6]

In the light of this a rather fundamental question emerges: Is not what is good enough for Jesus good enough for Christians today? If Jesus – the one final, unique self-revelation of God – took to himself the Jewish form of prayer and worship, how are Christians now to claim at worship with other religious traditions, and the Jewish tradition in particular, is unacceptable or compromising or both?

It may be objected that it is not fair to concentrate on some of the basic facts of the life of Jesus in isolation from the later confession of Jesus as the Christ of faith. Jesus is, after all, the 'new Temple'. Devotion to him as Christ and Lord inspired a new and eventually distinct community of worship. In order to do justice to Christian thinking it is essential, it may be claimed, to examine some of the subsequent reflection on the work and person of Jesus which gave rise to Christian orthodoxy as we now know it. The Jesus of history, it may be protested, is also the Christ of the cosmos.

This latter idea of Christ as Lord of, or Logos within, the cosmos is one early and important strand of Christological reflection found especially in Ephesians and Colossians. Here are the well-known texts in full:

> Blessed be the God and Father of our Lord Jesus Christ, who has blessed us in Christ with every spiritual blessing in the heavenly places, even as he chose us in him before the foundation of the world, that we should be blameless and holy before him. He destined us in love to be his sons through Jesus Christ, according to the purpose of his will, to the praise of his glorious grace which he freely bestowed on us in the Beloved. In him we have redemption through his blood, the forgiveness of our trespasses, according to the riches of his grace which he lavished upon us. For he has made known to us in all wisdom and insight the mystery of his will, according to his purpose which he set forth in

Christ as a plan for the fullness of time, to unite all things in him, things in heaven and things on earth. (Eph. 1:3–11; RSV)

He [Christ] is the image of the invisible God, the first born of all creation; for in him all things were created, in heaven and on earth, visible and invisible, whether thrones or dominions or principalities or authorities – all things were created through and for him. He is before all things, and in him all things hold together. He is the head of the body, the church; he is the beginning, the first born from the dead, that in everything he might be pre-eminent. For in him all the fullness of God was pleased to dwell, and through him to reconcile to himself all things, whether on earth or in heaven, making peace by the blood of the cross. (Col. 1:15–20; RSV)

Reflection upon these verses will certainly serve to underline the view emphasized in the Open Letter that Jesus Christ is of central saving significance for the whole world. We encounter here the phenomenon – observed by Moule – as the 'extraordinary concept of the Lord Jesus Christ as a corporate, a more-than-individual personality'.[7] Signatories to the Letter may well point out the specific relationship here envisaged between Christ and believers. Christ stands, in both accounts, in a special relationship to those who believe in him and confess God's providential purposes. Moreover, he is 'head of the body, the church'. Those who claim an exclusivist understanding of Jesus Christ have half of the truth here.

But it is at best only half of the truth and the less important half at that. For the confession of Christ as head of the church can be comprehended and rendered intelligible only by the corresponding, if not prior, confession that Christ is also the indwelling Christ of the cosmos. What we have in these reflections are attempts to describe in the most dramatically macro-cosmic way possible the centrality of Jesus to God's work of reconciliation and redemption. But it would be a mistake, as some exegetes seem to do, simply to note this point and pass on. For the significance of Jesus Christ in both texts is that he crystallizes, embodies and enables God's will. And what is this will? It is nothing less than the summing up of all things. As Moule comments: 'When Luther affirmed this principle of scriptual interpretation, he was going back to the primitive Church.'[8]

God's will is achieved through Christ because he is the Logos, the agent of co-creation – '*all* things were created *through* him and *for* him... *in* him all things hold together' (Col. 1:16–17). But if this is true, the Gospel proclamation is not and cannot be just about the proclamation of the coming of Christ but the real and existing presence of Christ in every part of the created world. Whatever is true about Jesus is true because not one part of creation came into being without him, can exist without him, and there is no part of creation where Christ is radically absent. If we take these Christological reflections to heart, it seems to me that we are confronted not with an *exclusive* vision of Christ but a wholly *inclusive* one. What is most staggering in these early reflections is the way in which Christ is seen to hold together all the varieties and diversities of the created order. Nothing is excluded. Everything has its part to play in the eventual triumph of reconciliation.

If this is true, it follows that there must be something of Christ not only in the fragments of created existence but even and especially in those religious traditions that proclaim the existence of God and worship him or her. There is something paradigmatically wrong therefore in the assumption – as displayed in the Open Letter – that members of all other faiths must respond to our proclamation of the gospel of Jesus Christ in order to be saved. The living risen Christ is certainly witnessed to in Christian preaching and proclamation. But preachers and clergy do not bring Christ into the world; Christ is already present within every stratum of created life.

The question that must be asked therefore by preachers and clergy and others in this Decade of Evangelism is not: To whom shall we proclaim Christ? – but rather: Where shall we celebrate the life of Christ in our world? Once this question is asked, it will be seen immediately that a different attitude must be taken to other religious traditions and especially to the reality of worship. For worship is not just a God-inspired activity – though it is certainly that; there is also a radical sense in which, judged by Christian orthodoxy, worship *is* God's activity within us.

This idea requires some amplification. At one level it seems perfectly obvious that what with all the paraphernalia of bells, candles, incense and service books, worship is a human affair – sometimes an all too human affair. And, of course, in one sense it is. But to understand worship theologically we need to embrace the paradigm offered by St Paul: 'Likewise the Spirit helps us in our weakness; for we do not know how to pray as we ought but the Spirit intercedes for us with sighs too deep for words' (Rom. 8:26). The picture presented here expresses the conviction that prayer is, to say the least, a co-operative venture with God. The Spirit of Christ gives utterance – makes real and intelligible – our deepest longings for God even though in our weakness we know not even how to pray. I suggest that as we survey the created order of which Christ is the Logos, it is in the activity of worship that we most obviously encounter the Spirit of Christ. It must follow then that to take an attitude of indifference, antagonism or even hostility to worship in its non-Christian forms is to turn from Christ who is the one for whom all creatures – however imperfectly – long.

I anticipate three kinds of objections. The first is that my thesis devalues the significance of Christ himself. It may be claimed that I have turned Christ from being a saving messiah into a principle of worship and that, in consequence, I have failed to grasp how Christ's work is uniquely salvific.

The proper response to this objection consists in the rejection of the notion that we can oppose the salvific work of Christ to his universality. It seems to me that it is precisely because Christians came to see Christ's work as salvific that they were also compelled at one and the same time to confess Christ as universal and cosmic. In other words, as Christians came to reflect upon the reality of forgiveness and new life that Christ mediated to them through his death, they also came to see that Christ could only be such in relation to them if it was also true that the Christ of the Cross was also the Christ of the Cosmos, that is, the source of *all* illumination and light and creativity for *all* people, indeed for the whole earth. The logic of inclusivity follows inexorably from the confession of Christ crucified and risen. In the end the Christian confession consisted of a radical rejection of the view that Christ existed only for Christians and could be apprehended only through self-consciously Christian means. In this, we do no more and no less than offer commentary on the Prologue to John's Gospel: 'He was in the beginning with God; all things were made through him, and without him was not anything made that was made. In him was life, and the life was the light of men' (1:1–4).

The danger of mainly or exclusively emphasizing the salvific work of Christ is that we run the risk of becoming fundamentally untrinitarian. Our Jesus thereby becomes rarefied, literally too small for the cosmos of God: Creator, Sanctifier and Redeemer. In short: if we are to do justice to Jesus Christ we must save him from the hands of the fundamentalists in which the life of Christ in our world is turned into a package which is the possession of an exclusive religious sect.

A further response to this by fundamentalists may nowadays be heard. It is that there can be and is a 'general revelation' of God in creation but only a 'saving revelation' in Jesus Christ. This position is not as satisfactory as is often thought. We need to ask the simple question: What is revelation or, rather, what is revealed in revelation? Here the thought of Karl Barth illuminates the issue decisively. God can only reveal himself or herself. If this is true, then it must follow that all revelation is revelation; all revelation is self-revelation or it is no revelation at all. It is impossible therefore to separate 'general' revelation from other forms. To offer a two-tier system of revelation actually detracts from the grace of God in

Jesus Christ: God as Trinity always and everywhere offers him/herself as Father, Son or Holy Spirit. In sum: there is no revelation that is not God's revelation of his/her very self.

The second objection is that my thesis devalues specifically Christian worship, and that in consequence I put all worship on the same level.

This objection seems to have force. I do not believe that Jews who pray in the synagogue or Muslims who perform the daily salat worship any other God than the only God, the God who Christians describe as Father, Son and Holy Spirit. As David Brown – the former Bishop of Guildford who thought and wrote extensively about non-Christian traditions – was fond of reminding his hearers: 'All prayer is prayer.' From a Christian perspective we must risk one further step: All prayer is Christian prayer. I mean by this that if all movements towards God are, at least to some extent, God inspired, it has to be concluded that they are the result of the indwelling Christ in creation itself.

Does it follow then that we can make absolutely no distinction or preference between one form of worship or another, whatever its kind or whether it involves satanic ritual, animal abuse or other such practices? Help here is again at hand from what some would regard as a most unlikely source, namely the thought of Karl Barth. It is well known that Barth made a distinction between 'religion' and 'revelation'. On one hand, revelation was defined as 'God's self-offering and self-manifestation'. Religion, on the other, was 'the attempted replacement of the divine work by a human manufacture'.[9] This led Barth to define all religion, Christian or non-Christian, as 'sin'.[10] At first sight this might appear wholly unhelpful but I want to suggest that Barth's distinction between religion and revelation is quite fundamental here. Whereas Barth, in the end, appeared to endorse evangelical Christianity as the only true faith, it seems to be quite possible to extend Barth's thought so that it can provide a significant critique of all forms of religion and therefore of worship.

From this refashioned Barthian standpoint what we should say is that all worship, Christian or non-Christian, contains both elements of revelation and religion. Both, in other words, are the result of God's self-revelation on one hand, and sheer 'human manufacture' on the other. This does not mean that we can immediately say that some forms of worship are true and others false, but it does mean that within each religious tradition (Christian, Jewish, Muslim) we have to be alive to what is of God and what is not. I do not pretend that this work of discernment is anything other than profoundly difficult, even within the Christian sphere alone with all its manifold varieties and methods of worship. But however difficult to establish, the distinction seems to me absolutely crucial. Worship is the work of the Holy Spirit and therefore God's self-manifestation and offering, but not everything that constitutes the practice of worship is of God.

If this is true, it follows that Christians can never be in the position of holding that their own form of worship is always God-inspired whereas the worship of non-Christians is not. Rather we need to be aware of how each and every religious tradition may contain genuine revelation of God as well as sinful human manufacture. All religion, as Barth would have it, is under the judgement of God, and therefore

> it is our business as Christians to apply this judgement first and most accurately to ourselves: and to others, the non-Christians, only in so far as we recognize ourselves in them, i.e. only as we see in them the truth of this judgement of revelation which concerns us, in the solidarity, therefore, in which, anticipating them in both repentance and hope, we accept this judgement to participate in the promise of revelation.[11]

The third objection is that my thesis devalues evangelism. If non-Christians also worship the one true God and if even non-Christians may be responding in their own way to the divine self-manifestation, what can be the point of evangelism?

I take it that the point of Christian evangelism is to share with others the divine truth that has possessed us in Jesus Christ. But it is vital to see that the truth which possesses us is not our possession. Early Christological reflection speaks of how believers are 'in Christ' or 'of Christ'. They do so in order to convey the proper sense of how Christ made himself known to us and claims us as individuals. But these concepts should not be pressed into a language of possession as though what God has given us is ours, and only ours, and that others can share it only on our terms. The point is elementary but needs to be constantly before us, and for this reason especially: the work of witnessing to and sharing the good news of Jesus Christ is pre-eminently the work of the Holy Spirit. Although all Christians have some obligation to share with others what their experience of the new life of Christ may be, it is vital, even and especially here, that Christians do not conceive of witness to Christ as exclusively or even primarily as their own human activity. Sometimes we may gain the impression that evangelism is simply the means whereby the Church itself tries to gain more adherents. This may or may not be a worthy intention, but it can never be theologically what we mean by evangelism. Sharing the good news can never just be about filling the pews. It is rather about how God makes his or her truth known in the world, and if we are to have the temerity to claim or proclaim anything at all in God's name we do well to ask ourselves whether it is not we who are part of the problem rather than part of the solution.

We conclude by stressing, in Barthian like terms, the reality of divine freedom. The Open Letter holds that gatherings for interfaith worship 'imply that salvation is offered by God not only through Jesus Christ but by other means, and thus deny his uniqueness and finality as the only Saviour'. I think that the precise reverse may be the case. If we are to be true to Christian convictions, our belief in the uniqueness and finality of Christ requires the fullest possible sharing and communion with other religious traditions. We shall recognize that not all in their traditions is good, honourable and true – as we shall be the first to say this of our own. But we shall be unafraid to stand together before God and worship him or her, not through any proper or exaggerated sense of interfaith togetherness – but because the risen Christ himself will be in our midst.

5 EVANGELIZATION AND OTHER FAITHS: the Motivation for Mission
Michael Barnes

I want to try to bring together two themes: the Decade of Evangelism and the topic of our course – the Ignatian anniversaries. I would like us to think about one of the most important aspects of the mission of the contemporary Church: the interfaith encounter. Jesuits have always been great missionaries, great evangelizers, responsible for much of the great post-Reformation Roman Catholic revival, not only in Europe but throughout the world. Ignatius himself hardly moved outside Rome after the foundation of the Society in 1540, 'but his companions went to the ends of the earth. We remember particularly the extraordinary voyages, the incredible energy of Francis Xavier, the greatest of all missionaries. We think of men like Matteo Ricci in China and Roberto de Nobili in India whose efforts to adapt the gospel message to different cultures are almost legendary. And today we are aware of Jesuits in every part of the world, serving the Church, preaching the gospel, teaching in schools, working with refugees, at the forefront of the struggle for justice in many Third World countries – some of them, as recently in El Salvador, paying the ultimate price for their beliefs. Why do these men do what they do and what can we learn from them for this Decade of Evangelism?

I shall not spend much time on definitions.[1] I want, rather, to begin with the perhaps rather obvious point that mission defines the Church, not the other way round. The Church is not a gathering of people who *then* decide to 'do' something. Basically the Church is that community empowered to share the Good News of the Resurrection of Jesus Christ. The Church is missionary first and foremost – which is not to say that Christians do not have to listen for the Word, that they do not have to be evangelized themselves. They may have been awakened by the experience of God's love but they still need to go on learning about how that Good News is *already* present in the world.

The Good News begins with the Incarnation of Christ. But it is the coming of the Holy Spirit on the first disciples, which establishes the Church as a people whose very identity is to be missionary: people with a special experience and a message to share. The Church's mission is to evangelize in the broadest sense: to bring the values of the gospel to bear on the reality of contemporary society. The form which that mission takes depends on particular circumstances but, more importantly – and this is the point I want to dwell on – it will also depend on how Christians interpret the key experiences which form the Church: their source of motivation.

More particularly, however, it will also depend on how they value the way in which that motivation is recognized and made explicit in actual lives and actual situations. It is spirituality, the forms of prayer and religious practice, which shape attitudes to the world and to others. Here there is a great richness. Even within the Roman Catholic Church there are different spiritualities. A Benedictine monk, for example, whose life is very much dominated by a regular rhythm of daily prayer, will have a particularly contemplative mode of showing forth what he believes. The Benedictine tradition emphasizes study, teaching and hospitality, and has been particularly influential in the development of many aspects of Catholic tradition, liturgy and spirituality.

The Ignatian tradition is also contemplative, but, because it does not emphasize the recitation of office in choir, it has a very different way of mission. In a short space it is impossible to do more than illustrate my point with a couple of examples; these, I hope, will show that Ignatian spirituality has developed the Christian motivation for mission in a particular way – enhancing the vision of the Incarnation, of how God makes himself present to the world. In so many cases, Jesuit missionary endeavours have been characterized by an extraordinary broadness of spirit. With these examples in mind we may get some idea of how today's missionary Church, living and working in a pluralist society, needs to regard its own mission towards people of other faiths.

Everybody today is familiar with David Puttnam's film *The Mission*, about the famous Paraguayan reductions which eventually brought the Society of Jesus into a destructive clash with the colonial powers of Europe. But perhaps the most instructive example of Jesuit missionary endeavour is in China, not in South America. It's one of the great 'if onlys' of missionary history: if Matteo Ricci, Adam Schall, Ferdinand Verbiest and others had received support from Rome the history of the Church in China might have been very different. At the beginning of the seventeenth century Jesuits from all the countries of Europe were spread around the world. Ricci was a mathematician and an astronomer: it was his interest in these subjects which gained him a favourable hearing at the Emperor's court in Peking. Schall and Verbiest followed him and were appointed to the Chinese civil service to use their mathematical skills in the calculation of the imperial calendar. Ricci was also a scholar of Confucianism and strove to reconcile the traditional teaching of the native Chinese social philosophy,

Confucianism, with Christianity. Understood correctly, he argued that the early Chinese believed in a universal God and that their rites of 'ancestor worship' were merely a formal token of respect paid to the past. Converts were allowed to continue to participate in these rites.

The missionaries ran into controversy and opposition at regular intervals. What the Jesuits regarded as a legitimate adaptation to the religiosity and customs of local people, others saw as pandering to superstition, little short of pure idolatry. Eventually, after a long and at times unedifying debate, Rome came down against the rites. The Jesuits appealed to the Chinese Emperor himself who agreed that the nature of the rites was purely civil and not religious. A papal legate was despatched to deal with the matter but got holed up in Macao. The Chinese took grave exception to the implicit insult to their time-honoured institutions; the Portuguese, anxious not to jeopardize the position of their Chinese colonies, tried to deter the Pope. To no avail; in a strongly-worded decree of 1715 the rites were condemned. The Emperor wrote in reply:

> After reading the decree I can only say that the Europeans are small-minded people. How can they talk of China's moral principles when they know nothing of Chinese customs, books or language? Much of what they say and discuss makes one laugh. Today I saw the papal legate and decree. He is really like an ignorant Buddhist or Taoist priest, while the superstitions mentioned are those of unimportant religions. This sort of wild talk could not be more extreme. Hereafter Europeans are not to preach in China. It must be prohibited in order to avoid trouble.

That response says it all – what happens when people refuse to dialogue with a sophisticated culture. The story does not end there, of course. Jesuits remained in highly influential positions at the imperial court in Peking right up until the suppression of the Society in 1773, by which time the number of native Christians is estimated at 300,000. But I do not want to dwell on the past and what might have been. The aim was definitely to make converts for Christ but what of the strategy, the theology of mission, more particularly: the motivation for preaching the gospel? Let me take up these questions with another, and much less well-known, example of Jesuit missionary endeavour.

Recently I have been reading an account of the first Jesuits to Tibet.[2] They were part of the mission to India and travelled over the Himalayas to Lhasa in the early seventeenth century. The terrain proved to be too difficult and that first mission was unsuccessful. About a hundred years later another Jesuit, Ippolito Desideri, went back. He left behind him an account of his journey, giving an immense amount of careful detail about the state of the country, the customs of people, and his encounters with lamas, monks and rulers. In many ways what emerges from his journal is typical of the missionary theology of the time; he very rarely speaks personally of his feelings or even his motives. He does, however, refer to the king being impressed by their 'disinterested zeal and devotion'. He says that his only concern was to 'disseminate Truth and the Gospel of salvation solely for their good, as all I longed for was their eternal happiness, for which I was willing to expend all my strength'.

At another point he talks about a book which he is writing 'in the Tibetan language' which he hopes to present to the king at a public audience.

> When the King and the Minister heard that I was preparing this work, [writes Desideri] they were impatient for it to be finished. Indeed, constantly, until their tragic death, they seemed unable to talk of anything but different points of religion. Moved by Divine Grace, far more powerful than any words of mine, they inquired over and over again whether there was any difference between our Holy Faith and their Sect or Religion. Partly not to diverge in any way from Truth, and partly not to discourage them, I explained that in every religion there were two principal facts, firstly, principles, maxims, or dogmas, to be believed, and secondly, precepts, counsels, or instructions as to what to do or not to do. As regards the first, our religion and theirs were absolutely different but in the second the difference was very slight. This explanation consoled and encouraged them greatly, and they showed in many ways that Divine Grace was gradually animating and inciting them.[3]

One could quote more extensively but that must suffice. Even in this short extract we find two references to the work of Divine Grace among the Tibetans; there is no question of these people being totally estranged from God. Secondly, we should take note of two principles of missionary practice: being faithful to the gospel and deliberately encouraging, that is to say, building bridges. It is this tension between faithfulness or integrity and openness which is the key: the firm conviction that God is at work within the Church, based on Desideri's own experience of God's grace, coupled with a recognition of the *possibility* of God's work outside the Church.

In other words, Desideri can see in the Tibetans something of that experience of Divine Grace which he knows all too well in himself. If God has shown such generosity to him then surely that God must also be ready to be generous elsewhere, to others. How come that Desideri thinks in this way?

One of the things that many of these early missionaries show us is that there are many ways of witnessing to the love of God; in fact, there can be no end to the number of ways in which the Church seeks to share its joy in the Risen Lord. The disciples at Pentecost, for example, find to their astonishment that they are communicating the truth of the Resurrection; the metaphor of the many languages reverses the confusion of Babel and speaks eloquently of the world-wide mission of the Church to proclaim the Good News. But note what the apostles are really doing: they are proclaiming their own experience of becoming alive through the Risen Lord. This is the experience of the Church: a community of people which finds itself overwhelmed by an experience of the love of God which cannot be confined; it has to be shared with others – somehow.

Ignatian spirituality is a particularly effective way of focusing on this mystery of the love of God made manifest in Christ. The members of the Society of Jesus are first and foremost companions of Jesus, co-workers with him. Nowadays this experience is shared by all those people, lay and religious – and by no means just Jesuit – who have been through the experience of the Spiritual Exercises, Ignatius of Loyola's little handbook of Christian formation.[4] One of the most important of Ignatius's mystical experiences occurred at a little place called La Storta, outside Rome. There he had this vision, as he recalled, 'that God the Father placed him with Christ his Son, that he would not dare to doubt that the Father had placed him with his Son'.[5] Some years ago I had the opportunity of visiting the little chapel on the Via Cassia; it really is *on* the Via Cassia – noisy, grotty and rather undistinguished. Somehow I could not but feel that this spoke eloquently about the way in which God is present in our world: at the heart of all our messy humanness. It is there that Christians encounter God and hear the call to be 'companions'.

Ignatius's Spiritual Exercises are the formal expression of his experience of God and what he consistently taught. They are often regarded as spiritual asceticism, deliberately building up people's enthusiasm for the mission, making them full of zeal. No doubt there is something in that: Ignatius is full of ideas on how to help people to make generous life-decisions. But there is another side to it. This is the recognition that before we work God is at work; without letting God work at the heart of our world of sin and selfishness our efforts are in vain. In other words it is important not just to build the motivation to work (that is comparatively easy, especially where you have a good teacher who can fire your enthusiasm) but to get the motivation right. Christians, even the most generous-hearted Christians, have to learn to *see* things correctly.

In the Exercises there are many different forms of prayer and many different meditations, a number of which are crucial to a proper understanding of the dynamic of the four-week pattern. At the end of the first week the exercitant is filled with a sense not so much of sin but of the goodness, the forgiving mercy, of God.[6] At the beginning of the second week he or she is ready to follow, but it is important that a generous response be developed in the right way, that the effects of sin are overcome. In this process two meditations are crucially important. The first is entitled the 'Call of the King'. Just as a temporal king, much loved and respected, asks his followers to endure all sorts of hardships in order that they might enjoy the fruits of victory, so Jesus invites his followers to follow him in pain that they may share in his glory. If the former, the temporal king, excites the Christian's admiration and willingness to become a companion, how much more so the latter, the King eternal?

It is important to note, however, that no attempt is made to elicit a definite response. The exercitant is asked to make a prayer which asks to make the suffering Christ the normative model – '*if*', as the text puts it, 'thy most Holy Majesty wants to choose and receive me to such life and state'.[7]

The 'if' is important. There is no attempt to force a particular response; what is asked for is openness to the possibility that God is calling and a willingness to respond when the time is right. The real commitment comes with a second key meditation, on 'Two Standards', that of Christ and that of the devil. It is not a picture of two enemies locked in battle: a sort of Christian *Bhagavad Gita*. Rather, it is something of a repetition of what has gone before. Only this time the exercitant is to consider the way in which the two leaders work: one is open and honest, the other devious and deceitful. The prayer is to 'ask for knowledge of the deceits of the bad chief and help to guard myself against them, and for knowledge of the true life which the supreme and true Captain shows and grace to imitate him'.[8] Desire for riches is contrasted with desire for poverty; the vice of pride is set against the virtue of humility. Why? The exercitant knows now from experience, brought home forcefully in the first week, how much he or she is prone to such vices. In the second week, the call of Christ proposes a remedy. With the meditations on the example of Christ, it becomes clear that the only way to be really sure of avoiding all the subtle ways in which evil works is to ask to follow Christ generously. This, however, is not something which the exercitant can do; too often the dark side of human nature perverts God's work. Selfish and petty prejudices all too often make people *think* they are doing God's work, when in reality they are working for themselves. How can they be sure that they are doing *God's* work? Only when they go deliberately against *all* human desires by asking God to 'place us with his son'.

This idea is not, of course, Ignatius's, though it was his genius to incorporate it in a systematic way into his Exercises. It is at the heart of the gospel. Take the example of Peter. He thinks he knows it all; he remonstrates with Jesus at Caesarea Philippi when Jesus tells the disciples that he will enter into his glory only through suffering (Mark 8:27ff.). And he learns true humility and self-knowledge the hard way – by first claiming he would follow Jesus to the end and then denying him three times.

Returning to the Jesuit missionaries, we find – quite simply – that for them evangelizing is God's work. Really to understand the gospel, in other words to become 'evangelized', is to understand with humility what God has done in them – and can do in others. In other words, it is to realize that God is at work in the world not *because* of what his disciples are doing but *in spite of* them. God is alive and active in the world; this conviction is what leads to the Ignatian contemplative ideal – that of finding God in all things. This is what Ignatius says to the novices in his Constitutions: 'they should often be exhorted to seek God our Lord in all things, stripping off from themselves the love of creatures to the extent that this is possible, in order to turn their love upon the Creator of them, by loving him in all creatures and all of them in him, in conformity with his holy and divine will.'[9]

That is the ideal which is consolidated throughout the Exercises: to see the creator in the creatures. Gradually a vision is developed which recognizes that all things are created by God and are re-created by God, in Christ. What is the part of the companion in all this? It is not a sort of contemplation of the eternal mystery of evolution or emanation and return into the Absolute, but, rather, an attitude of wonder, praise and thanks for all that God does. This is summed up in the final meditation of the whole process – the 'Contemplation to Attain Love'. This begins with the realization that all we have and are comes from God; it is pure gift. When Christians talk about the love of God they are not, as St John puts it, speaking of their love for God, what *they do*, but God's love for them, something which they receive; to love God is to return something which is already there, something already received. The exercitant is asked to

> bring to memory the benefits received, of Creation, Redemption and particular gifts... to look how God dwells in creatures... to consider how God labours and works for me in all things created on the face of the earth... to look how all the good things and gifts descend from above, as my poor power from the supreme and infinite power from above.[10]

This is a wonderfully contemplative vision of God inspiring the whole of the created order, yet inviting the one who contemplates to take an active and responsible part in making that vision known.

But how to become properly contemplative and to lose all those subtle little ways in which human beings subvert God's purposes and fail to follow the way of the Divine King but are deceived by the wiles of the devil? That too is God's action; Ignatius's conviction is that God will act because he is the creator. Indeed, God has to act if the Christian companion is to get the mission right; to think that the work of mission is a human work is to fail to understand that it is, first and foremost, a work of co-operation in which the Christian looks to build on what God is already doing. He or she is motivated to be a companion of Christ through developing the broadest vision of the way in which God makes himself present in the world. That vision begins with God and with God's witness to God: a God who is always seeking to reveal himself to humankind. The Christian is one who recognizes and rejoices in the signs of that revelation and takes responsibility for co-operating with the Spirit in making that revelation more and more explicit.

This perspective on mission and evangelization arises from the vision of God already and always at work. The particular form of missionary encounter with which I started – the dialogue with other faiths (but the same applies to all forms of dialogue) – is based on an attitude of speaking and listening, witness and humble waiting on the word of the other, for the other may also be the Other, the voice of the Spirit. Both are necessary aspects of the response to the call of Christ the King: following yet noting all the time the way in which human beings can unconsciously and thoughtlessly let their selfishness or weakness or ignorance, even their best intentions, get in the way.

To return, then, to ourselves and our question about the motivation for evangelization: once this idea has been grasped – that God may already be there before we respond to the call of the King – our attitude to the other will be one of respect and a healthy reticence. True evangelization begins with ourselves, that is to say with our joy in the Risen Lord, and continues with a real humility – for we may well be treading on holy ground.

6 CHRIST AND THE SCANDAL OF PARTICULARITIES
Alan Race

The 'scandal of particularity' is a theme running through both ancient and modern Christianity. As an evocation of the absolute uniqueness of Christ, it has functioned as a rallying cry to the Christian faithful, fundamentally safeguarding their identity on theological and political fronts. Theologically, it has protected the *sui generis* nature of Jesus Christ as a saviour figure on the stage of world religious history. Politically, it has provided ideological-divine sanction, at one extreme, for Christian separatism (e.g. as in Karl Barth's 'Barmen Declaration' against the rise of Nazism) and, at the other, for exploitation, domination and imperialism (e.g. as in some of the manifestations of the European politico-missionary expansion of the last two centuries). The *scandal* of Christian particularity relates therefore to the sense of *exclusiveness* regarding the truth of its religious claims and the political use that has been made of those claims. Yet no matter how pervasive the evocation to the absolute uniqueness of Christ has been, at least three developments during this century signal the need for its careful scrutiny.

First, new encounters between people of different world faiths are demonstrating how each religious tradition provides a living context for religious aspiration, unswerving faithfulness and vibrant spirituality outside the Christian circle. Growing positive respect for these world faiths is leading some theologians to re-evaluate the concept of the absolute uniqueness of Christ in relation to other perceived revelatory visions of the divine life.

Second, historical and philosophical currents of thought have demonstrated how religious truths are more humanly constructed than we once imaged. Doctrines and patterns of meaning are not inviolable, but have been linked inextricably to the needs, institutions, perceptions and religious assumptions of a society at any one period. Historically, reality as 'a continuous connection of becoming' (Troeltsch), leaves little room for the older view of religious truth which was grounded in a supernatural interventionist account of divine activity. On the philosophical level, religious beliefs now tend to be held less as direct descriptions of the divine life, than as provisional pointers to truth using symbolic and metaphorical forms. Clearly, the doctrine of Christ is not so readily or easily circumscribed under these conditions.

Third, awareness of the ideological function of the absolute uniqueness of Christ in the missionary exploitation of other cultures and religions has rightly attached strong criticism on moral grounds. Now while the religious and political abuse of the uniqueness of Christ does not discredit the concept of Christ's absoluteness as such, there is no necessary connection between the 'scandal of particularity' and the Christian refusal to acquiesce in State power when the latter shows pretentions to divine triumphalism. This was even true of Barth's opposition to Nazism through the Confessing Church. In other words, the act of Christian resistance to State power is not dependent on espousing belief in the Christian 'scandal of particularity'.

If there is an assumption that the 'scandal of particularity' is synonymous with Christian faith, it has become an ambivalent blessing. It might even run the danger of becoming a 'scandal of obscurantism'.

The 'scandal of particularity' was eventually protected in the history of Christian thought by the doctrine of the Incarnation. In the light of new encounters and developing critical consciousness, dare we ask whether this hallowed term also deserves careful scrutiny? Conceptually, the Incarnation is certainly more elusive than is generally imagined, as the variety of its historical linguistic forms could demonstrate. Yet no matter what the form of words has been, the idea of the Incarnation has been taken to furnish Christian faith with a clear criterion for evaluating its relationship to the other world religions. Augustine, for example, could rejoice after many years of religious searching that he had not found elsewhere the unique doctrine that 'the word became flesh'. This was the distinctive message of the Christian faith which separated it from other religious possibilities.

If the concept of the Incarnation both forms the distinctive heart of Christian faith and also provides the central criterion for judging Christianity's relationship to other world religions, then it is small wonder that the christological issue remains central in the debate about the Christian response to today's religiously plural world. What I wish to do here is first to trace some of the internal criticism being made of the doctrine of the Incarnation by Christian theologians, and second to show how christology relates to differing stances within the changing Christian response to the world religions. There is a dialectic between these two endeavours. Modifications within christology allow for a more open approach to the world faiths than has traditionally been assumed; and the growing demand for positive recognition of the world faiths in turn places a strain on inherited assumptions that protect the uniqueness of Christ.

Christology in Internal Christian Debate

The variety of the linguistic forms of the doctrine of the Incarnation is a clue to the complexity of the problem of christology. In its classical Chalcedonian form (451 CE), the difficulty is usually posed as how to combine the divine and the human natures in the one person of Christ. The legacy of that Council has been that it set the parameters for future discussion. But today this specification for christology is too narrow, as a number of factors have arisen to force a shift in perspective. It is worth rehearsing them in order to demonstrate why the critique has proved so far-reaching. While all of the points remain controversial, by presenting them fairly bluntly (for reasons of brevity) I hope to sharpen up the issues as I see them.

First, the philosophical assumptions and categories of antiquity are no longer current coin, and cannot be reinstated. What it means to speak now of 'person', 'nature', 'substance', and so on, is entirely different from the technical thought-patterns of the patristic era. Not many theologians therefore are prepared simply to repeat these early centuries. But more is at stake than this linguistic difficulty: the story of the Chalcedonian definition involves intellectual assumptions and political manoeuvres which disclose its full historical character. The hermeneutical use of scripture, philosophico-theological assumptions about cosmology and divine activity, and the role of political will are just three extensive elements in a story that with hindsight it is impossible to endorse as a way of believing today. Historical change has fractured any easy continuity with the ancient formulae: Chalcedon's putative achievement strikes us not so much as a mystery to be adored, but, outside of its own historical setting, as a puzzling *coup de théâtre*, dazzling yet incapable of conveying any real theological meaning. As it is, no satisfactory coherent interpretation of the 'Chalcedon problem' has been forthcoming, and suspicion that it was inherently incapable of acknowledging the real humanity of Jesus is well-founded. The later Second Council of Constantinople (553 CE), for example, stated that the 'personhood' of Jesus was exclusively divine in origin. And Christian history supplies abundant evidence of a kind of quiet or implicit Docetism running through the church's christology since those early councils.

Second, the revolution in New Testament study with the critical historical method has brought about a fundamental shift in the manner by which we are able to approach the earliest interpretations of the figure of Jesus. Basically, the New Testament horizon was one of eschatology, not ontology or incarnation. The writers are thoroughly theocentric, in that they view Jesus as the one from God, who fulfils the promises of God after the pattern of preparation-fulfilment through Israel's history. Even the sporadic elements of incarnational language, found particularly in Paul and John (e.g Col. 1:15–20; Phil. 2:6–11; John 1:1–18), require to be interpreted in the context of each writer as a whole, and it cannot be assumed that these texts necessarily indicate what later orthodoxy took them to be. Even John's Gospel is far from clear about whether Jesus is seen as God's agent or simply as God. Besides, incarnational imagery is one thing: incarnational doctrine another. The fact that the Fathers found John's Gospel a rich resource for incarnational belief should not over-influence us now: anachronism in the reading of biblical texts comes too easily in theology. To be sure, incarnational doctrine may represent a reasonable evolutionary development from the eschatological biblical basis; but it would need some crafty hermeneutics to demonstrate this. Moreover, the Fathers cannot be blamed for treating the biblical text the way they did, for they did not have present-day critical tools available to them.

Third, New Testament study has demonstrated the diversity of the first reaction to the person of Jesus. The titles used of him – Son of God, Son of Man, Messiah, Word, Wisdom etc. – spring from experience and commitment, by whatever route it came to them, and not from some wooden arrangements in the purposes of God. That is to say, the titles are not free-floating, carrying the same fixed meaning wherever they are applied. Each writer interprets Jesus according to his own community response, background circumstances and available theological apparatus for 'receiving' him, with all the richness and limitations that imposes. Jesus is transformative of a writer's whole outlook – whether as Mark's enigmatic and disturbing Son of Man, or Matthew's bearer of the new messianic way, or as Paul's 'Son of God whose death and resurrection ushered in the new era of eschatological hope, and so on – such that the interpretation could not avoid subjectivity. Diversity indicates vitality. One implication of this development is that we ought not to award higher marks to some writers over others. For example, John's 'logos' christology need receive no higher appreciation than Mark's 'Son of Man' view. They are different, simply that, and historical and literary criticism can give us a reasonable estimate why it turned out so. Constructively speaking, recognizing this early creativity can spur us on to find our own estimate of Jesus appropriate for our own missionary circumstances. As we do so, of course, we will take full cognisance of the New Testament process itself, as a critical partner in the endeavour.

Fourth, it is possible to acknowledge candidly the myth-making tendencies of early Christian doctrine, beginning in the New Testament itself and stretching out from there through the metaphysical assumptions of the first centuries. What seems to have occurred at the earliest period is what has been called a 'Christian mutation' of the Jewish approach to God.[1] In the Jewish background there was a role for divine agency which was of broadly three types: divine attributes and powers (e.g. Wisdom, Logos), exalted patriarchs (e.g. Moses, Enoch), and principal angels. Given this background, the Christian devotion to Jesus led implicitly to the assertion of his pre-existence, which itself later became part of a religious story of 'God the Son' coming to earth or of a metaphysical theory of two natures in one person. But what we are to make of this myth-making capacity today remains deeply problematic. The following judgement, by the English Anglican theologian John Robinson, captures the heart of what is being affirmed: 'To register the conviction that in this man was fulfilled and embodied the meaning of God reaching back to the very beginning, they proclaim him as his Word, his Image, his Son, from all eternity.'[2]

Jesus conveyed the power and presence of God through the impact of his whole personality; in his sense he embodied the love of God through the impact of his whole personality; in this sense he embodied the love of God for the world. Put empirically: the creative impact of Jesus initiated a new style of relationship to God, one with its own particular parameters of divine offer and human response. Eschewing pre-existence in this manner has at least the advantage of acknowledging the full humanity of Jesus.

Fifth, the doctrine of the Incarnation has acted as a theological mould for the concept of the 'finality' of Jesus outside of the latter's original Jewish framework. But under the influence of critical historical thinking it is precisely the validity of this concept of 'finality' which has come under serious questioning. As this was attached to Jesus, 'finality' has its roots in the Jewish apocalyptic view of history with its expectation of a messianic figure at the end of days. Critical thinking, while not being dogmatic about history as a closed or open system, is none the less more likely to view history as an interwoven process of cause and effect, with little room for the notion of a 'final' age and therefore of a 'final' saviour figure. As it is, looking to 'the end' is reminiscent of mythological thinking. Even Christianity's retention of the theme of the 'now and the not yet' of the coming Kingdom, given the failure of that kingdom as Jesus preached it to arrive, remains basically untouched by changing perceptions in historical thinking. But if Jesus is no longer 'final' in the strict sense, this need not imply that what he stands for is not decisive in some way. Distinguishing between the creative impact of Jesus on the one hand, and the interpretation of him in terms of 'finality' on the other, opens the way for new interpretations of that impact in the changed climate of a different historical consciousness and positive religious pluralism. It is worth noting, moreover, that even a writer such as Jurgen Moltmann, who leaves metaphysical speculation on one side in favour of a return to biblical categories in christology, fails to follow through the critical method at this point.[3] What it means to talk of christology in *messianic* dimensions outside of the New Testament's own assumptions about the nature of messianic expectation remains puzzling.

Sixth, christology is parasitic on the experience of 'salvation' or 'liberation'. Incarnation was intimately linked with views about 'salvation' which strike us today as deficient. In particular they depended on a literal interpretation of the story of the 'Fall' of Adam and Eve as the first historical couple. Remove that background, and the necessity for Jesus to be the God–Man reversing the 'Fall' is undermined. What exactly we might mean by 'salvation' varies in Christian experience and theology, but it is likely to have both individual and corporate, this-worldly and after-worldly references. In other words, christology now begins with questions of human need under God, asks first how the impact of Jesus meets those needs, and second how his – and therefore ours – relationship to God is to be envisaged as a result. In these circumstances many theologians have turned the christological question of the Fathers – 'How can God become man?' upside down. In a historically and humanly conscious world we no longer have 'christology from above', but 'christology from below': 'What does it mean to speak of the human Jesus as also divine?' Value is placed on Jesus's connection with humanity, not on his difference.

These six points could each be expanded at greater length. Yet I believe they reflect a fair account of what is taking place within christological debate, certainly within a European context. Inevitably I have reflected my Anglo-Saxon bias! Taken together, however, they amount to a substantial dent on received tradition; and they pave the way for a shift in the work of the Christian theology of religions. I wish now to point out some of the issues within those shifts, before drawing an interim conclusion.

Christology in the Christian Theology of Religions

The concept of the Incarnation has had an ambivalent history in relation to other world faiths. While its undoubted implication is that God intends all to follow Christ as the absolute saviour, and therefore that the Christian Way represents the finally true Way, this has been expressed either as a confrontation with the other faiths or as the fulfilment of the evidence of divine life within them. Neither view takes the above critique of christology with the full seriousness it deserves. But we need to examine the effects of the doctrine in both cases, and in the light of a changed context and new encounters. As we do so, we shall discover that the work the Incarnation has been required to do cannot meet the new circumstances. The new encounters and the new context place a different additional kind of strain on the merits of incarnation doctrine.

Let the early Karl Barth be representative of the confrontational view: 'It is because we remember and apply the christological doctrine of the *assumptio carnis* that we speak of revelation as the abolition of religion.'[4] Barth was here taking religion to mean the humanly misguided attempt by sinful creatures to reach God through unaided effort. He was not initially speaking of other faiths as such, but of the abject failure of human beings to rely on the initiative of God's grace. In the background was the liberal outlook of his former teachers who, it seemed to him, had lost hold of the sovereign transcendence of God and had turned to the human sciences for faith's intellectual and religious justification. Nevertheless, he followed through his position when he said of Christianity that the reality of grace known in the Christian story 'differentiates our religion, the Christian, from all others as the true religion'.[5] The strong distinction between 'revelation' and 'religion', the former indicative of grace and the latter of human grasping, enabled Barth to drive a wedge between Christianity and the other faiths, and to promote Christ as the absolute saviour of all. In relation to the doctrine of the Incarnation, which encapsulated this absoluteness, the Kierkegaardian fascination with paradox was not far from the surface.

As has often been pointed out, there is majesty in Barth's relentless resolution to 'let God be God'. There is also an invulnerability, which is less convincing. The crux issue is not the legitimacy or otherwise of paradox in theology, but to what extent theologians are prepared to allow their constructions to be open to criticism. Barth allowed a limited role for criticism, secondary to biblical assumptions, but a generation later we have come to see the difficulties in sustaining that limitation. Once we have grasped the role that the human imagination plays in theological endeavour it is difficult to set boundaries to the effects of criticism. This means that the strong distinction between 'revelation' and 'religion' was really an attempt to circumnavigate the human element in interpreting Christian faith.

In so far as the Incarnation was intrinsically bound up with this whole scheme, that doctrine too was held to be inviolate. Yet the encounter between Christianity and other faiths shows this inviolability to be simply a hidden form of *arbitrariness*. In other words, the truth of Christ's exclusive uniqueness is so because the Christian theologian says it is so: it requires no grounds other than the decision to claim it so! Some might complain at this point that I have forgotten that Christianity is its own self-evident truth. My response to that rejoinder is to say that there is a distinction between authentic religious truth discovered by living and believing it, and sheer prejudice for the absoluteness of this truth in relation to other religious paths. The gospel's character as *sola fide* need not be jeopardized by recognizing divine truth outside the Church. The distinction between 'revelation' and 'religion' can run just as easily *through all* faiths as between Christian faith and the rest.

The *arbitrariness* of Barth's confrontational exclusivism is further highlighted by his inability to allow that the theme of grace known elsewhere, for example in some strands of oriental religion, could modify his *a priori* approach. So the Pure Land of School of Amida Buddhism speaks of putting trust in the saving love of Amida, thus echoing the structure of faith remarkably similar to the Reformation Christianity Barth espoused. Barth's response, that 'only in Christ' is salvation forthcoming, further compounds the *arbitrariness* of this view. Again, the Incarnation is unable to sustain what is being asked of it.

If Barth narrowed the Incarnation in an exclusive direction the alternative possibility within the tradition has pursued its universalist trajectory. This is the view that the uniqueness of Christ does not entail a negative judgement on other faiths, but is a fulfilment, gathering up clues, hints, pointers and responses to the presence of God discerned within them. Expounding the 'logos' language of John's Gospel, the Roman Catholic Federation of Asian Bishops' Conferences, in their seven theses of interreligious dialogue from 1987, expressed this view thus:

> In presenting Christ as the 'Word' mediating the mysterious reality of God's presence to the word, John is implicitly admitting the presence of God's self-revelation in other religious traditions. The fact that John presents the Christ-event as an experience which is not reduced to the compass of his individual and ecclesial experience but which transcends any particular form of expression and can be identified in the universe at large, shows that the Johannine Church was prepared to enter into dialogue with the surrounding religious traditions.[6]

Whether in reality John's community was so open to dialogue as this interpretation believes we cannot tell; there are other features of that gospel which suggest otherwise. But the theological point is clear enough: the Incarnation means that God is so committed to the world that we should not deduce from it that God's presence is precluded from being known elsewhere in the world. Yet it would be wrong to conclude from this that God's universal presence is such that all responses in faith to it are the same or equal in quality. Christ remains the crowning glory.

If Barth's confrontational scheme highlighted the *arbitrariness* of the Incarnation, this second fulfilment strategy brings out the *ambiguity* of the Incarnation in relation to other faiths. This ambiguity refers to the double sense of the relationship that the Incarnation sets up in relation to other faiths – with one hand the Incarnation speaks of the solidarity of Christ with other human beings, and therefore other saviours; yet with the other hand it continues to affirm Christ's absolute uniqueness. It is therefore likely to be less helpful than many Christian groups assume. Whether Christian fulfilment is mediated dogmatically ('from above') or historically ('from below'), the ambiguity, which is manifest differently in either mediation, is worth further reflection in order to clarify the point being made.

Karl Rahner's theory of 'anonymous Christianity' stands as an example of mediating the supremacy of Christ 'from above'. Although he accepted the thrust of historical consciousness – so that he viewed the Incarnation as 'the (free, gratuitous, unique) supreme fulfilment of what is meant by "human being"'[7] – he nevertheless, out of loyalty to received tradition, retained belief in the qualitative difference between Jesus and the rest of humanity. 'The truth of a divine humanity would be mythologized,' wrote Rahner, 'if it were simply a datum of every person always and everywhere.'[8] Only with the one man, Jesus, has the eternal Word been identified. The consequence in the theology of religions is that Christ is somehow the origin of 'salvation' anonymously mediated through the world's religiously varied communal life. Thus, what Rahner opened up with one hand, he took away with the other. Positing Christ as the historical goal (fulfilment) of human and religious aspiration creates an ambiguity in christology, for the determining factor at root is really the dogmatic premise that it is Christ who is defined as the original cause of 'salvation'.

The other route of ambiguity, mediating the supremacy of Christ 'from below', can be demonstrated by referring again to the theological work of John Robinson.[9] Here Jesus was accepted not as the exception to the human race, but as its true representative: in Jesus the intended goal of creation comes to fruition. But Jesus is so, not because he was the unique cause of 'salvation' in the whole world, as was the case with Rahner, but because he is 'decisive' as the true representative. Within an overall model of complementarity between the faiths, God's presence in Jesus remains always open to 'completion, clarification, and correction' in dialogue with others. Yet Robinson also went on to confess Jesus as the 'profoundest clue to all the rest', thus retaining hold on his uniqueness at least on the basis of implicit historical comparisons. By way of additional support for his confessional stance, Robinson went even further and claimed that Christian faith had the capacity to deal better with those factors religions have found to be most inimical, and which he named as evil, the impersonal and the feminine. But there is a difficulty in knowing what value to attach to Robinson's suggestions at this point. If such a claim is to be substantiated it will require detailed historical comparisons and unusual hermeneutical skills. Many would think it is not possible to make these claims anyway, for religions are not open to that kind of comparative valuing. Once again, even the method of historical comparison is unable to overcome the yearning for Christian supremacy which is revealed at the heart of inclusivist christology. In the theology of religions the 'dogmatic lag' of the doctrine of Jesus's uniqueness gives way to an unsatisfactory ambiguity.

As a result of this kind of analysis, my contention is this: both the internal shifts within Christian thought about the person of Jesus and the inappropriateness of the belief in final supremacy (expressed either as exclusive-confrontation or inclusive-fulfilment) attached to Jesus in a culture which values religious pluralism positively, point to a profound need for reinterpreting what tradition came to call the 'scandal of particularity'. *The doctrine of the Incarnation cannot bear the weight which Christian thought has put on it, and nowhere is this more highlighted than from within the whole modern debate around the Christian theology of religions.* Therefore the 'scandal' now is the refusal to take the necessary steps in Christian theological reconstruction in the light of changed perceptions. This is not to say that simply because Christians are learning to value the religious experience of their neighbours, therefore Christian thought about Jesus ought to change. It is claiming, however, that the factors of *arbitrariness* and *ambiguity* compound the problematic nature of traditional christology in modern debate, once the relationship between Christianity and other faiths is brought into the open.

Pointing out problems in theology is always easier than constructing solutions. Yet there are some suggestions available. Within a 'pluralist' framework in the Christian theology of religions, basically two broad approaches to the place of Jesus, which are sensitive to the concerns of critical consciousness and religious plurality, have emerged. Both are prepared to use the more relaxed language of the 'centrality' of Jesus as mediating the purposes of God for the world, rather than the specialized language of incarnation which carries so much cultural specificity from the early centuries.

The first view is more metaphysical in tone and accepts Jesus as different 'in degree', not 'in kind', from the rest of humanity and therefore from all other saviour figures. Following a general process-evolutionary-historical outlook, in which creation is seen as the field of the self-expressive activity of God, the intended goal of humanity has come to fruition in Jesus as the climatic moment where God's activity and human response achieved perfect pitch. Incarnational and inspirational language are collapsed into a single form: God as spirit is ever energizing the process of creation from within, ever seeking incarnational embodiment. Thus the divine–human potential is capable of emerging in differing degrees and forms across many cultures and histories. The 'Christ-event' was one paradigm moment in history where the realization of this potential occurred, but it does not preclude other paradigm moments.

The second view is more metaphorical in tone, and speaks of the impact of Jesus using parable, symbol and metaphor. It believes that Jesus is both a metaphor of God's love and care for the world and also a door of human response to the divine mystery. It is not 'mere metaphor', as some commentators might put it, for it recognizes that metaphor bears both instrumental and representational power. The objectivity of its power lies in its ability to evoke the perception that with Jesus a new paradigm account of God's relationship with the world is possible; and its subjectivity honours the fact that it is *our* perception that Jesus's way can be trusted as salvation-bearing. Once again, there are other possibilities, other parables and symbolic occasions which have initiated different patterns of the divine–human relationship throughout the world.

Both accounts here spring from the concern to root christology in the commitment to Jesus as a historical figure through whom we encounter the power and presence of God. The 'salvation' or transformation of human living which he has opened up has come to us in a particular form, stemming from the mixed culture of middle eastern Palestine of the first century CE. Yet Christian faith views him as no less a universal figure than a particular instance of religious response to the divine summons within life. His saviourhood is not so much 'unique', 'final', or 'absolute', as *'intentionally universal'*. That is to say, while Christ is obviously the named saviour figure for Christians, he is not confined to the Christian communities: his significance is *for* the whole world. This acclaim provides Christian faith with a foundation for mission, which in relation to other faiths now assumes a dialogical character.[10]

Viewing Jesus in this manner holds together both the reality of God that stems from discipleship of him and the vocation to witness to him in dialogue, without assuming him to be the 'final' truth of God prior to the dialogue itself. Jesus need not be the 'norm above norms', as other 'norms' also make their own contributions to the dialogical process. The purpose of the dialogue will then be to develop criteria whereby a world ecumenism, which respects differences and yet encourages mutual criticism can be pursued.

Of course the strangeness of this journey leaves it open to being easily misconstrued. Some might think that it amounts to a judgement on Jesus by a prior conception of God other than that found in the Christian tradition. But this is to miss the point. Once disentangled from outmoded perceptions, Jesus as saviour figure for Christians is freed in order to allow his impact to be felt afresh at the important level of religious experience. In this way the wider religious life of human communities is also challenged.

The kind of epistemology required to undergird this new venture in dialogue has yet to be fully realized. Meanwhile, the experience of persisting religious pluralism entails that truth in the religious interpretation of reality can no longer remain a function of one tradition alone. Of necessity it must embrace many traditions, as well as what we know from the natural and human sciences. In this process of 'dialogue for truth', the eschatological nature of truth, itself reflected pluralistically in the world's different religious visions of the divine life, can be a bridge to any epistemological framework that might emerge. Whatever form it takes, it is committed to the belief that the 'particularities' of the world religious traditions are not isolated islands, but territories deeply and necessarily related to one another. The 'scandal of particularity' has been superseded by the 'scandal of particularities'.

Christian theologians have long thought that they were handling stable tradition, but that era has now faded. The alternative reading of Christian history is one marked by change and innovation, according to shifts in cultural and historical sensibilities. Given hindsight, we can see how and why Christian faith has taken various forms at different periods in history. It is therefore open for us to make our own variation at our own time and according to our own partial vision and knowledge. If this is a new venture, the 'scandal of particularities' is bound to show itself as a vulnerable possibility. But for Christians, the life of vulnerability Jesus himself lived and the universalism he achieved can be our guide on the way.

7 DIALOGUE IN AN AGE OF CONFLICT
Michael Nazir-Ali

Dialogue is an aspect of the human condition and, in fact, all human societies presuppose a certain amount of encounter and of dialogue as the basis for their existence; 'as iron sharpeneth iron, so the countenance of man his fellow' as the Bible says (Prov. 27:17). We should not forget that today there are different ways in which communities and people continue to have dialogue with one another. There is, for example, dialogue which is *internal* to a society; how laws should be made, how a society is to be defended against its enemies, what will ensure a society's prosperity. At the same time there is dialogue *between* communities; how to promote trade, for example, or keep the peace or plan together for scientific research.

The Church too is engaged in dialogue on a number of fronts and its dialogue is not limited to that with people of other faiths. For example, the Church is and should be involved in dialogue with the scientific community about religious beliefs and the ever-changing perceptions of science and how the one relates to the other. The Church needs to be in dialogue with the arts and the ways in which perceptions of transcendence are appreciated by artists. A very significant book on this by George Steiner called *Real Presences* shows us the importance of dialogue with those in the arts; Steiner believes that all art raises profound issues regarding transcendence.[1] If this is true, it provides an important basis for dialogue between the Church and the arts. So as we talk about dialogue with people of other faiths, this has to be put in the context of the Church's call to dialogue with the world in its several manifestations.

On what is the Church's dialogue based? It is based first of all on the recognition that men and women everywhere are created in the image of God (Gen. 1:27). It is true that this image has to some extent been affected by human sin, both communal and personal, but nevertheless the image survives, it has not been destroyed and we have dialogue with people who are not Christians because we believe this image is there and that this image has something of God, both in communities and within individuals. Secondly, we recognize that the eternal word, the *logos*, incarnate in Jesus Christ, has illuminated all human beings everywhere, as St John tells us clearly at the beginning of his Gospel (John 1:4, 9). This recognition of the universal illumination of the eternal word was present in some of the early Fathers of the Church, in Justin Martyr and Clement of Alexandria, for example, who believed that some of the greatest achievements of their particular civilization, Stoic and Platonist philosophy, for example, were possible because of the presence of the divine word in them. At the same time, we need to note that Justin and Clement were much more reserved about the presence of the eternal word in certain, contemporary religious expressions of the time.[2] Now the presence and illumination of the divine word in human societies and individuals is obscured by human sin and although we recognize its presence we also recognize the obscuring and distorting effects of human sin. Then thirdly we base our dialogue on the presence and work of God's Holy Spirit in the world and not merely in the Church and once again in the Johannine writings we find teaching about the Holy Spirit as present in the world bringing the world to a knowledge of righteousness and sin and judgement (John 16:8). In the Pauline writings, we find a recognition that the prior work of the Holy Spirit is indeed necessary for conversion itself (1 Cor. 2:14–16; 12:3; 2 Cor. 3:4–4:6; Eph. 1:17–20; 3:14–19).[3] In other words that if the Holy Spirit were not working in the world, not working among men and women everywhere of all cultures, of all kinds, the recognition of the truth of the gospel would not at all be possible. So we base the possibility of dialogue with people of all kinds on these principles which we believe have been derived from the Bible.

More generally, we need urgently, I believe, to recognize that the Bible is a complex collection of documents written in a variety of situations and contexts and cultures and that although there is an underlying unity about the Bible there is also a great variety in the Bible's responses to many matters, including the question of people of other faiths.[4] Let us explore some of these approaches. There is first of all an approach, or a response, that is wholly negative. Let us put within such an approach the ways in which the Israelites treated the Canaanite city states when they arrived in Canaan. (I won't at this time examine whether they arrived by conquest or infiltration; perhaps it was a bit of both.) At any rate when they arrived their commitment to a theocratic egalitarianism made them destroy these city states. Those who are working in the sociology of the Old Testament see the egalitarianism of early Israel as a leading characteristic of this emerging people at the time.[5] Of course the Canaanite city states were very hierarchical and so one can see why Israel responded in this negative way to these city states. Then you have Elijah and the prophets of Baal, once again a negative response. Later after the exile you have the ways in which

Ezra and Nehemiah dealt with people who wanted to co-operate with the returning exiles in the rebuilding of the temple. In both these responses, both negative of course, there was a fear of syncretism, a fear that the pure worship of God would somehow be mingled with beliefs that were not consonant with God's revelation as it had been given to the Jews.

Against these we have to put some positive approaches, responses and events. Take the response to the Canaanite city states, for example. On the one hand there was the rejection of hierarchy, on the other hand there was a gradual assimilation of the religious symbols of the Canaanites. If you read a description of the building of the temple of Solomon this becomes clear, and the temple itself, as replacing the ark of the tabernacle as a focus for Israelite worship, indicated a shift from being desert nomads to being a settled people (1 Kings 7–9). But think also of Melchizedek encountering Abraham. We have to recognize that the story, as it comes to us, has been edited in different ways at different times in the history of Israel. It is not that there has been no reflection on the story, within the development of Israel itself there has been, and yet what we have clearly is a Canaanite priest king, the very thing that the early Israelites were concerned to reject, bringing bread and wine to Abraham the patriarch of all the faithful and Abraham making an offering to Melchizedek! (Gen. 14:18–20) Now who was Melchizedek? There is later reflection on him, as I say, not only in the book of Genesis but in the Psalms, 'thou art a priest forever according to the order of Melchizedek' (Ps. 110:4). It is clear that such an order was not Aaronic. What kind of order of priesthood was Melchizedek's? In the Christian tradition, of course, Melchizedek has been seen as a type of Christ himself and the priesthood of Christ, in the Letter to the Hebrews for example, has been related to the priesthood of Melchizedek (Heb. 7). Well there is a positive encounter with great potential for reflection by the people of God! Then there are others, there is Balaam, for example, and the fact that he was called to prophesy *for* Israel, on behalf of Israel, in the presence of their enemies (Num. 22–24). It is true that Balaam is shown as coming to a rather sticky end later (Num. 31:8), but that cannot detract from the fact that he prophesied in an authentic way for Israel. In more political terms, there is, of course, the figure of Cyrus and the way in which he functioned as a liberator for Israel (Isa. 45:1–6). In the book of the prophet Malachi, in the first chapter, there is that famous passage where the prophet is comparing the offerings of the people of Israel to the offerings of the Gentiles, to the disadvantage as it were to the people of Israel. There is inescapably some reference here to worship, though there may also be reference to ethical behaviour because the usual words used for the wholeness of sacrifice are not used in the passage; rather, words that are more generally used in the Bible for moral behaviour are used.[6]

But perhaps the most significant aspect of the biblical witness that we need to consider is the developing realization in Israel that their God was the God of the whole world, that he was the God of every nation, of every people. Again, responses to this realization vary in the Bible from a felt calling that God's universality needed to be expressed in terms of judgement on certain peoples. I mean this is, by and large, the witness of the books of Joshua and Judges, though not wholly so. This is replaced then by an approach that regards Zion as the centre of devotion to God, to Yaweh, and the other peoples are seen as eventually coming to Zion to make their submission to the God of Israel. The great passages from Micah and Isaiah which we read at Christmas about people streaming to Mount Zion, these belong to such a response. Yes God is the God of the whole world but if people want to respond to his universal lordship they must do so in terms of Israel, the way in which Israel has responded must also be the model for them. Later on this becomes known as the Judaizing tendency. If you want to respond to God's revelation, even in Christ, you must do so in the way the Jews have done so. Of course, we all know that the early Church rejected such an interpretation but it has been a strong element in the tradition and it affects some of our contemporary attitudes in this area.

The third approach has to do with a growing realization that God, if he is the God of the whole world, of every people, must be working in the histories of those people. Now, sometimes that may be seen as judgement but on many occasions it is seen as salvation. Sometimes that salvation is projected on to the future, the great visions in Isaiah, for example, where Egypt and Assyria are seen to be as much, at least potentially, God's people as Israel. It is right to interpret the nineteenth chapter of Isaiah as eschatalogical, to project it into the future, but that is not always the case with other passages. Sometimes God's work among people is about the past so that in Amos Ch. 9 God is shown to have a purpose, not only in the Exodus of the people of Israel from Egypt, but in the histories of the Ethiopians, the Syrians, the Philistines, all the neighbours that Israel had encountered. This is extremely important for our attitude to certain emphases in biblical theology. We are greatly indebted to those who have developed the paradigmatic concept of Salvation History, that is to say that God's revelation is not to be understood primarily as propositions about belief, but that God's revelation is about his activity among his people and in the world. The biblical Salvation History is very largely about God's action,

God's revelation to the people of Israel, that culminates, comes to a climax, in the Incarnation, though not of course to an end. But if this is normative Salvation History, if you like, why is it normative? What is its function? It can be normative only if it leads us to a recognition, to a discernment, of other salvation histories, that is to say, and I believe this to be the teaching of the Bible, that there is a salvation history among every people, every culture. It is not easy of course to discern such a salvation history, it is very problematic, but it is possible for us to discern this salvation history, with whatever difficulty, because of the normative Salvation History that we have of the people of Israel in the Bible.

I have not commented particularly on the attitude of Jesus himself but perhaps one or two remarks are necessary. One is that liberation theologians, as you know, have underlined the importance of what they call the Galilean option, that is to say the importance of the choice of Galilee by Jesus for his earthly ministry. Their point is that Galilee was chosen. It was not an accident that Galilee came to be the focus for his earthly ministry, this was a deliberate choice because Galilee was all that the religious and political and economic establishment was not. Jesus deliberately chose to be among people who were not powerful, who were not wealthy and who were not learned.[7] But from our point of view Galilee is important because Galilee is Galilee of the nations and it is possible to read this choice as a choice for pluralism. You will know that Galilee was among the first of the parts of the northern kingdom to be conquered by the Assyrians, depopulated through exile of its original inhabitants and repopulated by people from different parts of the Assyrian empire.[8] So by the time of Jesus it had a very mixed population, people of very different beliefs, and some of the encounters in the gospel are about that of course: 'Many will come from east and west and sit at table with Abraham and Isaac and Jacob' (Matt. 8:11). The Galilean option is an option then for pluralism against the orthodoxy of Jerusalem. Secondly, it is also where the risen Christ is present, ahead of his disciples. In the resurrection narrative in Matthew, the disciples are told to go to Galilee where Christ will meet them. It is possible to read this in two different ways. It is possible to say that what the risen Christ is saying is that he will *lead* the disciples into Galilee, that is to say, he will go ahead of them. The other is to read it in such a way as to say that he is *present* in Galilee ahead of them, before they get there. However you read it, the point is that when we approach people of other cultures, other communities, other language groups, we can be sure that Christ is ahead of us. Very often the unspoken, implicit assumption in a lot of mission work is that of taking Christ to people and that expression is used sometimes. Now I know what people are saying and it is not wholly incorrect to speak like that but we have to be on our guard lest we become, or think that we are, more than in fact we are. Christ is already ahead of us in Galilee. What then is dialogue in the rest of the New Testament and in the early history of the Christian Church? The words that are used in the New Testament, *dialegomai* and *dialogizomai*, both mean something like an argument for the sake of persuasion. This is the way in which the word is used in relation to the activity of the apostle Paul in the Acts of the Apostles (Acts 17:2; 18:4 etc.). This is also the sense in which the word is used in Justin, for example, in his dialogue with Trypho the Jew. A dialogue conducted so that the interlocutor may be convinced of the truth of the gospel. Indeed, we find this meaning still in use at the later end of the patristic period, by John of Damascus. Now John of Damascus is a very interesting figure because he came from a family which had opened the doors of Damascus to the Muslim armies. A Christian family, they had opened the doors of Damascus to the Muslims to get away from the oppression of Christian Byzantium. I think this is, if anything, a matter for profound repentance for Christians. Not only did he come from such a family, but for a while he held very important office under the Ummayad Caliphs. Apart from his great theological work which is the basis for a great deal of the theological method that we still use, he wrote two dialogues, or accounts of dialogues, with Muslims.[9] Now again the word as it is used by John means arguing with somebody, conversing with somebody, with a view to persuading them of the truth of the Gospel. This sense, this meaning of the word dialogue comes right down to modern times in the way in which Hume uses the word, for example, Hume's *Dialogues Concerning Natural Religion* are about convincing people of certain things that Hume believed to be true.[10] Nevertheless, in the patristic and perhaps the New Testament sense of the word, there is in the background something about the *dialectical method* that was used by the ancients a great deal to arrive at truth. Think of Plato's accounts of the dialogues of Socrates; conversations which result in a perception of truth that dogmatic teaching does not. The question-and-answer method results in genuine discovery of something new. Now this is very important of course for dialogue as it is today. While Christians will of course want to present truth as they see it revealed in Jesus Christ and in the Gospels, there is always a sense in which dialogue with people produces a new kind of appreciation of some aspect of truth, even Christian truth. For me, and this is a personal testimony if you like, my dialogue with Muslims over the years has resulted in a fresh appreciation of the doctrine of the unity of God which in some cases is seriously compromised by certain kinds of Christian trinitarian theology. It is very interesting to me to see how the western Christian theological tradition which in the past used to emphasize the unity of God, over against the diversity of the persons, has in this century gone completely over to a version of eastern Christian thinking without the safeguards of classical eastern Christian thinking. Now that perhaps is another matter, but just to alert you to the fact that dialogue can result in something new when it is conducted in this way.

How is dialogue practised? Professor Eric Sharpe, who is now a professor in Australia, has distinguished four different ways in which dialogue is conducted today. The first he calls discursive dialogue, that is to say when partners come together and exchange information about each other's beliefs. This is a necessary aspect of dialogue. From the Christian point of view it is an aspect of dialogue where Christians must be very attentive to their partners, talk less and listen more; of course, we are not known for this in the world, but when people are telling us what they believe we need to listen very attentively. Then Sharpe talks about dialogue which has to do with a common recognition of our humanity. Again this is a crucial area for dialogue today as we seek to discover each other's commitment to, for example, human rights and the rights of women. In the context of dialogue with Muslims, this is an area that bristles with difficulties. Both sides talk about human rights but when Christians and Muslims talk about human rights together they soon discover that their perceptions about human rights are very different. What are Christian perceptions about Qu'rànic penal law, for example, and what are Muslim perceptions? This is a matter for dialogue and it is something that is not easily resolved. Third, Eric Sharpe refers to dialogue that is for the building up of community: if we are citizens of a particular nation, if we are members of a particular community, we will all be committed to the building up of that community. Dialogue is very important to ensure that we are working together for the building up of one community and not engaged in activities that divide communities into Muslim and Christian sectors, Hindu and Muslim and Christian sectors and so on. Finally, Sharpe talks about the sort of dialogue which is about the sharing of spiritual experience. Once again to give an example from Muslim/Christian history, as it were, there has been for thirteen hundred years dialogue between Christians in the mystical ascetical tradition and Muslims in the mystical ascetical tradition. Sufism, as a phenomenon in the world of Islam, is glad in many respects to refer to encounters with Christians that have enriched the Sufi tradition. From the Christian point of view, a great deal of mystical terminology that is used by Christians in the Muslim world comes from the Sufi tradition. So this dialogue about the exchange of spiritual experience is important.[11]

The Vatican has recently issued a document which also attempts to classify kinds of dialogue, and once again it seems very like the division that Sharpe made all those years ago. The Vatican's divisions are the dialogue of life, the dialogue of deeds, the dialogue of specialists and the dialogue of the interior life. So you can see how they correspond with Sharpe's division.[12] Just a word about the dialogue of specialists because sometimes not enough value is given to it. In some cases this *has* been sterile; where it has been overly concerned with classical issues and there has been a danger in some respects of a merely antiquarian interest. But one way forward which is proving to be quite fruitful is a model which has been taken from intra-Christian ecumenical dialogue. That is a model of dialogue where a group of scholars from each side come together for a considerable period of time, say five or six years, correspond with each other, meet each other regularly and consider one theme such as the scriptures in Islam and Christianity – so that they may come to a common mind about the place of scripture in religion, for example. There has been a fruitful dialogue between French-speaking Muslims and French-speaking Christians in this particular area which has been very revealing about how far the Muslims are prepared to go in their understanding not only of their own scripture but of the Bible.[13]

Some remarks about dialogue, mission and indeed evangelism. The Church Missionary Society has been committed for many scores of years to the view that dialogue is the presupposition for Christian mission, for Christian witness, in other words there can be no authentic Christian witness without prior dialogue. Unless we understand people's beliefs, their culture, the idiom of that culture, their thought forms, the intellectual tradition, the artistic tradition, the faith tradition, unless we understand these we will not be able to witness to people authentically as Christians. This is behind the strongly incarnational approach that CMS has taken in the past and continues to take today. Mission is not hit and run. People these days are talking about 'non-resident missionaries'; well, in some cases these are necessary, of course. But that will never be, I hope, a model for CMS because mission must be incarnational and this is why so many distinguished missionaries – Temple Gairdner in Egypt, W.D.P. Hill in India, in our own days people like Roger Hooker and Christopher Lamb – spent years in incarnational situations learning about cultures and languages and peoples before they felt able to witness to them of Christian faith and Christian truth. This is absolutely essential. So mission cannot be hit and run. It cannot be at a distance. A great deal of time and effort is being expended in the world today in preaching the gospel to people through the mass media. Now in some ways this is necessary, some parts of the world cannot be reached in any other way. Think of the way in which the Bible was broadcast at dictation speed to the people of Albania. But again it can never ben an ideal way because of the commitment to incarnation and to dialogue as the presupposition for witness.

But dialogue is not only preparatory to witness, *it is also the means to witness* and here I have been somewhat distressed by the ambivalence in the ecumenical movement on this question. Some documents, such as the guidelines on dialogue produced by the British Council of Churches, say clearly that dialogue is a medium for authentic witness.[14] But other documents of the World Council deny this and make every effort to claim that the occasion of dialogue must not be an occasion for Christian witness.[15] I think the concern behind this is that our partners should not see our efforts at dialogue as efforts at proselytization and that concern is valid. On the other hand, I cannot see dialogue in its fullness without the opportunity for both sides to witness to their faith in trust that the partners recognize each other's integrity. For Christians, dialogue will always be about listening and learning; our partner's faith may shed unexpected light on our own. We must, however, also be committed to let the light of Christ shine through our conversation and reflection. Without that, dialogue remains unfulfilled for the Christian.

8 THE CASE FOR RELIGIOUS PLURALISM
Paul Badham

One of the most urgent needs in modern Britain is for our society to come to terms with religious pluralism. According to the Marc Europe Religious Census of 1991, which is the most detailed and exhaustive survey of religion in Great Britain, it seems that 65 per cent of the population describe themselves as Christian. 55 per cent being nominal Christians and 10 per cent being churchgoers. Thirty-five per cent of the population are not Christian. Of these 27 per cent are atheists or agnostic and 8 per cent describe themselves as religious, but as belonging to a religion other than Christianity.[1]

Statistics to do with religion are incredibly difficult to interpret, but one way of taking these figures would be to relate the 10 per cent of Christian churchgoers with the 8 per cent of people committed to a religion other than Christianity, and arrive at the conclusion that in Britain there are almost as many worshippers of other faiths as there are worshipping Christians.

On the global scene it looks as if religious pluralism is going to be a permanent feature of the human condition. At the beginning of the century many Christians believed, on the basis of nineteenth-century successes in the mission field, that the whole world would one day be Christian. At the same time many secular thinkers were predicting that with the advance of modern science and philosophy all religions would wither away. Both expectations have been disappointed. Islam has experienced revival, Hinduism has undergone a renaissance, Buddhism remains vigorously alive and has attracted growing interest among intellectuals, Sikhism and Judaism are holding firm, and new religions of bewildering diversity are coming into being in both East and West. In western Europe the decline in Christianity appears to have stopped, and in eastern Europe there has been a dramatic revival. In Africa, Latin America, the USA and Korea, Christianity is very much alive. At the same time, however, secular patterns of thinking continue to dominate intellectual life.

As far as any one can predict the future, it looks as if both religious and atheistic ways of interpreting reality will continue to co-exist and that the major world faiths will continue to play a significant role in all human societies. If this analysis is correct, then I believe that there is an overwhelming case for arguing that the academic study of religion should be religiously pluralistic and open, and should provide for the study both of individual religious traditions, and for the wide variety of traditions which now exist in almost every country of the globe.

I was fascinated to discover during a recent visit to the Russian Academy of Sciences in Moscow that this argument has now been fully accepted there. All their institutes for scientific atheism are being converted into institutes for religious studies and are now committed to a wholly open philosophy in which religious traditions will be studied from a wide variety of perspectives and interpretations and in which believers will form an important part of an ongoing dialogue.[2]

In Lampeter we are committed to a many-sided approach to the study of religion. We have a well-established degree in Christian theology as well as a joint honours in Church history so that the Christian heritage for which Lampeter has always been known can continue to flourish. We also have a unique joint honours degree in Islamic studies so that Muslim students and others interested in Islam have a parallel opportunity to explore the scriptures, traditions and heritage of this other great faith community. We also have our degrees in religious studies and interfaith studies which cover the whole spectrum of human religious experience. In this context we are delighted to have at Lampeter this year, Dr Xinzhong Yao of the People's University of Beijing to add Chinese Religion and Culture to our range of courses. We also have students from Japan, Malaysia, Turkey, Saudi Arabia, Pakistan, Germany, Kenya, Canada and Korea. Within the department at Lampeter, religious pluralism is not just an idea but a reality of living everyday experience.

So far I have treated religious pluralism in its basic matter-of-fact sense as a phenomenon of modern life to which an academic department should appropriately respond. But the expression 'religious pluralism' is also used to describe a particular theological approach towards world religions. This approach starts from a presumption of equality between the enduring religions of the world on the grounds that each of the major faiths represents a culturally conditioned human response to a single divine reality. The starting position for this view is that in each religion, experience of God, or the ultimate, is the initial starting point. This whole approach is absolutely anathema to a very vocal group of Christians who have recently sent an Open Letter to all clergy in the Church of England and in the Church in Wales. This Open Letter was originally signed by eighty-seven leading churchpeople, Theological college principals, archdeacons, and members of the General Synod urging clergy to resist all involvement with interfaith worship. Since then they have succeeded in persuading over two thousand clergy, one-fifth of the total number of Anglican clergy, to sign up. They want the House of Bishops to take an absolute stand against multi-faith services because they think such worship undermines the uniqueness of Jesus. They state uncompromisingly their view that 'Salvation is offered *only* through Jesus Christ', who is 'the only saviour' and 'the only way to God'. According to this Open Letter Group 'Interfaith Relations is *the* Issue of the Decade'.[3]

The position assumed in the Open Letter is the position known as 'exclusivism'. It is the view that both eternal salvation and knowledge of God can come only through Jesus Christ. Let us start with the idea of eternal salvation as available only through Christ. This may seem straightforward to many Christians, but I wonder how many think through its negative implications, particularly if they understand salvation in its classical sense as salvation from everlasting damnation. If salvation really comes only through accepting Jesus Christ as one's personal saviour, as many signers say they believe, it necessarily follows that those who do not turn to Christ are not saved, but presumably damned. In other words we would have to suppose that God, who according to Jesus Christ is best pictured as a loving Father, has so arranged things that the vast majority of his children are to be tortured for ever in hell because the only way to salvation, namely personal knowledge of Jesus Christ as Lord and Saviour, is not available to them in the cultural situation in which they live.[4] As Karl Rahner points out, this traditional view is 'senseless, cruel, and has no hope of being accepted by the man of today, in view of the enormous extent of extra-Christian history'.[5]

The case against such exclusivism is not simply from the appalling picture of God which it presumes, but also from the ethical implications which logically follow from such beliefs. Historically speaking, the first Council to teach explicitly such exclusivism was the Council of Florence of 1438–45 which declared that, 'No one remaining outside the Church, not just pagans, but also Jews or heretics or schismatics, can become partakers of eternal life; but they will go to the everlasting fire prepared for the devil and his angels unless before the end of life they are joined to the Church.'[6] The papal theological adviser at this Council was Cardinal Juan de Torquemada. It was no accident that his nephew Tomas de Torquemada became the Grand Inquisitor of Spain. If one seriously believes that all non-Christians will be tortured for ever in hell, then it really does become an act of charity to use all possible means to ensure that everyone is converted. The uncle's theology leads to the nephew's practice. And the evil potential of such teaching is thereby exposed.

Turning to the second claim that Jesus is the only way to God. I think this viewpoint depends on growing up and living in a solely Christian environment, where one never really meets people from other faith communities. This was certainly true of Karl Barth, the best known exponent of twentieth-century exclusivism. In 1935 Barth was in full spate denouncing Hinduism as a form of unbelief when he was challenged by the Indian Christian theologian D.T. Niles who asked, how he knew that 'Hinduism is unbelief?' [see p.33] Barth's answer, which took Niles by surprise, was quite simply, '*A priori!*'[7] Such *a priori* reasoning cannot withstand the knowledge that follows from personal contact. One of the great contributions that I think the establishment of Islamic studies in Lampeter may bring to religious harmony is that in the future no Christian student in Lampeter who gets to know a single devout Muslim will ever be likely to succumb to the exclusivist tradition that God can only be known through Christ. One advantage of personal knowledge is that prejudices are exposed for what they truly are.

What most disturbs me about the Open Letter is what it reveals about continuing racial segregation and discrimination in modern Britain. To sign a petition suggesting that about a third of the people in Britain who regularly worship God do not know him seems to betray a serious lack of awareness of contemporary life. It is very sad to think that almost a fifth of the clergy of England and Wales have never sat down for a serious conversation with anyone from another religious tradition and know nothing of their religious inheritance or culture. That is one reason why our society needs religious studies to help understanding and to break down prejudice.

Fortunately, however, the Open Letter Group are not typical of Christian thought today. Since all clergy were asked to sign this letter, the good news is that 80 per cent did not. Clearly one cannot assume that all the non-signers have a positive attitude to people of other faiths, but it seems likely that at least a significant majority probably believe that God is known in many traditions and that God wills all to be saved. For the most common Christian approach to other faiths is now not exclusive, but inclusive. The inclusive approach takes the question of ultimate salvation out of the equation. Most Christian theologians reason that if there is a God, and if God is as Jesus revealed him, then if there is a future life all will ultimately participate in it. From a Protestant perspective William Cantwell Smith summed up the position thus: 'A Buddhist who is saved, or a Hindu, or a Muslim or whoever, is saved and is saved only, because God is the kind of God whom Jesus Christ has revealed him to be.'[8] Pope John Paul II is likewise completely firm on this point: 'Every one without exception has been redeemed by

Christ.'⁹ Christians who adopt this inclusive approach recognize and welcome what Cardinal Bea describes as 'the spiritual and moral values to be found in the various traditions'.¹⁰

This inclusive approach was expressed most strongly in the Vatican II decree on the relation of the Church to Non-Christian religions. In view of the existence of the Centre for Islamic Studies at Lampeter let me quote what the Vatican Council said of that religion:

> The Church has a high regard for the Muslims. They worship God, who is one living and subsistent, merciful and almighty, the Creator of heaven and earth, who has also spoken to men. They strive to submit themselves without reserve to the hidden decrees of God, just as Abraham submitted himself to God's plan, to whose faith Muslims eagerly link their own. Although not acknowledging him as God, they venerate Jesus as prophet, his virgin mother they also honour, and even at times devoutly invoke. Further they await the day of judgment and the reward of God following the resurrection of the dead. For this reason they highly esteem an upright life and worship God especially by way of prayer, alms-deeds and fasting. Over the centuries many quarrels and dissensions have arisen between Christians and Muslims. This sacred Council now pleads with all to forget the past, and urges that a sincere effort be made to achieve mutual understanding.¹¹

I think this is an important statement and in so far as some Christians have questioned the appropriateness of Lampeter's expansion into Islamic studies, it is perhaps worth reminding ourselves that the most representative body of the largest Christian Church has spoken in these terms, and called for precisely that understanding of Islamic thought which our Islamic studies programme can provide.

The Document also has firm and positive statements on Judaism and on the great religions of the East, and insists that the universal love of God extends also to those who intellectually reject faith. As the Council document puts it: 'Nor shall divine providence deny the assistance necessary for salvation to those who without any fault of theirs, have not yet arrived at an explicit knowledge of God.'¹² All this is an immense improvement on exclusivism and intolerance but I am not totally happy with it. The tone has a slightly patronizing feel to it. There is a tendency to see other faiths as good in so far as they have points in common with Christianity. The inclusive position remains convinced of its own superiority, even though it recognizes how much it has in common with other faiths and with all people of good will. Inclusivism goes a long way but not far enough. What is required is more than Christian tolerance and understanding. It is a totally open-ended search for truth based on the assumption that all the major religions of humanity have insights to offer, and it must also accept that much of the secular critique of traditional religion is justified and needs to be taken on board also.

The pluralist position rejects both Christian exclusivism and Christian inclusivism and calls for genuine religious pluralism. This is the position that the various religions of the world represent different human responses to a single divine reality. It was the position pioneered in the last century by Rowland Williams, Professor of Theology at Lampeter. His book *On the Knowledge of the Supreme Lord in Christianity and in Hinduism*[13] was a groundbreaking work in this field. In our age this kind of religious pluralism is most closely associated with the writings of John Hick. As a distant successor to Rowland Williams and as a disciple of John Hick I am happy to associate myself with such views and shall now seek to spell them out.

The starting point for a doctrine of religious pluralism is acceptance of the view that we are living in a religiously ambiguous world. For there is a virtual consensus among contemporary philosophers that all the arguments for the existence of God fail to provide 'proof' of God's existence and philosophers of religion have come to recognize that the most that one can hope to argue for is that a religious understanding of reality can be recognized as at least a possible alternative to a naturalistic one. It seems that God, if he exists, has created us at an epistemic distance from himself (that is a distance in terms of our knowledge), in order that a response to him can be genuinely free. In this religiously ambiguous world both faith and non-faith may be equally valid responses. Hence the issue has to be decided on the basis of the individual's own experience, or non-experience, of transcendent reality. The person of faith may feel justified in believing as she or he does, because that is how they experience some of their most precious experiences. They see these 'peak-experiences' as pointing to a transcendent God. All the pioneers of faith in the Judaeo-Christian-Islamic tradition, such as the Old Testament prophets or Muhammad the Prophet of Islam, all believed in God, not on the basis of an overwhelming call. Since their experience of God was for them as much a part of their lives as their experience of the perceptual world they were as justified in taking for granted the 'givenness' of divine existence as they took for granted the objective reality of the external world. For in the final analysis, the way we interpret our experiencing is the basis of for all our thinking about the nature of reality.[14]

This centrality of religious experience was the starting-point for Rowland Williams way back in the mid-nineteenth century in his books on *Rational Godliness* and *Lampeter Theology*. Rowland Williams's position was that genuine faith is not based on either the authority of the Bible, or on the person of Christ, but rather on the individual experience of the believer. He sought to demonstrate this by pointing out that in the Bible itself Enoch walked with God, Melchizedek blessed Abraham, and Abraham's faith was counted to him for righteousness centuries before the earliest of our sacred books took their present form.[15] In his book on Hinduism he urged the need to accept that many Hindus had a profound knowledge of God, and in his contribution to *Essays and Reviews* he argued for the view that all the Bible should be seen as the record of human religious experience, as the product of the Christian spirit and not its cause.[16] It was for this understanding of the Bible and the Christian faith as the product of a human response to the divine that Williams was brought to trial for heresy in 1862 and 1864. And it was through his total acquittal by the Judicial Committee of the Privy Council that academic freedom for Theology was won. Yet it seems to me that to argue for an experiential base for religion is a matter of crucial significance to understanding its true nature.

The experiential base of all the different world religions can be demonstrated if one looks at the nature of the human response to the divine. In almost all cases it manifests itself in worship. However much religions may differ, one is never really in any doubt that religious buildings have more in common with each other than with other buildings. Christianity and Buddhism are very different and yet when I stood in the temple of Amida Buddha in Tokyo I felt an overwhelming sense that I was in a familiar kind of place. If a person could visit earth from a planet of some distant star and stand at the back of a temple, a gurdwara, a synagogue, a mosque or a church he or she would have little doubt in sensing that in an important sense the same kind of activity was going on, however much cultural differences led to differing modes of expression. The similarity can be further demonstrated by reading through the hymns, prayers and religious readings used in different traditions. Provided that one removes the specific names which occur one would often be at a loss to know from which tradition the prayer or hymn came, for the overlap of expression is so striking.

If one starts from the various religions predominantly represented in Britain the similarity in modes of worship is such that it might appear one could settle the issue by saying that 'God has many names'.[17] But this language is adequate only in contexts where religions share, or appear to share, a comparably theistic understanding. In particular, the personal overtones of much Christian usage of the word 'God', would appear to exclude

Vedantic and Buddhist approaches to ultimate reality which tend to adopt impersonal understandings of this. On the other hand, dialogue with members of these traditions does seem to suggest that their very different forms of expression may equally be a response to the same transcendent reality. Hence it seems crucial to search for some hypothesis which will do justice, both to the supposed common source, and to the very different ways in which that source is apprehended and described in different human traditions.

In his recent Gifford Lectures John Hick has argued that religion can essentially be described in two ways; as a purely human phenomenon to be accounted for in wholly naturalistic terms, or as a human response to a transcendent reality. Because of the 'pervasive ambiguity of the Universe' it is not possible to refute either possibility.[18] And indeed the two hypotheses are not mutually exclusive because even religion is deemed to be a human response to a divine reality, the mode of that response remains embedded in the cultural, social and intellectual world of the believer. This latter consideration is crucially important to Hick's thesis, because he seeks to account for the differences between the various concepts of the divine reality to be found in the religions of the world as the product of these factors.

The problem for a pluralist understanding of religion has always been the need to reconcile the notion that each religion is some sense an authentic response to the one divine reality while at the same time facing up to the immense diversity in the ways that reality is pictured. Hick's solution is to emphasize the way in which each of the world's religions have drawn a distinction between the Real as such, and the Real as perceived by us. He is able to show that leading thinkers in each of the world's traditions, whether Jewish, Christian, Islamic, Buddhist, Taoist or Hindu, have all been vividly conscious of this, and have insisted that all the ways we image God, Brahman or the Dharmakaya are all ultimately misleading.[19] He suggests that the distinction Kant drew between things as they really are in themselves, and things as we perceive them within the categories of our thought structures, might be a useful analogy to help us to appreciate this distinction.

What Hick claims is that the world religions are a response to a single divine reality, and that their differences in describing that which they claim to encounter are culturally conditioned human projections which seek to image that reality. Each 'name of God' represents a different *persona* of the divine reality as responded to in human history. Hick takes as examples of his thesis the character of Krishna as worshipped in the Vaishnavite tradition of India, and the character of Jahweh as believed to be disclosed in the life and experience of ancient Israel. Although these are perceived as quite distinct *personae*, they are both experienced as the focus of religious experience within the cultural and historical traditions to which they belong. Hick believes the same to be true of 'the heavenly Father of Christian faith, known through the distinctively Christian response to Jesus of Nazareth; the Allah of Islamic faith, known as self-revealed in the Qur'àn through the prophet Muhammed; and Shiva, known and intensely experienced within the Shaivite cults of India'.[20]

What is the ontological status of these *personae*? That is, are there actually distinct deities? Virtually all contemporaries who seriously consider this question would answer 'No'. All the philosophical arguments which suggest the possibility of God do so on the assumption that we are living in a universe which may perhaps point beyond itself to a divine creator. Polytheism is incoherent in this context and this is explicitly acknowledged in all religious traditions as soon as they reach any kind of maturity. Nor is it justifiable to say that one only kind of worship corresponds to reality and all the rest are simply worshipping human projections, for there are no adequate criteria to make such a distinction. From a phenomenological perspective each appears equally 'real' to its believers.

Hick's conclusion therefore is that the one God is differently described because experience of God, like all other human experience, is necessarily coloured by the differing cultural traditions and historical experiences of particular human groups. Hick believes that this perspective also applies to those religious traditions which reject the notion of a personal deity and think of the Real in impersonal terms as the Absolute. This Absolute is also differently signified in different cultures as Brahman, Nirvana or Sunyata. Once again these should not be perceived as descriptive of different realities, but rather as alternative culturally conditioned apprehensions of the one supreme reality. It should also be noted that personal and impersonal concepts of God co-exist in many religions. The God and Father of our Lord Jesus Christ is also the impassible, incomprehensible unmoved mover of Aquinas's thought. In Pure Land Buddhism, Amida Buddha the heavenly saviour, is one with the empty void of Sunyata. And even in Islam the intensely personal response of the Sufis may be contrasted with the religious austerity of the Wahhabis.

The great value of Hick's pluralist hypothesis is that it enables one to do justice to two equally important 'facts' about the religions of the world. The first is that there do seem to be valid grounds for supposing that they may each be responding in their different ways to a common underlying reality. But the second equally true fact is that the world religions are different. And indeed that they hold mutually incompatible beliefs about the way the world is, and of the relation between humanity and the ultimate. John Hick's theory does suggest how these two facts of human experience can be held together. The similarity coming from the fact that each is a human response to a genuinely transcendent reality, the difference coming from the fact that this experience is filtered through very different cultural and intellectual traditions. Clearly Hick's attempt to hold these two truths in harmony raises many problems. But I think we should note that these problems are not peculiar to interreligious dialogue but that very comparable problems arise also within each of the great religions. Think of the difference between the Christian exclusivist and the Christian inclusivist we considered earlier. Both may kneel in worship together in the same Church and yet they hold utterly different and mutually incompatible pictures of God in their minds. The exclusivist thinks in holy awe of a God of such implacable wrath that the vast majority of humanity must be tortured for ever in the flames of hell. The inclusivist has a picture of God as a loving heavenly Father always ready to forgive his prodigal children and whose will is that all shall be saved. Yet strange as it may seem both may feel the presence of God with them in the same communion service. It is hard to think of many differences *between* world religions which are wider than these two incompatible images. To accept the actuality of human religious experience while recognizing the tension of mutually incompatible belief-systems seems to require some such solution as Hick's; not only for interfaith dialogue, but also to do justice to the experience of everyday worshipping.

Hick believes that in trying to find a common term for that to which all religions respond, the phrase 'the Real' is particularly useful. The advantage of this term is that instances of its use can be found in almost all religious traditions. As Hick urges, 'without being the exclusive property of any one tradition, it is nevertheless familiar within all of them'.[21] Hence it would seem a 'name' acceptable to all and repugnant to none. An outstanding example of the usefulness of the term can be seen by considering the discussion of the world's major religious traditions by Keith Ward in his *Images of Eternity*. Ward makes a detailed study of the principal writings of Sankara, Ramanuja, Asvaghosa, Maimonides, Al-Ghazzali and Aquinas (the leading philosophers of Buddhism, of the two main traditions of Hinduism, of Judaism, Islam and Christianity), and makes a very powerful case for claiming that behind the differing concepts used lie complementary approaches to one supreme reality.[22]

However, I suggest that there are advantages in continuing to use a wide variety of 'names' in interfaith dialogue. The mainstream religious words like 'God', or its Arabic translation 'Allah', or the Hindu concept of 'Brahman', or the Buddhist understanding of 'the Dharmakaya', are helpful in dialogue precisely because they are so rich in meaning within the religious traditions where they are habitually used. If, in addition, reflection is further stimulated by the use of less specific terms such as 'The Real' or 'The Transcendent' or the 'Ground of Being', then this may challenge believers to explore more deeply what their tradition really affirms about, the Ultimate. On Hick's concern that the word 'God' is too identified with a personal theistic understanding to be the general term, I believe it would be positively helpful to interfaith dialogue if contemporary Christians were reminded how modern the dominance of such a personal understanding of the term is within their own tradition. The essentially impossible God of the Christian Fathers with his aseity, incomprehensibility and infinity would seem much closer to Buddhist concepts of the Dharmakaya than the anthropomorphically conceived divinity of much contemporary Christian devotion. Hence, using the term 'God' in non-personal contexts in interfaith dialogue might help Christians to rediscover that awareness of the complexity of talking about God which was so strong an element in the apophactic and mystical traditions of both eastern and western Christianity.

It seems to me impossible to accept the reality of such a concept as 'the religious experience of the human race' without affirming that in some sense there is an underlying unity in the human response to the transcendent. But human cultural diversity and the system-building capacity of the human mind has left us with a bewildering multitude of 'names' for that to which the religious experience of humanity can be regarded as a response. Each of these names has a richness of its own and can enlarge our understanding. John Hick's distinction between the Real as such as the various *personae* and *impersonae* of the world's religions seems to be one way in which we can come to terms with the diversity of the human response while continuing to affirm the essential unity of that to which human beings respond.

Part II
THE CHALLENGE OF INTERFAITH

9 THE MEETING OF RELIGIONS TODAY
Geoffrey Parrinder

The religions of the world today face a completely new situation, and this is particularly significant for the West. Never before this century have there been such close contacts as now obtain in religious organizations, practices and thought. The 'one world' in which we live, with its close communications makes nonsense of religious isolation. Whether it is agreeable or not, the fact is that men and women can and do now compare religious ideas with one another and often mix them together. This situation presents challenges to traditional forms of theology.

The challenges are acute for the Semitic or western religions of Christianity, Judaism and Islam. They have been accustomed to think of themselves as supreme, in religion and culture, possessing the highest truths and the oldest and best philosophies. Many histories of philosophy, or of other aspects of culture, have considered only European or Near Eastern forms as if they were the only ones that mattered. In a popular history of philosophy, Bertrand Russell agreed that our culture must be defective as long as it is purely European, yet he stated that philosophy began in Greece in the sixth century BC. But some of the greatest Indian philosophers, whose works are still studied and now translated, lived centuries before that.

We have been accustomed to speak of the rest of the world, say India or China, as isolated until our explorations in the sixteenth century and colonization in the nineteenth. In fact it is the West that has been isolated. India has long been a meeting-place for some of the greatest religions. Christianity appeared there in the early centuries and the Syrian Church has persisted along the Malabar coast, while new churches have sprung up in many parts of India. Islam entered India from the eighth century and eventually spread over much of the sub-continent, so that today rather less than one-sixth of Indians are counted as Muslims. There have long been small communities of Jews and Parsis in western India. Although the great majority of Indians are counted as followers of some form of Hindu religion there are other ancient and powerful indigenous Indian religions; as well as relatively small numbers of Jains and Sikhs. Buddhism arose in India, prospered for a thousand years, and then dispersed to take Indian religion and culture to much of the rest of Asia. So the meeting of religions today is but an acceleration of India of age-long processes. India has been used to many religions, so that Hindus tend to regard other faiths as different ways to one goal with unusual tolerance.

Western Christianity is emerging from its isolation and slowly adjusting its thinking to the fact that not only do other religions exist, but that they persist. Even more, that they are not far away, to be the subject of missionary attention, but are close at hand. The Jews have of course been long in Europe, but they have often been treated to indifference at best, and to shameful persecution at worst. Grudgingly it might be admitted that Jews had a form of religion to which they strangely held fast; their past was sacred history, but it was rarely thought that their present religion could teach anything.

Christianity has faced Islam too, especially eastern Christianity, but relations have not been the happiest. The western Church sent the ill-named Crusades, from the eleventh to the thirteenth centuries, in a mixture of zeal, greed and cruelty. When the first crusaders captured Jerusalem in the name of God they massacred most of the inhabitants, chiefly Muslims but even some Jews and Christians, and the fourth Crusade sacked and desecrated the Christian city of Constantinople. Misrepresentations of Islam were common in the West, even if all did not reach the depths of ignorance shown in the medieval miracle play which depicted Turks worshipping an idol called Baphomet (Muhammad!). Even Dante in his *Divine Comedy*, while willing to see Muslim philosophers like Avicenna and Averroes in Limbo like other non-Christian thinkers, yet consigned Muhammad and Ali to the ninth chasm of Hell as 'sowers of scandal and schism'. Until modern times there were virtually no attempts to meet Muslims on an equal footing or engage in religious dialogue with respect to both sides.

But now not only Judaism and Islam, but most other religions are our neighbours. Hinduism, Buddhism and Sikhism, in particular, demand the attention of Christian thinkers and speak in our own streets. Many Europeans and Americans are aware of this, for they have travelled to the East and have seen for themselves something of the strength and beauty of oriental religions in mosque and pagoda, temple and monastery. Some went as missionaries, and were impressed despite themselves; others were traders and administrators; and many more went in the armed forces during and after the world wars. They can no longer be put off with stories about heathen darkness, for they often know more than their own clergy about the Asian religions that may receive passing reference in the pulpit on a missionary Sunday. This is not surprising, since most theological colleges for training the clergy give little or no time at all to consideration of any other religion than Christianity. Ministers of religion may know nothing of subjects that interest many laymen and laywomen, such as reincarnation, karma or nirvana.

Further, Asian religions are not only practised in another continent, they are here in our midst. Many Europeans and Americans have been to Asia, but orientals come to the West in increasing numbers. The modern phenomenon of multi-racial society is also multi-religious. There are hundreds of Muslim mosques in Britain and other western lands, many Hindu and Buddhist temples, and smaller numbers of places of worship and instruction for Sikhs, Parsis, Bahais and other religious movements of Asian inspiration. Priests, monks and various teachers and yogis serve their communities here, and so the East returns the compliment and sends missionaries to the West.

In addition to contacts with religious organizations, there is a great flow of books and leaflets which bring hundreds of thousands of people into touch with oriental religious teachings. Many books have a large sale. A Penguin on Buddhism, by the president of the English Buddhist Society, sold tens of thousands of copies, and a translation of difficult Buddhist texts sold out in a few weeks. Reputable publishers print popular series of eastern texts in reliable though not always easy translations. There is also a good deal of 'occult', and sometimes cranky, literature. But anyone who wishes can buy good texts of eastern classics cheaply and paperbacks flood the market.

Some of the earliest translations of Asian religious texts were the work of missionaries, a small but important minority which had become interested in the languages of the people and their sacred classics. William Carey, Baptist missionary and great linguist, produced one of the first English translations of the great Hindu religious scripture, the Ramayana. Legge translated the Tao te Ching, Soothill the Analects of Confucius, Saunders the Buddhist Dhammapada, and so on. But today there are many new versions of these and other scriptures, and there are over fifty of the Bhagavad Gita in English.

The wide sales of these books testifies to the interest of the western world in eastern religions. They show a concern with religion in general, perhaps even a revival of religion, if the Spirit is recognized as blowing where it listeth. Certainly there is a meeting of religious people and ideas, and that requires a re-examination of traditional attitudes to other faiths.

It has been said that the open meeting of religions is a modern phenomenon for the West, but some other major religions have long faced both this problem and the challenges of modernity, and it may be helpful to consider their situation briefly.

Islam has been confronted with different religious traditions in the past and with western thought and practice today. A Semitic faith, and almost wholly Asian and African, it has not been isolated to the same degree as western Christianity. In India and China Islam settled alongside other faiths, and in Persia (Iran) it fused Muslim, Christian, Zoroastrian and Hindu thought in Shia sects and Sufi mysticism. Very different from early Christianity, Islam was a success religion from its first century. Muhammad and his followers endured persecution until the Hijra (Hegira), the 'migration' from which Muslim years are counted, brought the support of the community of Medina, the growth of an army, and the subjugation of Mecca and the Arabian tribes within ten years till Muhammad died. The amazing success of the Muslim armies in subjugating much of the known world is almost unparalleled. Within a century Mesopotamia, Syria and Persia had fallen, India had been entered, North Africa and Spain overrun and France invaded. Not only was there political and social success, but new forces created new Islamic cultures, incorporating and transforming much of that of classical times. It was all integrated by religion, Islam being the driving force and religious law regulating all spheres of life.

That was the classic period of Islam which future ages looked back to with pride. It came to an end in 1258 with the fall of Baghdad to the Mongols, but even then Islam converted the conquerors, and after the Arabs new forms were given to Muslim culture by Persians, Turks and Indians. The Turkish empire lingered on till the present century when 'the sick man of Europe' collapsed under the pressures of the West and Balkan and Arab nationalism. The Arab countries eventually succeeded in throwing off the colonizing efforts of the West also, but they found themselves regarded as backward, client-states, or subject to 'coca-cola-nization', suffering under the offensive superiority of British and French, Americans and Russians. The Islamic peoples, conscious of a great culture and monotheistic religion, find themselves despised as ignorant, dirty or lazy.

There is a profound religious crisis in the Muslim world, no less profound for not being easily recognized by outsiders. Since Islam is the best religion, held to be the latest and crown of the three monotheisms, and the Arabs seemed to have been historically the people of God, why are they so low down in the modern world, and why do infidel nations flourish? The problem of Western superiority and technical success is a religious problem, for it implies that either the world or Islam must adapt itself. With a tradition of success, rather than suffering as in early Christianity, the problem is acute.

The most drastic adaptation to modern ways was made in Turkey itself, and it involved radical reshaping or limitation of Islamic tradition. Under Kemal Ataturk's revolution the Caliphate was abolished, the religious orders dissolved, western legal codes substituted for Islamic sharia, the Latin alphabet adopted, women unveiled, the Turkish replaced Arabic in the call to prayer. There have been uneasy revivals over the last seventy years, Arabic has come back, the pilgrimage has increased in numbers, and many people hold to the old religion. Moreover, not only have the oil-rich states wielded enormous power through their wealth along with adherence to traditional Islam, but there have been powerful reversions to 'fundamentalist' or conservative applications of Islamic tradition to all areas of life, demonstrated in states from Iran to Sudan, and from Pakistan to Algeria.

It is sad that the West is often blamed for the low state of Arab lands, and that 'West' tends to be identified with Christianity. Few are conscious of western attempts to understand the East, even in the political sphere let alone in the religious. It must be admitted that western missions have made little impact and there have been few converts from Muslim lands. A head-on attack, now being advocated again by some in the Decade of Evangelism, has patently failed. Tolerance and dialogue are more hopeful and some small, very small, beginnings have been made at understanding Islam in western terms, and in discussing with members of the monotheistic faiths some of the common problems of modern times, secularism and materialism.

India suffered invasions of armies and religious ideas for over four thousand years. About 1500 BC, before the Hebrew exodus from Egypt, the Aryan invaders with their chariots and weapons destroyed the cities of the Indus valley peoples, calling them black, snub-nosed and irreligious, and imposing their own Vedic practices. In time, however, the ancient religion reasserted itself and many features of it survive in modern Hinduism.

The Muslim invasions of India destroyed thousands of temples and countless images in idol-breaking zeal. Yet the great Mughal emperor Akbar in the sixteenth century favoured Hinduism more than his ancestral Islam, and then he went on to invent his own eclectic religion after listening to Jesuit debates on Christianity. The influence of the West came in the British empire, though as a political entity it was relatively short-lived. The most extensive empire the world has known was also one of the most brief, lasting about a century.

Hinduism, a loose name for the major religious complex of India, now faces both the secular and the religious challenges that confront other religions. In such a profoundly religious country the scientific secular outlook comes as a check to traditional preoccupation with the spiritual. Many young people are more concerned with material and social welfare. The political and social struggles of this century which led to Independence, brought women into the open and required reassessment of human relationships. The sense of nationalism and community, joined to a desire for progress and world peace, sought the inspiration of religion. There have been many social reforms, sometimes under the stimulus of Christianity or imposed from above by government, but more deeply led from within by political leaders who were also religious, like Mahatma Gandhi.

The effect of Christianity in India has been powerful in education and social reform, but less in the religious sphere. Christianity destroyed no temples, as Islam did, and it was not spread by force except indirectly. Its greatest successes were among the outcastes, banned from some Hindu temples but welcomed into churches. There has probably been more dialogue of Christians with caste Hindus than with Muslim or Buddhist leaders elsewhere, but even so it has been small. For over a century there have been Hindu intellectuals who have sought to modernize Hinduism, or make a synthesis of Hindu, Christian and Islamic teachings. It is recognized that there are different ways of salvation and the edge is taken off confrontation. Others have adapted Christian methods, with an emphasis on 'missionary work', previously foreign to Hinduism, but active in Ramarishna missions, and now in Hare Krishna and similar movements which carry Hindu teachings and practices to Europe and America. In the other direction, revivals of traditional Hinduism, 'fundamentalist' and militant movements not only oppose 'foreign' missions, but revive communal tensions, as in attempts to replace the Muslim mosque at Ayodhya with a rebuilt temple to the god Rama. Similarly, militant Sikhs, in the Punjab and elsewhere, seek both political and religious independence and oppose those who sought a synthesis of Hinduism and Sikhism.

Relationships between religions in India have not always been sweetness and light, on the contrary, communal riots and tensions have often resulted from the arrival of new religious forces into the traditional situation. Islam came to India as a monotheistic, idol-breaking, international and missionary religion, encountering a Hinduism that was polytheistic or pantheistic or monotheistic by turns, and in any case indigenous and resistant to change. The one-sixth of India that is Muslim today, along with Pakistan and Bangladesh, demonstrates the considerable success of Islamic missions. Yet the mass of Hinduism remains resistant; it has traditions, scriptures, and holy men and women to provide distinctive life. Indeed, modern Hindu revival movements seek to make India a Hindu state, in which Christians as well as Muslims and others would be barely tolerated. So far, the 'secular' state means not that it is materialistic, but neutral between the religious forces.

Two other products of Indian religion may serve to illustrate ways of reacting to religious pluralism. The Sikhs, 'disciples' of Guru Nanak in the Punjab and beyond from the fifteenth century, seem to provide a synthesis of Hindu and Muslim devotion. Certainly the basic scripture, Adi Granth, contains verses from Hindu and Muslim holy men in addition to many from the ten Sikh gurus. But Sikhs maintain that they are distinctive, with their gurus as supreme, indeed all incorporating the same spirit, and they seek to convert other people to their own belief in one God who dwells everywhere and is acceptable to all castes and races.

Much older was Buddhism, which arose in India and became the earliest of the great international and missionary religions. From about the sixth century BC Gautama, who became the Buddha, 'enlightened', for this present era, and his followers, wandered around north and central India teaching and seeking to convert people to their way of life. The early Buddhist scriptures, which reject the Hindu scriptures, are full of stories of the Buddha meeting Hindu and Jain teachers and defeating them in argument. Many Hindu gods appear in Buddhist stories, but the Buddha is superior to them all, 'teacher of gods and men', not a god, or God, yet like a functional deity and the object of countless devotions.

Although Buddhism flourished in India for over a thousand years, as one of many religions, it finally declined and almost disappeared, largely due to the destruction of its monasteries and temples by invading Muslims. But in the meantime this faith had spread throughout south-east Asia, and right up into China by the first century and to Japan by the sixth. In Sri Lanka, Burma and other southern lands Buddhism became the dominant religion, encountering no scriptural rival, and here the Theravada or Hinayana (Doctrine of the Elders, or Small Vehicle) form of Buddhism prevails and still shapes the religion and culture of the people.

In China Buddhism met the indigenous and literate Taoism and Confucianism and, despite some conflict, it became one of the three Ways or religions of China. Similarly, in Japan it met Shinto, indigenous though less literate, and worked alongside and with it. Statistics of Japanese religions have claimed 85 millions for Shinto,

84 millions for Buddhism, out of a total population of 110 millions. That is because most Japanese follow both Shinto and Buddhism, and so that latter missionary religion learnt to accommodate itself to the Japanese, and partly to the Chinese, situations by synthesis rather than confrontation.

In modern times contact with the West and Christianity has had a similar upsetting effect as on other religions, though more in northern Buddhism than in south-east Asia. British and French administrators in the latter areas, in colonial days, welcomed Buddhism as apparently a rationalistic and materialistic religion, ignoring the innumerable images, pagodas, and scriptures which were marks of religious faith. But efforts have been made, from within Buddhist communities, to reform and spread their faith, translating scriptures into western languages, and taking their practices to Europe and America. Buddhist of the 'Dispersion' are now an important factor, as with other Asian religions.

The fate of Mahayana (Great Vehicle) Buddhism in northern Asia has been less happy, except in Japan where in addition to its links with Shinto it has broken out into new sects. But in China, and even more in Tibet, Buddhism, has been subject to harsh persecution, and to the attacks of Marxist materialism. With this latter ideology, bringing the latest brand of Western fanaticism, Buddhism has been in sore straits. Its emphasis on monastic life has not made it easy to fit into a society where productive labour is the rule for everyone. In Tibet especially, but also in China and Mongolia, monasteries have been destroyed and their inhabitants killed, enslaved or deported. Buddhism has undergone persecution before in China, particularly under the Tang dynasty in the ninth century, but it rose again and there are signs that some relaxation of oppression may bring Buddhist revival. But its future depends more on the devout and informed laity rather than on the monks.

That other religions besides Christianity are suffering from the materialism and secularism of modern times is worth noting, and their attempts at reformation. They are also facing the challenge of other religions, usually Islam or Christianity. But such a challenge is relatively new for Christians. Whereas with exploration, trade, imperialism, and missions, emanating from the West in the past four hundred years, other religions have undergone what is called culture-contact or acculturation, now the confrontation comes back to the West. We live in a multi-cultural context in which we are one element among others. The religions of Asia are not safely far away beyond Suez, they are here in Southall or Bradford, in Paris or Amsterdam, in California or Oregon, and countless other places.

This is a hard lesson to learn. For a long time the West has been supreme, regarding other peoples as inferior. But now with independent states of Asia and Africa, and the great blocks of China and Japan, all emerging, this can no longer be assumed. And it applies in religious affairs as in political. In the past Christians have often thought of themselves as secure and dominant; there were few obvious religious variants, Jews were a minor group and other religions were distant and unobtrusive. In language and in colour dominance was assumed, and minorities were to be dealt with in one way or another, or ignored.

The resurgence of Asian nations and religions brings home another fact: that Christians are in a minority. Statistics of religions are hard to establish, because of different ways of conducting a census, or not conducting one at all by assuming that all people in a country follow the same faith or ideology. Many wild guesses are made, but from careful and reliable sources general estimates have been made in the *World Christian Encyclopedia*, edited by David Barrett: Christians, of all denominations, 1,600 millions; Muslims 820 millions; Hindus 650 millions; Buddhists 300 millions; Shinto we have seen, Jews and Sikhs about 14 millions each, and smaller numbers of Jains, Parsis, and Bahais.

Christianity is the largest religion, if its different denominations can be regarded together, but even so it is in a minority situation, as with all other religions. Though it is hard to recognize that we are in a minority, when we have been used to ruling over large areas of the world, with all the advantages of power and education, yet the facts of modern social and religious diversity should bring adjustments of understanding and attitudes.

A consequence of the religious minority situation, or even a simple recognition of diversity, should bring respect for other religions and their followers. Exclusive attitudes of the past, which considered their own opinions as supreme and others not worth discussing, or to be safely ignored, should no longer have a place in this one world. The theological gulf between those who believe in our way, and those who believe in some other way must be bridged. As we ourselves are in a minority it is no longer valid to divide humanity into 'we' and 'they'. Somehow the gulf must be closed and those who care for spiritual things should recognize each other's strivings in a community that turns into a 'we'.

The meeting of peoples of different religions today is a universal phenomenon, but the presence of Asians in the West has presented Christians with new problems, of which two may be mentioned here from my own experience.

Many Asians came as workers, the men first of all, to be followed later by their families. Before long they sought the communal practice of their faith and eventually many mosques and temples were built to provide quite new varieties to urban scenes. Before such buildings were constructed, however, groups of believers looked around for buildings that they could rent or buy, and empty or little used church premises seemed the obvious choices.

Debates were held in church committees as to the proper procedure. Some churches were willing to rent or sell their buildings to any applicant, and others refused outright to loan or sell them to 'idolators'. They often seemed unaware that Muslims, Sikhs and Jews have no idols, and indeed are more opposed to any form of imagery than some of the major Christian churches. Some maintained that 'consecrated' buildings could not be used by members of any other religious body than the consecrating authority. It appeared at times that the church was less hospitable than the British Legion Hall, and it was a sad situation when devout strangers could not find a welcome, despite the parable which said that 'I was a stranger and you did not take me in.'

Some churches compromised by allowing the renting of 'ancillary buildings', school halls and the like which were not regularly used for worship. Even then the condition might be imposed that they should be used for purely 'secular' ceremonies, such as marriages, though these are usually not secular but religious. It seems strange to impose a veto of religious worship on members of another faith. For these and other reasons Asian communities have bought or built their own temples as soon as it became financially possible. Generous supporters were found in eastern countries, giving their names to buildings, such as the Saddam Hussein mosque.

There is an interesting historical example. In the eighteenth century Protestant Huguenots fleeing from persecution in France were able to build a church in Brick Lane in the East End of London. They worked hard and prospered and in due course moved up to the West End. The church was sold to poor Methodists, who also worked hard and prospered and moved westwards. Then this church was sold to be a synagogue for Jews escaping persecution in Europe, who also worked and prospered and moved to Hampstead. This church–synagogue is now a mosque for Bengalis, who will also undoubtedly work and prosper and move on. Who will be the next occupants? It is a listed building, a religious building, and it is better that it should continue to be used for worship than turned into a warehouse or brewery. It remains a parable of the diversity of religion in this country, a building which has heard prayers in French, English, Hebrew and Arabic, from men and women who have struggled to worship God, each in their own way, and it may serve those yet to come.

The question of interfaith worship, which has recently been challenged, arises out of the variety of religious communities and the desire of some to join together in prayers with other believers in God. The World Congress of Faiths has held such services for many years, chiefly in churches and synagogues of liberal traditions. But interfaith services became larger and more prominent in celebrations of the unity of the British Commonwealth.

The Commonwealth is multi-racial and multi-religious, and as its head the Queen has attended these services. In one way this is following the tradition of Queen Victoria who, when she became ruler of Ceylon, became the protector of Buddhism, in succession to previous rulers of that State religion. When the Commonwealth service was to be held at St Martin-in-the-Fields in London, I was consulted by Ian Trethowan and a colleague from the BBC which was to broadcast this service. The programme included readings from the scriptures of different religions which I was able to identify for them. But after the service objections were made to the uttering of 'heathen' words in a Christian church. The diocesan bishop was persuaded to forbid such mixed religious worship in St Martin's and the Commonwealth service moved around annually till it found a home in Westminster Abbey. The Abbey is a 'royal peculiar', not under the authority of any bishop, and if the dean is agreeable he is solely responsible for the permission.

Several questions arise, practical and theological. Should the scripture readings or prayers be general, acceptable to any faith, or should they include specific items and names from particular religions? Clearly it would be useful to have a common policy, and this could be worked out in the preparation for the service.

Theologically, if the names of God are Father, Adonai, Allah, or Nam (for Sikhs), they may be claimed as variants of a common faith, comparable to Dieu, Dios or Gott. But if the names of Krishna, or Buddha, or even Christ, are used might this not bring offence to some believers?

No doubt those who attend interfaith services expect and accept that different religions have different ways, names and beliefs. Acceptance of this fact is an ingredient of modern life. But theologically it may be understood more profoundly. The cosmic Christ can be seen as inspiring and embracing all expressions of sincere faith. This cannot be put better than in a favourite passage from the great Archbishop William Temple. In his devotional commentary on St John's Gospel he wrote on the verse that speaks of the logos as 'the true Light, which lighteth everyone'. Temple commented: 'By the word of God – that is to say by Jesus Christ – Isaiah and Plato, Zoroaster, Buddha, and Confucius, uttered and wrote such truths as they declared. There is only one Divine Light, and every man in his own measure is enlightened by it.' Therefore Christians need not be afraid, as if the ark of God were trembling, when they hear other names and concepts, even in churches, for these can be taken as inspired by the one divine light.

There are some who would have no sharing or dialogue with members of other religions, regarding them as 'pagans' and 'lost' unless they submit to particular organizations and doctrines. But a better example of sharing in prayer, in a church, was given by Pope John Paul II in 1986 when he joined with hundreds of leaders of world religions, Christian, Jewish, Muslim, Hindu, Buddhist, Sikh and Shinto, to pray for peace in the basilica of St Francis in Assisi.

Further, it is always open to lay people or their leaders to observe interfaith worship in the buildings of particular religions. Synagogues and churches, temples and mosques, are usually open to visitors of any faith or none. There the specific doctrines and practices may be witnessed and studied in the full context of faith, and religion may be seen not only in writings but in the commitment of worship. To observe how other people pray may give insight into the depth of attachment to religion.

10 MODELS OF INTERRELIGIOUS COMMUNICATION: Reflections on Interfaith Dialogue
Ursula King

Dialogue is a relatively modern concern and its usage requires some clarification. Besides the words interreligious and interfaith dialogue one finds such terms as trialogue, multilogue, 'transtraditional dialogue' or 'intra-religious dialogue' as distinct from 'interreligious dialogue'. We have to inquire into the meaning of interfaith dialogue to find our way through all this conceptual confusion.

Dialogue seems to be primarily a very practical activity of listening and sharing and, at its best, it might imply an in-depth participation in another mode of thinking, believing, praying or worshipping. How then to theorize about it? It may be helpful to introduce here Margaret Chatterjee's concept of 'interreligious communication' which she describes as the communication between an individual of one faith and an individual of another faith, a personally direct communication which takes place in a social and historical context, but at the same time it also takes place in spite of that context and involves mutuality. This communication can take place at a behavioural level by sharing one's festivals or other activities but it often occurs at the verbal level where language poses a special task to understanding and where we have to reflect on the difference between the language of devotion and worship as distinct from the language of theology (Chatterjee, 1967-68).

The experience of dialogue will affect our mode of theologizing. If one understands different theologies as using different models by which they interpret and interconnect a wide variety of experiences, we are able to perceive the plurality of existing theological forms of expression, for the concept 'model' in theory formation presumes a multiplicity, a plurality of models which need not indicate a competition but allows none the less for the possibility of alternative ways of expressing and reflecting on experiences.

It has been said that our experiences in the contemporary world have undergone profound changes but that the theoretical expression of these experiences, the way we theologize about them, has not kept up with these changes so that our level of expression does not match our level of contemporary experience. This is true of many fields of theology. To develop an adequate theology in a radically new religious situation we need a hermeneutic of past and present multi-religious encounter. If dialogue is conceived as a process of 'baptismal immersion', this presupposes an open faith in the sense that my faith needs to be re-conceived in the light of encountering the faith of another, rather than seeing another faith in the light of my own. Thus dialogue presupposes equal partners and it also presupposes the acceptance of other religions as genuine religions equal to my own. In that sense true dialogue expands the range of common concerns and helps to evolve a shared vocabulary.

In what follows, I shall reflect on interfaith dialogue from a number of different perspectives. I shall begin with the challenge of religious pluralism, then consider the nature of interfaith dialogue, and finally discuss the importance of this dialogue for contemporary theologizing. I also want to include one particular example by looking at the significance of Christ in the light of Hinduism.

I. The Challenge of Religious Pluralism

We live today in a world of unprecedented ethnic, social, cultural and religious pluralism. This is a new situation with new opportunities and new difficulties. Instead of simply acknowledging our different religious histories in terms of diversity and plurality, we need to ask religiously about the religious meaning of religious pluralism. We have reached a new historical moment in terms of a new 'critical corporate consciousness' where we can discern a unity and pattern in the religious history of humankind. This has been recognized by several twentieth-century thinkers, for example the Muslim Mohammed Iqbal, the Hindu thinker Sri Aurobindo and the Christian Teilhard de Chardin. More recently this theme has been imaginatively explored by Wilfred Cantwell Smith in his study *Towards a World Theology* (1981). Not only does Cantwell Smith emphasize the centrality of faith and its transforming powers in human life, he also examines the historical, academic and theological dimensions of contemporary religious pluralism. Like others, Smith strongly underlines the current 'shift from unawareness and insouciance to the new recognition of our global interdependence... in spiritual matters' (Smith, 1981:43). If approached with the right attitude and searching reflection, religious pluralism can become an important source for mutual enrichment rather than a cause for further communal tension. If we honestly seek to answer the challenging question of how we can meaningfully recognize and learn from each other in mutuality and trust, we must explore together the specific insights, moments of revelation and spiritual treasures which our respective religious traditions have accumulated and handed down from one generation to the next, and whereby the lives of countless people in the past and the present have been nourished, sustained and transformed.

Immersing ourselves into that process we come to recognize our profound diversities and the wounds we have inflicted on each other, and this is a deeply painful experience. There is not only the extraordinary pluralism between our different traditions, but there is also the challenging pluralism within each of our own communities, an extraordinary variety and richness of different historical and theological strands. It takes courage and humility to acknowledge this diversity which can be regarded as a rich spiritual resource rather than a cause for confusion and competition.

The discovery of the true nature of pluralism implies what has been called the 'demonopolization' (de Souza, 1986) of any particular religion and the refusal to act in a monopolistic, imperialistic and triumphantly exclusive manner towards religions other than one's own or, rather, towards religious people outside one's own community, however large or small. (This negative, exclusive attitude can be found within different strands of the same religious tradition as well as between people of completely different traditions.) If we are open and perceptive, and sensitive to human needs and historical transformations, we can recognize an irreplaceable spiritual heritage in each tradition, a specific message and distinctive identity which are of tremendous importance for all of us, for each faith provides a powerful matrix for ultimate meaning which can help us in the process of shaping a meaningful global community. We must be humble and sincere enough to concede that there is incompleteness in each of our traditions, that none is static and complete but continually in the process of becoming, that there is room and need for further growth in all of them. However, the recognition of pluralism poses intellectual, moral and theological problems. It is particularly the latter with which I am concerned in this paper and much work still needs to be done in all these areas.

To develop a richer, more differentiated and universalist theology of pluralism we need to reflect on the dynamic of dialogue between people of different faiths.

II. Interfaith Dialogue and a Theology of Pluralism

In historical terms dialogue is a very recent development. The World Council of Churches has actively promoted interreligious dialogue since 1967 and the Roman Catholic Church since the Second Vatican Council, although many religiously committed individuals pursued dialogue long before that. Dialogue has different dimensions and can take place at different levels; by now the various experiments in interreligious encounter, interfaith movements and dialogue have come a long way and helped many people to realize that faiths other than our own are genuine homes of the spirit to be discovered rather than fortresses to be attacked.

Dialogue can considered an ongoing process which involves mutual discovery, living, working and worshipping together so that empathy grows and relations are strengthened. This process must be undertaken in a spirit of openness and mutual trust, without any tacit schemes of displacement, absorption or conversion. However, without giving up the particularities of one's own faith, one can think of a certain 'reconception' of each faith through the experience of encountering another. The four 'Guidelines for Dialogue' of the British Council of Churches (1983) state that:

(i) dialogue begins when people meet each other
(ii) dialogue depends upon mutual understanding and mutual trust
(iii) dialogue makes it possible to share in service to the community
(iv) dialogue becomes the medium of authentic witness

Much work has gone into thinking and working out the implications of closer relations between people of different faiths, so much needed in our multi-cultural societies and cities; but central to the whole process of dialogue is the realization that people from different faiths are not 'competitors' but partners and fellow pilgrims. The fuller implications of the four 'Guidelines for Dialogue' have been presented more recently in the *Report Towards a Theology for Inter-Faith Dialogue* (Anglican Consultative Council, 1988) submitted to the 1988 Lambeth Conference, and the 'Guidelines' themselves are being republished in a revised form.

Interreligious dialogue is not only a 'Christian ecumenical concern' (Eck, 1985), but a global ecumenical concern. It has to be carried on at the interreligious and the intra-religious level (Panikkar, 1978), that is to say, between the different communities as well as within them, and within each of us. While such different forms of dialogue will help to make our institutional and mental boundaries more flexible and less rigid, they will also help to strengthen the bond between us so that we can build together a larger community.

Dialogue has to be perceived in a larger dimension still, for it is not only needed between people of different faiths, but also between religious world-views and secular cultures. Theological reflections often remain in static and inappropriate categories since they do not always sufficiently take into account contemporary developments in global society and in the growth of human knowledge. If dialogue is to be effective, it will also have to take place between religion and science as well as between religion and politics.

Because we share a common humanity and a common responsibility for life on earth, we can and must learn to move towards greater mutuality by encouraging and taking part in different kinds of dialogue. In a different context, namely that of feminism, Letty Russell (1974) has emphasized the capacity of dialogue for community-building. She describes three forms of dialogue which are currently being explored and tested:

(i) mutual interpellation as a way of thinking one's way together in action
(ii) dialogical action where people act their way into thinking together
(iii) shared world in which people can not only think and act but also experience the same environment together.

Perhaps we need to experiment with all three of these forms when people from different faiths meet to think, act and share together – and then go away transformed to think and act in a new way.

As to the theological implications of such a transformation process, one must first recognize that most theological thinking – and I mean by this the critical intellectual reflections arising out of any faith – still occurs within narrowly confined cultural and conceptual ghettos characterized by far too restricted a vision and far too exclusive a language. Today, under the growing influence of interreligious encounter and dialogue, each religious tradition requires a new kind of reflective theology which is responsible to the situation of religious pluralism. There have been various attempts to develop a 'theology of religions', but these have largely been explorations of how to approach, from within the perspective of Christianity, the existence and message of 'other religions' (see the essays in Hick and Hebblethwaite, 1980, *Christianity and other Religions*). We have not yet developed a generally accepted theology of pluralism or what Wilfred Cantwell Smith has called a 'world theology' (1981). His own work, however, has laid an important basis and provided many helpful directions for this. In his life-long scholarly endeavours Smith has also highlighted again and again that all believers, from whatever faith, share the strength of a religious approach to reality, the support and sustenance drawn from the vision of a living faith.

Today, by acknowledging our situation of religious pluralism not only as a fact, but by theologically reflecting on it and by engaging in dialogue with others and within ourselves as individuals and communities, we can enlarge that vision, strengthen it and perhaps feel at home in more than one vision of faith. One might say, as I have said elsewhere (King, 1986), that perhaps we have 'to become not so much spiritually multi-lingual as perhaps spiritually multi-focussed'. It is not only a 'world theology' we need, but perhaps also a growing number of 'world believers'. Like the 'world citizen' who feels at home in different countries and cultures, but is rooted in a particular one, so also the 'world believer' will have roots in one faith and yet be able to relate to that of many others. The experiences of religious pluralism and interfaith dialogue invites us to a global vision which requires a new mode of theologizing.

III. Some Theological Implications of Interfaith Dialogue

Theology is grounded in experience; it is also contextual and cumulative. Particular theologians do not always take sufficient account of the pluralism of theological thinking within their own religious tradition. Thus theological language is often expressed in a normative, absolutist manner while it is in fact much more helpful, and much more conducive to greater openness and better understanding between people of different religious traditions, to think of different 'models' of theology, of different ways of expressing the root experience of faith. While our experience of interfaith dialogue and of a new awareness arising out of it has undergone and is undergoing much transformation, our models of expressing, of reflecting this experience have not yet caught up with this process. The first implication of interfaith dialogue thus affects *theological methodology*: theological reflection can no longer be based on one religious tradition alone by proceeding deductively and exclusively from the premises of one faith. The only viable mode of doing theology in contemporary society is by the inductive method (Berger, 1980) based on contemporary experience which is one of pluralism. This implies the experience of common fellowship, of fellow pilgrims recognizing each other as called by the same spirit.

The experience and practice of interfaith dialogue also raises the question of each person's and each community's *faith commitment* (Nirmal, 1980). This is not called into question; it may in fact be strengthened and enhanced. But our attitudes and the formulation of our beliefs arising out of our faith commitment will be changing as they are always tentative and provisional, always in need of further clarification and growth. Theology is a verbal–conceptual symbol system of a particular kind, conveying something of profound importance about the meaning of life and transcendence. As Cantwell Smith has stated:

> Theology is critical intellectualization of (and for) faith, and of the world as known in faith; and what we seek is a theology that will interpret the history of our race in a way that will give intellectual expression to our faith, the faith of all of us, and to our modern perception of the world... In giving conceptual articulation to our faith, the faith of all of us, it must not dilute Christian faith – the faith of some of us – but transcend it. (Smith, 1981:125)

Each tradition will have to explore the implications of religious pluralism and interfaith dialogue for its own theological thinking. From the perspective of the Christian tradition, in which I am personally rooted and with which I am most familiar, one could summarize the theological task as one of reformulating the traditional teachings on 'God, man and the world' (or more specifically 'God, the human being, nature and society'). Or what Teilhard de Chardin (1969, 1975) in his inquiry into the spiritual energy resources of eastern and western religions for 'building the earth' called the problems of 'God and his transcendence; the world and its value; the individual and the importance of the person; mankind and social requirements', all of which have found particular formulations in different theologies, but so far no overall synthesis and integrated approach have been attempted which are commensurate to our contemporary experience of history, society, and new consciousness and realization of the common destiny of humankind (a fuller discussion of this is found in King, 1980).

It is impossible to explore all these aspects in detail, but central to them all is the question of God or, rather, of *the nature and structure of the concept of Ultimate Reality, of our language and thought about transcendence.* Any dialogue must struggle with this question, and any 'in-depth-dialogue involving deeper participation and sharing of one's vision will make the participants realize that no conceptual and symbolic model for understanding this reality can encompass its richness nor the richness of religious experience in encountering the signs of divine life and grace at all levels of human life. Theology is quite literally 'talk about God' or, more generally, 'about the transcendent dimension of human life and of the universe to which the history of religion (the history of man's spirit) bears witness and which it elucidates and to which Christians have historically given the name "God"' (Smith, 1981:151).

The Indian theologian Arvind P. Nirmal (1980) has argued that different theologies are model discourses about ultimate reality. In his view, religious pluralism implies that ultimate reality is indeterminate and capable of many different manifestations in human history and consciousness. From this perspective, different world religions can be seen as 'economic gifts' to humankind, as the outpouring of the spirit on earth. This does not mean that all religions are paths to the same goal and thus primarily human attempts to reach the ultimate but, on the contrary, it implies 'that the very structure and nature of Ultimate Reality is such that it contains within itself a rich and inexhaustible capacity for different and ever-new manifestations'. In Christian theological terms this also implies a 'process-view' of God.

Interfaith dialogue can lead participants to the existential realization that each religious tradition has received a valuable glimpse – some perhaps more, some less – of the total vision, and in dialogue we can learn to complement each other's insight and disclosure of the Divine. It is thus not a question of competition, but of the complementarity of different visions which, when related to each other, can grow into greater fullness. Without losing our respective identities, the task of integration, of relating our respective visions to each other, can enlarge and enrich us all together and give us access to greater splendour and deeper understanding.

Another important theological question arising out of interfaith dialogue is the question of truth or, as it is often put, of the respective truth claims of different religions. This is not a very satisfactory formulation, however, as it represents already a specific theological perspective whose premise one might wish to question. It relates more to a propositional than to an experiential approach to truth; religions are not like territories in which one stakes 'claims' but rather like maps with well-tried paths to meaning, liberation and transcendence. Each faith community is sustained by a particular paradigm of ultimate reality and by multiple ways and pointers how to approach, embrace and love it. Too often we are tempted to make universal 'truth claims' on behalf of that reality which we have only partially apprehended and understood. Instead of analyzing the respective 'truth claims' of different religions, we need to discover the search for truth in all of them, for truth is truly 'thousand-eyed', to use an Indian image rich with symbolic resonance.

Arvind P. Nirmal (1980) has emphasized the twofold character of all theological statements in being 'truth-claims' and 'faith-affirmations' at the same time. This is true of the theological reflections of all religions. They are primarily of an experiential nature and not 'empirical' truth claims which can be universally validated. In Nirmal's view, none of our faith-affirmations or truth-claims has a one-to-one correspondence with the reality we seek to affirm. All theological language is necessarily analogical, symbolic, metaphorical and model-oriented. He also thinks that one of the postulates of interreligious dialogue should be that 'truth' emerges only in the actual process of dialogue – but even this 'emergent truth' is never to be regarded as 'final truth'.

Or, as Cantwell Smith has written:

> With regard to the question of truth internally within the religious field, and among its potentially bewildering diversities, perhaps the primary lesson to be learned is this, if one is to be discriminating but not sit in judgement: that the rigorous and unrelenting search for truth can be combined with a profound respect for others and for variety provided that one recognizes the truth that one seeks as to be found not in the history of religion but through it... In so far as truth is apprehended by persons, it is apprehended within history; yet in so far as it is true, it transcends history (and any particular formulation). (Smith, 1981:190)

To develop a new 'global theology', whose outlines we are just beginning to discern, will require a new corporate effort and imaginative vision born from the insights of a living faith, often different in form and intensity, but not in kind. To formulate such a theology 'it is necessary to advance beyond confessional forms of theology to a universal, truth-centred position. A major difficulty in developing theology of this sort lies in our undeveloped ability to enter the various world-views as personal sources of insight' (Hughes, 1986:173).

Members of different faiths have to learn to see through each other's eyes and feel with each other's senses. Perhaps the term 'global theology' still sounds too absolutist, too unacceptable to people outside the Christian tradition, too much like a grand synthesis which leaves no room for internal differentiation. Perhaps another term has to be found – 'multilateral theologies', or something similar – to reflect at the linguistic and conceptual level the pluralistic complexities, the variety of approaches to truth and ultimate reality in their historical and contemporary forms. Such a theology must be free from any apologetics and imperialistic claims; it has to remain open-ended, always open in the search for further truth. It has profound implications for what is traditionally called the 'theology of missions' and also what is currently termed 'theology of religions'.

More and more contemporary theologians are beginning to reflect on interfaith dialogue. Starting from a Barthian position David Lochhead (1988) has developed reflections on what he calls *The Dialogical Imperative* which necessitates a new theology of mission and of the Church, rather than a theocentric shift in christology, as argued by Hick and others. In a more recent volume entitled *Religions in Conversation: Christian Identity and Religious Pluralism* (1989) Michael Barnes analyzes the conceptual and practical constraints placed on the understanding of a theology of dialogue through the categories developed so far and argues for the liberation of theology through the practice of dialogue. At the practical, as distinct from the abstract theological, level several helpful publications have become available for use in discussion groups, for example the BBC study guide 'Unfamiliar Journey; Christians and Inter-Faith Dialogue', Sargant and Sugden, 1986) or its regular journal *Discernment – A Christian Journal of Inter-Religious Encounter* or the Methodist publication God of all Faith – Discovering *God's Presence in a Multifaith Society* edited by Martin Forward (1989).

For Christians, one of the greatest challenges of interfaith dialogue arises out of the question about the universality of Christ and his mission, and how to understand the Incarnation in the context of religious pluralism. Some recent writers have addressed this question (Anderson and Stransky, 1981; Race, 1983; Knitter, 1985) but further theological work still needs to be done in this area. To finish with an example, I would like to end with some reflections on the meaning of Christ raised by dialogue with Hinduism.

IV. Questions about the Universal Significance of Christ Arising out of Hindu–Christian Encounter

What questions, new experiences and perspectives arise when we approach the mystery of Christ while being immersed into and passing through the Hindu way of seeing the divine? What can Christians learn about the central mystery of Christianity through an encounter with Hindu faith?

Can we be truly open to the otherness of this experience which breaks through our accustomed frames of reference, especially as Hinduism is not a single religion focused on a central event, but consists of a pluralism of beliefs and practices? Or are we so steeped in our own concepts, our own history of doctrine and expression of faith-experience in the West that there exists from the beginning a theoretical repression of new and different experiences made inadmissable by our very way of framing the question which we ask?

It seems to me that a question about the universal significance of Christ is initially a question about us – how we have learnt to think about Christ, both as a faith community and as individuals, and how we have become accustomed to associate this question with a number of ideas and concepts which from a different theological position and faith experience can be misunderstood and interpreted as too narrow and inclusive. The first question which therefore arises is: what are our presuppositions and parameters in exploring the Christ-event in the cultural and religious context of our contemporary world? How fully inclusive, how far-reaching, how comprehensive, how truly universal is the meaning of *'universal'* when we speak of 'universal significance'? Does it include all people, past, present and future? Does it include people of all faiths and none? Does it include all forms of life, not only human? Does it reach out to the whole cosmos? These are all questions which have been asked about Christ – and they are emphatically asked again when Christ is approached from a Hindu perspective.

Another, second question arises out of Hindu experience: why speak of universal *significance*, as we are wont to do? This way of speaking points to the Christ-event as a decisive, central sign, a symbol of far-reaching power and meaning, a universal point of reference. But subjectively it can also mean that to which we have assigned such meaning. While such assigning is an existential act involving the whole person, as a confession of faith it is often understood in a narrower sense as an intellectual act of assent relating to specific concepts and rational explanations. This is evident from the abstract theological language used about Christ in treatises of systematic theology which often more resemble highly complex intellectual games than they convey insight, enlightenment or wisdom – the life of grace and spirit. The religious language about Christ – as distinct from theological abstractions – the language of prayer and ritual is far more direct, concrete, personal and evocative of response. It does not define or explain significance, but is a direct expression and mediation of it. It would seem more honest, more humble, more true perhaps to speak not of universal significance, but of the *universal mystery of Christ*, as the early Church did too – a *mysterion* whose fullness we can never exhaust but only approach in reverence, with a sense of ever new discovery and wonder. New aspects may be revealed and new insights disclosed when we approach this mystery from a Hindu perspective.

While questions about the significance of Christ raise important historical and theoretical issues relating to a differentiated theological methodology and hermeneutics, we must not forget that much of western Christian theology needs to be freed from what has been called its 'Latin captivity' or bondage. We need to examine our traditional theological modes of thinking from a critical distance: how far has the western theological mode too much insisted on conceptual distinctions and separations, with an emphasis on otherness and exclusiveness rather than on the relatedness of all things, the connections between different levels of reality and experience? Here too Hindu perspectives can provide a wholesome corrective. (For a wide-ranging exploration of historical and contemporary aspects of Hindu–Christian dialogue see Coward, 1989.)

It is important to realize that, due to the colonial situation of political dominance and the intense missionary activity of various Christian denominations during the nineteenth century, certain Hindus have been thinking far longer about Christ and Christianity than Christians have taken serious note of Hindu religious experience. In that sense Hindus might say that the understanding of Christ is a greater problem for Christians today than it is for Hindus.

During the nineteenth and twentieth centuries Hindu religious reformers have been especially attracted to the ethical and moral teachings of Jesus, his self-negation and surrender to God, the supreme example of his life and of his precepts. They saw in Jesus primarily a great human teacher, perhaps an *avatar* or master yogin, but they were less interested in Christ as pre-existent logos within a wider trinitarian or cosmic context. Some spoke of 'Jesus the Asiatic', the 'Oriental Christ' or 'Christ the Ascetic' and, as M.M. Thomas has shown, 'the acknowledged Christ of the Indian Renaissance' became an important reality in modern Hinduism while Christianity as a religion was rejected. But can one thus divide Christ and Christianity? Historically speaking, one would not have come into being without the other, but perhaps they need to be clearly separated in order to recover the original meaning and mystery of the formative Christ-event which the Hindu might find much more accessible and less questionable than what has been made of it throughout the centuries of western Christianity.

Mahatma Gandhi saw in Christ above all the greater teacher of non-violence, the supreme *satyagrahi* (working through 'soul-force'), while Radhakrishnan spoke of the 'mystic Christ'. During the nineteenth century some Hindus saw Krishna as the 'Hindu Christ', a comparison perhaps originally rooted in the early translation of the *Bhagavad Gita* into English (1785) and used many times since by both Hindus and Christians.

A possible rapprochement between Christian and Hindu experience seems much easier on the level of prayer and worship than that of theological reflection. One also arrives at different kinds of insight and understanding depending on whether one focuses one's quest about meaning primarily on the person of Jesus or on a fuller theological reality which includes the symbol of the cosmic Christ. This theme could long detain us but cannot be developed here. I would like to touch briefly upon a few other aspects (see also Hooker, 1989, for other comparisons between Hinduism and Christianity). Given the absolute priority of *Brahman* in Hindu theology – *Brahman* as the inexhaustible, unapproachable, ultimate mystery of the One that has been called by a great variety of names – the Hindu would insist on the tension between this One and its many forms, of which Christ cannot be more than one. If a Christian approaches the mystery of Christ as an ongoing, but in some way uniquely significant, Christ-event, a number of questions arise from Hindu experience, which I can only list here:

1. *Immanence/transcendence*
   How does Christ's presence in the world, the Church, the sacraments, the human heart relate to God's ultimate transcendence? Does the Christian take divine immanence sufficiently seriously, or is it always outweighed by divine transcendence? Is Christ's work and significance still immanent with us here and now, or is it mainly seen as something in relation to the past?

2. *History/cosmos*
   Is Christ's coming a unique historical event or has God revealed him/herself at other times and places? Does God's revelation occur through significant actions in history or equally well through processes and events in the cosmos (as experienced by the Hindu in Vishnu's universal form, the *vishvarupa*, or through Shiva's cosmic dance)? Given the significance of the cosmos in Hindu theological speculations, it is perhaps not surprising that Christian theologians in India have shown a special interest in developing the theology of the cosmic Christ.

3. *Suffering and transformation*
   Most challenging of all is the theology of the cross. However enchanting and appealing the comparison between Krishna and Christ, however enriching in that it touches on aspects not easily experienced in Christianity, there is no easy contact between Hindu experience and Christ's redemptive suffering on the cross which brings healing and new life. Seen from the perspective of *karma* and *samsara* the Hindu must abhor and question the insistence on suffering in the redemptive work of Christ. The Hindu idea of liberation – *moksha* – involves freedom from suffering and transformation too, and one must ask how far the Christian focus on Christ's suffering has often been more destructive rather than truly redemptive and transformative.

4. *The central question about incarnation*
   Is the uniqueness of Christ's Incarnation too narrowly understood by Christians, too exclusively related to a one-time event? The Hindu religious tradition is particularly rich in the symbolic realm, and that also applies to the understanding of incarnation.

Could some of its symbols relating to God and his energies, actions and presence in the world help us to reformulate central aspects of christology? Hindu Vaishnava theology knows five different types of incarnations, from the highest, full incarnation of God over several cosmic forms to manifestations at the human level, plus manifestations in each human being as inner guide and controller, to the presence within an icon used in worship. Through all these different forms God becomes accessible to human experience – with an incredible closeness and immmediacy.

5. *The female expression of the divine*
In the Vaishanvite tradition the female divine form, *Shri*, is personified as the consort of Vishnu, and is seen as mediator and 'mother of all beings'. Some Vaishnavas consider *Shri* as originally human, but elevated to divine status, while others, emphasizing her role as mediator and saviour, consider her as co-eternal with Vishnu. A Hindu author has pointed out that the status of *Shri* functions somewhat similarly in Vaishnavite tradition as the status of the incarnate Lord in the Christian tradition and argues moreover that *Shri's* co-eternity with Vishnu can make a Vaishnava Hindu appreciate the co-eternity implied in the Christian doctrine of incarnation and trinity (Sundarajan, 1978–79).

In her discussion of 'Christology and Feminism' Rosemary Ruether (1981) has pointed out that the construction of christology has often occurred through symbols which have made it an instrument of patriarchal domination, and that we need to look for alternative models of christology. Here again, the rich Hindu resources of the female expression of the divine could provide helpful resources of renewal for exploring the meaning of Christ today.

6. *The understanding of the presence of the Spirit among us*
The experience of Christ as a living symbol and reality relates to an ongoing event disclosed through the presence of the divine Spirit among us here and now. One may consider it as part of its work and guidance that we have to seek for a fresh approach to the meaning of the central Christian mysteries in the context of a bewildering religious and theological diversity. Here the experience of Hindu faith may encourage us to ask: Are we sufficiently attentive to the workings of the Spirit? Are we sufficiently humble, honest and reverent to recognize the signs of divine revelation and disclosure in our own time among the peoples of the earth?

To conclude, we have to learn to live in and respond creatively to a completely new context of religious and social complexity which poses a tremendous intellectual challenge to our traditional mode of doing theology. It is not our task to affirm the sheer plurality of religious experiences and revelations and then let them stand by side. On the contrary, we need to pursue a genuine theological probing of the religious meaning of pluralism by relating our seeing, feeling, thinking, acting and praying to more than one mode of being. Hinduism has a rich tradition in dealing with complexity by approaching all realities from more than one perspective. Perhaps Christians can learn from Hindu experience that the very richness of the mystery of Christ consists precisely in allowing us to fathom its significance in many different and hitherto unknown ways.

It will not be easy to develop new theological modes of thinking and new modes of interreligious communication. All the powers of our intellect and imagination and the resources of our faith are called upon to bring to fruition the spiritual insights of our world religious heritage, to develop a theological vision which can help to build a world community on earth. Interfaith communication and dialogue can also help to remove unfavourable intergroup images and stereotypes, wrongly grounded philosophical categories and evaluative theological statements which hinder rather than help understanding. Dialogue is linked to openness and tolerance, but it develops at the deepest level only if it is transfigured by love. Interfaith dialogue has tremendous theological implications whose details have still to be worked out in full, but in and through it we can learn that its occurrence and further development are not only a task of philosophical and theological reflection, but also a religious event of tremendous importance for our future.

11 A RELIGIOUS UNDERSTANDING OF RELIGION: a Model of the Relationship Between Traditions
John Hick

A large part of the academic study of religion consists in its objective study as a range of forms of human thought and behaviour. It deals with the history of religions; with the interactions between religions, societies and cultures in the past and present; with the historical and literary analyses of religious texts; with the sociology of religious practices and organizations; with the psychology of religious experience and belief. And all such study is, in principle, entirely dependent of the question whether or not there is any transcendent reality of limitless value such as religious people affirm when they speak of God, Brahman, the Dharmakaya, the Tao, and so on.

The objective study of religion is thus a branch of anthropology in the broadest sense of that term, and is as such of profound interest and importance as a contribution to the study of humankind.

But distinctively religious ideas and practices differ from others in referring intentionally beyond humankind and beyond our natural environment. There is accordingly a fundamental difference between non-religious understandings of religion as a human phenomenon, and religious understandings of it as our response to the Transcendent. The relationship between these two points of view is asymmetrical. A non-religious study of the religious aspects of human life cannot refer to the Transcendent, although it must of course refer to human ideas of and beliefs in a transcendent reality. On the other hand, a religious understanding of religion must, as part of its essential discourse, refer to the Transcendent, although it can also, and indeed certainly should, also be interested in the human character and material conditions of the response, in its varying forms, to the supposed transcendent reality itself – or herself or himself.

If we set aside any naturalistic prejudice, we must acknowledge that religious understandings are intrinsically as legitimate as non-religious understandings of religion. They are also of course of particular interest to that large number of men and women who are religious practitioners or believers or – to use a truly horrid word – religionists. Now, in the past, religious interpretations of religion have normally been restricted in their scope to a single tradition.

There has been Christian discourse concerning the Holy Trinity and the history of human response to the Trinity. There has been Buddhist discourse about Nirvana, the Dharmakaya, Sunyata, and the history of human awakening to this reality. And there has been Jewish, Muslim, Hindu, Taoist discourse; and so on. Each of these constitutes a religious (as distinguished from a non-religious or a naturalistic) account of one particular stream of religion, but not of religion around the world and across the centuries.

There is of course no such thing as religion in general: religion exists only in its many concrete forms. But because there is a plurality of such concrete forms, a religious interpretation of religion over this wide range will inevitably differ from the particular self-understanding developed within any single tradition. The latter will see religion as a response specifically to the Christian Trinity, or to the Qur'ànic Allah, or to Brahman, or the Dharmakaya, and so on, whereas a global religious understanding of religion will see it as the range of forms taken by our human response to the Transcendent. We must not, then, expect a comprehensive religious understanding of religion to be identical with a Christian, or a Buddhist, or a Muslim, or any other one confessional interpretation of it. In spite of this rather obvious point, whenever a global interpretation is proposed there are always some who criticize it for diverging from the belief system of their own tradition. In doing so they are in effect rejecting the whole project of a religious interpretation of religion in its world-wide multiplicity of forms.

Because religion is concretely plural, a global religious interpretation of religion has to be approached through one or other of its particular concrete forms. We start from within one of the religious traditions – which in my own case is Christianity. From within any one of these traditions the believer is committed to the fundamental faith that this stream of religious experience is not purely a human projection but is at the same time a response to the presence of a transcendent reality. But a believer must today be aware that in addition to her own religion there are also other great world faiths, as well as many smaller religious movements both old and new, all likewise seeing themselves as responses to the Transcendent. At this point she may opt for the exclusivist claim that her own religion is an authentic response to the divine but that all the others are fundamentally different in nature, as products of the human imagination. In other words she can follow Karl Barth in accepting Feuerbach's projection theory as applying to all forms of religion except one's own. But this is, naturally enough, a position that will prove convincing only to other members of the same tradition. It is thus arbitrary in a way that must worry any reasonable person. Suppose, then, that instead we follow an analogue of the Golden Rule by granting to others the same basic faith assumption that we have made for ourselves, namely that religious experience within one's own tradition is an authentic response to the Transcendent. At this point a further choice opens up. One option is the inclusivist position that while other traditions are also responses to the Transcendent, our own is the purest or fullest or most direct such response, including but transcending all that is valuable in the others. However, this is only a modified version of the absolutist claim, and suffers from the same arbitrariness. The alternative option is the pluralist view that the great world religions all seem, so far as unbiased human observation can tell, to be more or less on a par as salvific responses to the Transcendent. Of course, no comparative judgement in this area is capable of being proved. There can be endless debate between, on the one hand, a Christian version, or a Buddhist version, or a Muslim or any other version of inclusivism and, on the other hand, a pluralism that acknowledges the rough parity of the great traditions as human responses to the Transcendent. However, I am not going to stage those debates here. For my concern at the moment is only to see how the great traditions, despite their immense differences, may nevertheless constitute alternative responses to the same ultimate transcendent reality; and whether or not they constitute more or less equally full and authentic responses is a further question that could only be settled – if indeed it could ever be settled – by extensive historical research into the religions of the world, studied both synchronically and diachronically. I have argued elsewhere that the historical data are so complex that one can at present only come to the negative conclusion that no one tradition stands out as soteriologically supreme; but I am not going to argue that here.

Our present question, then, is whether the great religious systems of the world can all have been formed in response to the same divine reality. And it must be admitted that the initial appearances are against this. For the intentional objects of the different traditions are so clearly different. Phenomenologically (i.e. as describable) the Holy Trinity of Christianity is obviously not identical with the Allah of Islam or with the Jahweh of biblical Judaism or the Vishnu or Shiva of theistic Hinduism. Jahweh, for example, is depicted in the Hebrew scriptures as living in close interaction with the children of Israel, but not as showing any interest in the life of India; while Krishna, as the incarnation of Vishnu, is depicted in the *Bhagavad Gita* as living in close interaction with some of the tribes of India but not as showing any interest in ancient Middle Eastern history. Further, the religious ideas and assumptions expressed by Krishna reflect a distinctively Indian background while those expressed by Jahweh are distinctively Hebraic in character. And neither these nor any other of the gods is depicted as being at all like the non-personal Brahman of advaitic Hinduism, or the Tao, or the Nirvana of the Theravada, or the Dharmakaya or Sunyata of the Mahayana.

Should we then opt, as regards the theistic religions, for polytheism, and as regards the non-theistic traditions, for what we shall have to call polyabsolutism? We should then be saying that Allah is a real divine being who is strictly unitary and who has never become incarnate; and that the Holy Trinity is another, more complex divine being, one aspect of whom became incarnate as Jesus of Nazareth; and that Jahweh, or Adonai, is yet another divine being, specially related to the Hebrew people; and Vishnu yet another; and Shiva another; and so on. And also that Brahman exists, as the unlimited consciousness, *sat-chit-ananda*, which in the depths of our own being we all are; and that in addition to this there exists the universal Buddha nature, which is the ultimate Dharmakaya, embodied in the interdependent flow of existence when one selflessly participates in it, experiencing it as 'wondrous being'; and that there is also the ineffable state of Nirvana which manifests itself in human spiritual enlightenment.

However, such a plurality of ultimates would reduce itself to a plurality of penultimates. For the monotheistic concept of God is that of the creator and ruler of everything that exists other than God; and clearly there can only be one such being. If there are two or more, then none of them is God, conceived as the truly ultimate reality. The Adonai of Judaism, the Heavenly Father of Christianity, the Allah of Islam and the Vishnu of the *Bhagavad Gita* is each said to be the ground and lord of the entire universe; and clearly not more than one of them can in fact be this. Further, none of these monotheisms is compatible with the ultimacy of a non-personal Absolute. Again, if the ultimately real is the immutable universal consciousness of Brahman, it cannot also be the Dharmakaya, which is not a consciousness; and nor again can the unchanging Brahman be identified with the ceaselessly changing process of *pratitya samutpada*. Thus if the God-figures of the great monotheisms, and the Absolutes of the great non-theistic religions, are all of them real, no one of them can be the sole ultimate reality which it is said to be. The reality of any one of them must reduce any one of them to a co-ultimacy or a penultimacy which its tradition firmly denies. I believe that we therefore have to consider attributing to each of them a status which is different from that attributed to them within their own tradition.

But before taking such a radical step let us ask if we could instead see them as different names and descriptions of the same referent – as, for example, the names 'Morning Star' and 'Evening

Star', which were once thought to refer to two different heavenly bodies, are now known both to refer to the planet that today we call Venus. On reflection this does not seem to be a viable way of escape. For in order for different descriptions to have the same referent they must, although different, be mutually compatible. But the description of the Holy Trinity, one aspect of whom became incarnate as Jesus of Nazareth, is not compatible with the description of the Qur'ānic Allah, who has emphatically never become incarnate as a human being. And neither of these is compatible with the description of Brahman or the Dharmakaya or Sunyata or the Tao. And indeed, although there are certain limited compatibilities within the total range, the general picture is clearly one of differing descriptions which cannot possibly all, as they stand, refer to the same reality.

Could these differently identified realities, however, perhaps be different aspects of one larger and more complex reality? Again, on reflection: No, not as they are currently described within their respective traditions. For in each case their descriptions do not allow them to be regarded as aspects of something greater than themselves. The God of developed monotheism is conceived, in Anselm's famous phrase, as that than which no greater can be conceived, and thus by definition not as an aspect of anything greater. And the non-personal Absolutes are likewise each presented within their own tradition as truly ultimate and thus not as an aspect of some yet larger reality. Nor for the same reason can they, as they are described within their respective traditions, be regarded as different *parts* of a greater reality, as in the ancient allegory of the elephant and the blind men.

We are driven, then, to the conclusion that if the Gods and Absolutes of the great traditions are not purely products of the human imagination, neither on the other hand can they all be simply identical with the transcendent reality itself.

Where can a religious understanding of religion go from this apparent impasse? I suggest that the way forward involves some kind of distinction between the Gods and Absolutes of the different traditions and a postulated ultimate transcendent reality in which they are all somehow grounded and of which they are all somehow expressions. For we want to say that in responding to the Gods and Absolutes, men and women are indeed responding to the ultimately real, and yet that these experienced God-figures and non-personal Absolutes are not themselves the ultimate as it is in itself but are nevertheless genuine manifestations of it to human awareness. We thus need a distinction such as is suggested by Joseph Campbell's phrase, 'the masks of God'. This implies a transcendent ultimate, which as westerners we call God, and a plurality of masks, or faces, or manifestations, or appearances of that divine reality as Jahweh, as God the Father, as the Qur'ànic Allah, as Brahman, as the Dharmakaya, and so on.

In further considering such a distinction we can begin by noting that some form of it is already familiar within the thought of each of the great traditions, though occurring with varying degrees of prominence. In advaitic Hinduism it is the distinction between *nirguna* Brahman, Brahman without attributes because beyond the entire network of human concepts, and *saguna* Brahman, Brahman as humanly thought and experienced as a personal deity known under many aspects and names as the gods of the different strands of Hindu devotional life. In Mahayana Buddhism it is the distinction between the Dharmakaya as it is in itself, which is *sunyata*, emptiness, empty of everything that the human mind projects in its acts of awareness, and on the other hand that emptiness as given form within human awareness. As one classical Buddhist thinker, T'an-luan, put it: 'Among Buddhas and bodhisattvas there are two aspects of dharmakaya: dharmakaya-as-suchness and dharmakaya-as-compassion. Dharmakaya-as-compassion arises out of dharmakaya-as-suchness, and dharmakaya-as-suchness emerges into [human consciousness through] dharmakaya-as-compassion. These two aspects of dharmakaya differ but are not separate; they are one but not identical'.[1] In Christianity the distinction is between God in God's eternal self-existent being, 'before' and independently of creation, and God in relation to and as known from within the created realm – God *a see* and God *pro nobis*. In mystical Judaism and in Sufi Islam the distinction is between *En Soph*, the Infinite, or *al-Haqq*, the Real, and the self-revealing God of the scriptures. And, again, the *Tao Te Ching* begins by saying that 'The Tao that can be expressed is not the eternal Tao.'

This distinction between the ultimate divine reality as it is in itself and as manifested within human thought and experience, is in line with the distinction familiar within western epistemology between an object – say a wooden table – as it is in itself, unobserved, and that same table as it appears to different observers situated at different places or with different perceptual equipments. What is to us, at our particular point on the macro–micro scale, a table must be something very different to the fly which alights on it or the woodworm that burrows within it, or to a dog, who perhaps experiences it as much in terms of odour as of colour. Further, the same entity may be differently perceived and responded to in terms of different conceptual systems. Thus stone-age persons suddenly transported into the twentieth century would not see the table as a table, because they would not have the concept of a table, or the wider system of sortal and practical concepts that surrounds it and in terms of which we ourselves inhabit the world as our life environment. This distinction between things as they are in themselves and as they are for different perceivers, although first introduced into western thought by the philosophers, has been confirmed more recently by cognitive psychology and further enlarged within the sociology of knowledge. Again, we are familiar from contemporary physics with the idea of a dynamic field of quanta of discharging energy in incessant motion, which is experienced by us as a single solid static coloured object; and, more fundamentally, with the idea that the perceived world is relative to the location of the observer, and that the act of observation makes an important difference to the observed world. Indeed it is today virtually universally agreed that the mind is not passive in awareness but is always active, being conscious of the environment, not only as it has been heavily filtered by the limitations of our perceptual machinery, but also as it is endowed by us with meaning in terms of the system of concepts embodied in our language.

It is this conceptual contribution of the human mind that is most relevant to religious awareness. It requires the distinction between reality as it is in itself and as it comes to consciousness in terms of different systems of human concepts. I want to suggest that this distinction may provide a clue to a religious interpretation of religion in its many diverse forms. I am still restricting what I say here to the 'great world faiths', because these have approved themselves as responses to the Transcendent over many centuries and in millions of lives; and when we go beyond them new issues arise which are extremely important and interesting but which I do not have time to tackle here. My suggestion, then, is that the great world religions should be seen, from a religious point of view, as having come about at the interface between the Transcendent and different human communities with their different sets of religious concepts. These concepts have made possible different modes of experience of the Transcendent, which have in turn given rise to different concrete forms of religious response. One could put this in terms borrowed from Kant's first *Critique*, as a distinction between the noumenal Transcendent or Real or Ultimate, and its plurality of phenomenal manifestations within human consciousness. In other words, something partially analogous to Kant's account of sensory experience may apply to religious experience. Kant held that the human mind actively contributes to the experienced world by fitting it into a categorial system at brings it within the scope of a unitary finite consciousness. Thus we never observe the world as it is in itself, unobserved, but only as humanly observed; and such observation is always both selective and creative. And the religious person's awareness of the divine is likewise not of the divine as it is in itself but always as thought and experienced within the framework of a particular human system of religious concepts and spiritual practices.

Our human contribution to the awareness of the Transcendent is in fact both conceptual and practical. Conceptually, our sense of the Transcendent comes to consciousness in terms of one or other of the two basic notions of deity, through which the Transcendent is experienced as personal, and of the Absolute, through which it is experienced as non-personal. The former is much the more widespread form of awareness, though it is not on that account to be regarded as superior. But of course religious experience is never of deity as such or of absoluteness as such, but always of a particular God figure or a particularly conceived Absolute. In Kantian terminology again, the general concept of deity or of the Absolute is schematized, or made more concrete, in actual experience in terms, not of abstract time, as in Kant's system, but of filled time, the time of human history and culture, including the rich particularities of the religious traditions. Accordingly, the ultimate, in being thought and experienced as a divine Thou, takes the form of a specifically male or female deity, living in relationship with this tribe or people or that, actively involved in this or in that strand of history, speaking through this or that prophet or guru. Thus the divine is known as the Jahweh of Israel, or as the Allah of the Qur'ānic revelation, or as the heavenly Father or Holy Trinity of the Christian Church, or as the Vishnu or Shiva or Vaishnavite or of Shaivite Hinduism, and so on. And the parallel concept of the non-personal Absolute is likewise schematized, though with a much lesser degree of concreteness, in terms of different philosophical conceptualities (which, however, may well also have their own historical and cultural roots) as the eternal unchanging Brahman, or as the Emptiness of Sunyata, or again as the ineffable Dharmakaya or Nirvana, or the Tao, and so on.

The associated practical aspect of our human contribution to the formation of the experienced Gods and Absolutes comes through the distinctive spiritual practices that have developed within the different traditions. Thus the conception of the Transcendent as personal is both elicited and reinforced by the practice of prayer. And correlated with conceptions of the Transcendent as non-personal are different forms of meditation, leading to illumination, awakening, or becoming one with the Infinite, whether in the depths of our own being or as the immanent ground of the incessant life of the universe.

Thus a religious conceptuality and its associated spiritual practice jointly make possible the particular form of religious experience that lies at the heart of each living religion. And together with the other aspects of a tradition – its sacred scriptures and its other classical writings; its myths, legends, creeds and confessions of faith; its history and sagas and its whole treasury of stories; its saints and community leaders; its music, architecture, sculpture and painting; its life-style and its ethics – it constitutes a complex living 'lens' through which those within that faith community are aware of the Divine. The particular 'lens' formed by each tradition is different and unique. But they are all human products, shaping and colouring in their own way what is perceived. Thus this 'lens' metaphor captures the idea of a variety of historically contingent modes of awareness of the ultimate divine reality. That reality is perceived as having different concrete characteristics which are joint products of the universal presence of the divine and a particular set of human concepts and religious practices.

What does this picture imply concerning the status of the particular Gods and Absolutes – Jahweh and Vishnu, Brahman and the Dharmakaya, and so on? Let us take the Jewish experience of the divine as an example, and then proceed to generalize it. The Jahweh who was experienced in the theophanies described in the Torah, who inspired a succession of prophets to declare his will, who was experienced as acting again and again within Hebrew history, and who is known today as an unseen presence on the high holy days and in the daily life of pious Jews – this distinctive divine figure, the Adonia of Judaism, exists at the interface between the ultimate transcendent reality and the Hebrew people. He is the Transcendent as seen through Hebrew eyes and as given form by the Hebraic religious imagination. And his laws are the particular way in which the practical difference that the presence of the Transcendent makes for human life has come to consciousness in Hebrew experience. But this particular concrete divine *persona* did not exist prior to and independently of the strand of history of which he is an integral part. What existed prior to and independently of that history is the transcendent reality itself, whose impact upon the stream of Hebrew consciousness has taken this particular experienceable shape. The concrete figure of Jahweh is thus not identical with the ultimate divine reality as it is in itself but is an authentic face or mask or *persona* of the Transcendent in relation to one particular human community.

This is, of course, the point at which a global religious understanding of religion inevitably differs from an exclusively Jewish one or, to an equal extent, from the particular understanding exclusive to any other tradition. But on the other hand such a global interpretation will add that in responding in life to the God of Abraham, Isaac and Jacob the Jewish people have been and are making their own authentic response to the Transcendent. Thus, on this view Judaism is emphatically a 'true religion'. But it is not the one and only true religion, and its distinctive awareness of the ultimate as Adonai is one of a plurality of awareness of different divine *personae*. For precisely the same has to be said of the heavenly Father of Christianity, of the Allah of Islam, of Vishnu, of Shiva, and so on.

If we now ask the same question about one of the non-personal Absolutes, or (to coin a term) the *impersonae* of the real, the answer will be essentially similar and yet also appropriately different. In the advaitic Hindu tradition, for example, the Transcendent is experienced as the Atman which is also Brahman, the universal non-personal consciousness which we become aware of being when we totally transcend individual egoity. For a global religious understanding of religion this universal mind, which we all are in the final depths of our own being, is a manifestation of the ultimate ground of the universe transcending the grasp of the finite intellect. But as in the case of Jahweh, the universal Atman did not exist prior to and independently of human life, but is a manifestation of the ultimate to purified human consciousness. Thus, on the one hand a pluralistic interpretation of advaitic Hinduism will deny that the Atman is simply identical with the transcendent reality in itself; and this is to deny something that advaitic Hinduism affirms in its identification of Atman with Brahman. But on the other hand it will want emphatically to affirm that in relinquishing egoity to become one with the Atman, men and women are making an authentically salvific response to the Transcendent. Thus advaitic Hinduism is a 'true' religion; but it, too, is not the one and only 'true' religion. And the same has to be said in turn of each of the other non-theistic streams within the great religious traditions.

When we say that in transcending egoity to become one with the universal Atman, or that in living faithfully in accordance with the Torah, or that in being filled with the spirit of Christ, one is making an authentic response to the Transcendent, what is meant by 'authentic'? An answer occurs only within the basic circle of faith which affirms that (within the great traditions at least) religious experience is not only a product of the human religious imagination but constitutes at the same time our human response to the universal presence of the Transcendent. For a religious understanding of religion, then, the great world of faiths are differing human responses to the ultimate. However, they are never perfect responses, but always human, all-too-human phenomena, with the ugly marks upon them of blindness, greed, cruelty and prejudice. As historical realities each is a mixture of good and evil. And so we have to look within their varied life to see, amid this mixture of good and evil, what kind of human change they centrally value as constituting a right relationship to, or within, the Transcendent. They all aim at a radical human transformation, which is variously known as salvation, redemption, peace with God, moksha, satori, nirvana, awakening. I suggest that this change consists at its core in a turning from the self and its ego-centred concerns to a new orientation centred in the divine. The 'saved' or 'submitted' or 'enlightened' or 'awakened' person has been liberated from the ego and has become to some significant degree 'transparent' to the Transcendent. Such a one is a servant of God who, in the words of the *Theologia Germanica*, is to the eternal goodness what one's own hand is to a human being; or again is an enlightened or awakened being in whom the eternal reality of Brahman, or the universal Buddha nature, has been realized. And so when we speak of a religious tradition as constituting an authentic response to the Transcendent we mean that the tradition is an effective context of this salvific transformation. Its religious authenticity consists in its soteriological power, its capacity to mediate the transformating presence of the Transcendent to human life.

It is I think a striking fact that those whom most people within each tradition spontaneously revere as being much closer than themselves to the ideal of humanity in true relationship to the Transcendent – the saints, gurus, jivanmuktas, awakened ones – exhibit a common basic profile as unself-centred servants or channels or realizations of the Transcendent. The fact that the systems of ideas and the images in their minds are so different, and that they have arrived in this state by very different spiritual paths, does not seem to negate what they have in common in a radical turning from ego to participate in the universal reality of the Transcendent. I cannot help think that if, *per impossibile*, we could bring together across the differences of time and space and language such persons as St Francis or Mother Julian, and Kabir or Ramakrishna, and al-Arabi or Rumi, and Dogen or the present Dalai Lama, and enable them to interact, they would arrive at a profound mutual recognition and respect. Thus, if we prescind from the metaphysical theories and the historical contingencies that distinguish the people of different traditions, and look at the actual human transformation that occurs within those traditions, we find that essentially the same salvific change is taking place within all of them. This is indeed the main reason for preferring the assumption of a single universal ultimate to that of a plurality of co-penultimates. Neither possibility is compatible with the claims of the different traditions as they stand; for as they stand each tradition holds that its own object of worship or focus of meditation is truly and uniquely ultimate. But whereas the polytheism and the polyabsolutism of the plural–ultimates theory has no compensating advantage, the single–ultimate theory is supported by the consideration that since the Gods and Absolutes all seem to produce essentially the same salvific human transformation, they are probably different manifestations of the same ultimate divine reality.

But let us now look further at this idea of a single ultimate reality underlying the plurality of divine *personae* and metaphysical *impersonae* – the Gods and the Absolutes – which are the intentional objects of worship and foci of meditation within the great world faiths. What the metaphor of 'lying behind' is meant to indicate is the relationship (in Kantian language) between a noumenal reality-in-itself, a divine *Ding-an-sich*, which lies outside the network of human concepts, and is accordingly not experienceable by us as it is in itself; and on the other hand the phenomenal appearances of that divine reality within human consciousness.

It follows that we cannot ascribe to the ultimate in itself the characteristics of its concrete manifestations. The real *an sich* is not subject to the conceptual schemas in terms of which it takes form and colour within our human experience. These schemes include the distinctions of personal/non-personal, purposive/non-purposive, good/evil, substance/process, even one/many – for the ultimate unity that we presume is the paradoxical non-mathematical unity that the Upanishads seek to express by the phrase 'the One without a second'. We cannot, then, apply any of these concrete characterizations to the ineffable reality in itself. This does not mean however that we cannot say anything at all about it. We can make purely formal statements, as for example when we say that it is ineffable. For it is logically impossible to refer to something that does not even have the attribute of being incapable of being referred to! But beyond such purely formal attributions we can make the positive statement that it is that which is humanly thought and experienced in the range of ways to which the history of religions bears witness. Thus it is known, in the mode of I–Thou encounter, as a loving or demanding, sustaining or challenging, personal presence; and, in the unitive mode, as the Buddha nature of all things; or again as the limitless consciousness that opens up when we transcend the boundaries of the separate ego. However, in itself the ultimate transcendent reality is not identical with any or all of these, but is that which is manifested in these different ways to different human mentalities forming and formed by different spiritual paths.

But may not some forms of mystical experience constitute an exception to the principle that we cannot experience the ultimate reality in a direct and unmediated way but only in forms that are shaped by our own human concepts? This is today a much debated issue. Steven Katz and others, for example in *Mysticism and*

Philosophical Analysis, argue that mystical experience always embodies the distinctive concepts of a particular tradition; while Ninian Smart and others argue for a core mystical experience that occurs within all the great traditions; and again Robert Forman and others, in *The Problem of Pure Consciousness*, argue that a pure contentless consciousness occurs within all the major traditions. I do not want to argue these questions here, because the basic hypothesis that the great world religions constitute alternative human responses to an ultimate transcendent reality is capable of being developed at this point in alternative ways that can accommodate either of these divergent understandings of mysticism. However, my own opinion, in brief, is this: granting the logical possibility of a rare and exceptional form of religious aware-ness constituting a direct and unmediated cognition of the real in itself, I nevertheless doubt whether we have good reason to think that this possibility is in fact realized. For the mystics who claim such a direct cognition of the ultimate produce incompatible accounts of it as personal or as non-personal, as unchanging or as in ceaseless process. It thus looks as though their experiences have been shaped by the basic concepts of their tradition, and are accordingly not experiences of the ultimate as it is in itself but rather as experienced from a particular human standpoint. Again, the pure contentless consciousness for which some contend may very well occur. But I am doubtful whether it can properly be said to be an experience of the ultimate, or indeed properly speaking an experience of anything. It rather seems to be a moment of blank consciousness. However, I am aware that I may be mistaken about this; and so I want to stress that the basic pluralistic hypothesis that I have been outlining does not in principle exclude such a possibility.

Let us now turn, finally, to the challenge that an unexperienceable ultimate is vacuous and otiose. Why postulate a reality that is not in itself humanly experienceable? Is it not a mere non-entity, such that it makes no difference whether it be there or not?

Let me first remind you that all of the great traditions have held that the divine reality is ultimately beyond the grasp of human thought. The finally mystery of God, of Brahman, the Tao, the Dharmakaya has always been affirmed by the deeper religious minds. For example, within Christianity, St Augustine said that 'God transcends even the mind,'[2] and St Thomas declared that 'by its immensity, the divine substance surpasses every form that our intellect reaches,'[3] and that 'The first cause surpasses human understanding and speech.'[4] And many of the Christian mystics have said similar things. St John of the Cross, for example, wrote that God 'is incomprehensible and transcends all things.'[5] The great Jewish thinker, Moses Maimonides, distinguished between the unknowable divine essence and the various attributes which God has in relation to us.[6] The Qur'an declares that God is 'beyond what they describe.'[7] The same theme is widespread within Hinduism. Shankara, for example, says that Brahman is that 'before which words recoil, and to which no understanding has ever attained', and the *Upanishads* declare of Brahman that 'There the eye goes not, speech goes not, nor the mind'.[8] And within the Buddhist tradition there has always been a strong insistence upon the radical inability of human thought to grasp the ultimate: all human teachings are instances of *upaya*, 'skilful means' to help the hearer towards the experience of awakening. However, this insistence upon the ineffability of the ultimately real has always been accompanied by an equal insistence upon the religious authenticity of the concrete ways in which the real impinges upon us in the form of revelation, enlightenment, or an experience of the divine presence in history and in individual lives. This dual affirmation of the final transcending mystery of the divine in itself, and of its genuine manifestations within human religious experience, is of course precisely the picture that I am advocating and am seeking to generalize across the entire field of the religions.

We can now directly face the question: Why postulate an ineffable and unexperiencable divine reality 'behind' the experienced Gods and Absolutes? The answer lies in the difference between a religious and a naturalistic understanding of religion. We all have to recognize today that there is a considerable human element in religion in all of its many forms. It has been evident and undeniable at least since the work of Max Weber, Émile Durkheim, and Sigmund Freud that geographical, climatic, economic, political, sociological and psychological factors have always influenced the development of religious ideas, beliefs, practices and modes of experience. The question is whether this is all that there is to religion or whether in ways shaped by these mundane circumstances religion constitutes our human response to the Transcendent. Is the religious projection a purely gratuitous or a genuinely responsive projection?

To affirm that it is responsive is to affirm the transcendent reality to which it is a response. But because of the plurality of religions, this cannot be simply identified with the distinctively Christian or the distinctively Buddhist or the distinctively Muslim or any other one particular conception of it. And to affirm the ultimate beyond these divine *personae* and metaphysical *impersonae* is to insist that they are not purely human projections but are the forms taken by our human awareness of the transcendent reality.

So far, then, from it making no difference whether we postulate an ineffable divine reality behind the experienced God-figures and the experienced non-personal Absolutes, it makes the greatest possible difference – the difference between a religious and a non-religious understanding of religion. Putting it another way, the central issue between a realist – not of course a naive but a critical realist – interpretation of religious language, and a non-realist and therefore naturalistic interpretation of it, hinges upon the affirmation or denial of an ultimate divine reality beyond the immediate objects of worship and foci of religious meditation. For since the fact there is a plurality of these international objects and foci means that they cannot each be simply identified with the ultimate in itself, the faith that they are not purely creations of the human imagination requires the affirmation of a transcendent reality that underlies them and is manifested to us through them.

12 RELIGION AFTER THE ENLIGHTENMENT
Keith Ward

The death of religion has often been proclaimed, but its funeral rites seem particularly protracted. Indeed, it seems to be particular forms of religion which die, only to be succeeded by progeny which, however rebellious they are, look remarkably like their parent. Religious faith may seem weak and politically marginal in parts of Western Europe; but throughout the world the impact of religion is immensely strong, both for good and ill. The growth of a newly militant Islam, the influence of Protestantism in the United States, the role of the churches in Eastern Europe and the erstwhile communist bloc and the rise of Sikh and Hindu fundamentalism – all these movements show the power of religion to influence human affairs. As this scattering of examples suggests, religion is closely connected to race and culture. As such, it tends to legitimate prejudice, intolerance and violence. Put in a different and more positive way, it focuses and motivates a sense of value and purpose in human communities, providing a positive vision for a society which is seen as just and free from oppression and in which can be realized the distinctive values of a culture. The major problem of religion in the modern world is how to retain such distinctive visions of value without bringing them into destructive conflict with one another.

But is such an ambiguous force really desirable, especially if one can create a liberal democratic society without the aid of religious faith? Has the time not come to outgrow religion, as a source of meaning and value, and rely on human resources alone? This is the proposal that, particularly since the eighteenth century, European intellectuals have repeatedly made – and with some success. Auguste Comte divided human intellectual history into three phases. The first, the religious phase, of myths and magic, is superseded by the second phase of metaphysics, in which people seek one coherent and rational system for understanding the universe, but still rely on non-empirical entities like God for their ultimate principles. This, he claimed, is being inevitably replaced by the third, positivist, phase, in which the scientific method will triumph and all beliefs will be based on the evidence of sensory experience and experiment. This is a view which still reverberates in some corners of European universities, though positivism in science itself is rather hard to find.

Positivism, in its technical sense, can, I think, be declared extinct. But there remains a fairly widespread view which asserts that all genuine factual knowledge is experimental, based on tests which are repeatable in principle and publicly verifiable (one of the main problems of Logical Positivism was that public verifiability was impossible to establish). All real entities are material; they exist somewhere in space. And all genuine explanations are non-purposive, or mechanistic, forming an ideally closed system in which measurable forces act in wholly predictable ways. In such a world, if religion survives it must be non-factual, not claiming to assert any alleged spiritual facts. It could have an emotive function, so that doctrines might be seen as instrumental in causing desired mental states or behavioural dispositions. But drugs might be quicker, given the appropriate technology; and the question of truth would be subsumed under that of causal efficacy.

It is clear that such a view does not replace metaphysics, since it is itself a form of metaphysics. It has an ontological component, stating the sorts of things which exist (indeed, claiming to specify exhaustively the sorts of things which can exist). It has an epistemic component, stating the proper way of knowing, or what counts as proper knowledge. And it has an explanatory component, laying down criteria for what counts as understanding (basically, one understands an occurrence when one can derive it from a general law and its boundary conditions, or preceding state). Moreover, this is a revisionary metaphysics, which does not agree at all points with common sense. The materialist ontology does not allow such things as dreams, thoughts, colours or feelings to have reality. Or, in more sophisticated versions, if they are real, they are aspects of physical processes which have no causal role and can be discounted as independent items of knowledge. Epistemically, no account is taken of human knowledge in art, morality or personal relationships. Knowledge of other people is usually participative rather than dispassionate; it is a matter of what Peter Strawson called reactive rather than objective attitudes. In our daily relationships we come to know other persons only if we establish some rapport with them, which will involve us in certain commitments and disclosures. What we find out about other people will largely depend on how we approach them; and it will never be free of that element of feeling and sympathy (or lack of it) which enables us to know them to any extent. As for understanding, the mathematical forms of understanding so important to the sciences are barely intelligible to most people. They normally speak of understanding such things as poems or works of art when they see what they are getting at, when they begin to see the viewpoint they are expressing and the insights which inform them. This is very different from understanding a mathematical equation expressing a law of nature; yet it is certainly a form of human understanding.

In brief, the materialist view proposes a rather abstract, austere and intellectually élitist metaphysics, compared to the complexity of ordinary experience. What it omits almost entirely is the realm of the personal; of the purposive, irreplaceable and unique; of the dignity and value of persons; of that which is known by introspection as well as by observation. As persons, we typically struggle from time to time to discern some pattern in our experience which may make sense of it; to grasp some enduring values, to do something worthwhile which will realize our distinctive potentialities. These are areas with which the arts and morality engage. It is here, too, that religion has its place. Religion, in its intellectual aspect, is concerned with the attempt to discern and realize some worthwhile purpose in life or discover some absolute values to live by. Of course religion, like philosophy, is an area where dispute is not only inevitable, but where it is an integral part of growth in understanding. So it may be denied that there is any one worthwhile value for human beings as such; or that the realization of it is a possible or profitable goal for humans; or that there is any authoritative disclosure of what it is, or any real power to help one discern and achieve it – all these typically religious assertions may very well be denied. But even such a denial, if it is serious, testifies to the fact that these questions are important and natural questions which arise about human existence. It is rational to ask them; and indeed materialism embodies one attempt to answer them, in so far as it suggests that publicly verifiable truth is an intrinsic value which overrides all others, and that introspective and participative knowledge – knowledge of oneself obtained by contemplation or of others obtained by reactive personal relationships – is of little or no significance in informing one what the nature of reality is.

Religion, in the main world traditions which now exist, answers these questions in a different way, by claiming to discern a supreme objective value which is to be personally realized by a process of self-discipline, and which has been found to be disclosed in an authoritative revelation. The distinctive ontology of developed religion is that *there is a reality of unconditioned value*, upon which in some sense all experienced reality depends. This may seem to be an impossibly general statement, given the huge number and variety of religions in the world. It may even be thought impossible to speak of 'religion' in general, as though all possible religions were the same. I am not supposing that all religions can be gathered under one heading; but there are some central characteristics which most religions share, and there are some typical developments in the history of religion which one can trace. Like

Auguste Comte, but in a different way, one might trace a historical development of religion through three main stages. The first stage is that of tribal or local religious practice, found in pre-literate societies or in societies which have not felt the need to systematize their thoughts about the nature of the world. If one looks at such religious practices, one finds that they are mostly concerned with obtaining good fortune (fertility, health, success or happiness), or palliating bad luck (demons, fate and unhappy ghosts) by ritual means (spells, mimetic magic, sacrifices or ascetic practices) or by the use of abnormal psychic powers (divination, spirit-possession and dream-visions). There is a basic concern with obtaining human good by some form of primarily mental or non-material means. When gods appear, they are conceived as spirit powers who may help or harm, appear in strange places or animals, and befriend certain holy pleasures. Anthropologists like Frazer, Tylor and Marrett gave varying accounts of the meaning and function of such practices, and it is now generally agreed that their own presuppositions coloured the selection and categorization of material to such an extent as to be misleading in many ways. Nevertheless, they did locate religious practice in the context of natural human behaviour, desire and concern to understand the world. The roots of developed religion lie in such practices, just as the roots of chemistry lie in alchemy.

The second stage of religious development lies in the construction of the great scriptural traditions, when rituals and narratives were codified and written down in canonical form, to form an authoritative basis for subsequent reflection and practice. It is important to see that the great religious traditions arose not only as a development from but also partly in opposition to the pre-literate forms of religion, either by excluding them, as in Hebrew religion, or by including them in a wider unifying system, as in India. The Hebrew Bible slowly developed the idea of one transcendent, ethical and providential creator, whom one must obey by striving for a society based on justice and mercy. The Upanishads developed the idea that all the gods are forms of one supreme reality of purity, intelligence and bliss, which one must realize by renouncing attachment and attaining higher states of consciousness. These two great traditions embrace most of the major religions now in existence, if one takes Buddhism to be a reaction against many aspects of the priestly Indian tradition while preserving its major elements of the renunciation of attachment to obtain a goal of purity, intelligence and bliss. There are obviously many variations in particular doctrines, but what is common to them is that they reject practices which make no moral demands on believers or which worship limited powers without total commitment, either by excluding them altogether or by relegating them to a lower level of importance. Developed religion becomes concerned with one supreme reality of intelligence and bliss, a being of supreme perfection which is beyond all finite limitations; which indeed in itself is beyond human comprehension, though it can manifest to us as a supreme Lord. One has to be rather careful of the Indian traditions here, since they may reject a supreme Lord, as in most types of Buddhism, or uphold an ultimate pluralism of souls, as in Sankyha. But even they speak of an ultimate goal of human realization which is described as all-known and supremely blissful, and to be obtained by self-renunciation and meditation. There may not be an objective being which instantiates supreme value; but there is a possible human state which instantiates such value, and it is the true goal of enlightened human endeavour.

Most of these great traditions accept one authoritative source as the bearer of final and definitive truth. The Indian Vedantin accepts the Upanishads as infallible and verbally inspired as much as the most orthodox Jew does the Hebrew Bible. The Buddhist (except for heterodox schools like Zen) accepts the teaching of the Buddha as infallible and as revealed by an omniscient mind, which is as near to divinity as a Buddhist can get. In other words, they share a view that the supreme human goal is disclosed in some authoritative teaching; and that it is a goal for all people, not an option for those who like that sort of thing. If religion makes an ontological or metaphysical claim – that there is a supreme objective value which is the true goal of human striving – it also makes a historical claim: that some one or a few rare individuals have seen and achieved this true human goal, which is obscured for most people by ignorance and passion. It is misleading to contrast the revealed religions of Judaism, Christianity and Islam to more experiential religions of Hinduism and Buddhism. Both traditions depend on a revelation of the true human goal by an outstanding person or series of persons, whether prophet or enlightened self, who has seen what most of us cannot.

It thus seems that developed religion is founded on the postulate of a reality of unconditioned value, of which finite reality is usually said to be a manifestation, disclosed in an authoritative source as the objective goal of human existence. The concept of God is just one formulation of such a reality, common to the Semitic religions of Judaism, Christianity and Islam. In the Indian traditions, the concept of Brahman, the supreme objectless intelligence which is pure bliss and with which all things are in some sense identical, plays this role. In other forms of religious thought, the ideas of the Dharmakaya, which might be roughly translated as the cosmic law, and of the Tao, as the unutterable unifying principle of all things, have a similar function of pointing to a supreme value which is unlike any conditioned being.

It has become quite popular in some Christian writing to speak of God as a person, albeit a supreme person. The reason for this is that God is spoken of as creating, acting, knowing and even feeling; and these are things which persons do. So a great deal of philosophical effort has gone into the project of articulating and defending the coherence of the notion of one supreme disembodied person who has made the world and relates to it in personal ways. When seen in the wider context of religious traditions from around the world, or even in the longer historical context of the Christian tradition itself, this idea of God as a person seems strangely inadequate. The eighth-century Indian philosopher Sankara puts it well when he writes that the supreme being can manifest as a personal Lord for the sake of finite devotees; but in itself it is so far beyond personhood that it is better to say nothing than to reduce it to such a category.

One can say that God is a person, in somewhat the same sense that one can say that I am an extended object in space. It is true, but it omits most of what is important about my distinctive mode of being, and it is misleading if taken as anywhere near an adequate description of what I am. A human person does possess materially extended properties, but it is very much disputed whether a person is necessarily a materially extended object. In order to bypass several volumes of philosophical argument, let me say that the possession of material properties is not essential to being a person (those who speak of God as being a person certainly agree with this). Then one could say that a person may possess material properties without necessarily being a material object; that is, without material properties being an essential part of being a person. In the same way, something may possess person-properties (properties of thinking, acting and feeling) without being essentially a person. It may be truly a person and yet not essentially a person; so that to call it a person would be to miss precisely what was important and distinctive about it.

What, then, is God if not a person? In the Christian tradition, a phrase of Boethius has often been quoted, and I think deservedly so, that God is 'the unlimited ocean of being'. Perhaps the best way to approach this is to think of those moments of human experience when one has a sense of the transience of all things, and a vague sense of a greater sustaining reality underlying and embracing them. If this is thought to be rather a Schleiermachean appeal to odd emotional experiences, one could turn to pure mathematics – surely an intellectual subject if ever there was one – and appeal to that sense of beauty and necessity which is apt to strike mathematicians as they explore their proper subject-matter. I have heard mathematical physicists testifying to a sense that such mathematical constructs as imaginary time are somehow more real than the one-dimensional process we seem to pass through. Behind the chaos of sense-experience lies the order and symmetry of the fundamental laws of nature; even the possibility of a uniquely consistent Grand Unified Theory from whose simple principles the whole world ensues. What I am focusing on here is not the detail of such highly speculative theories, but the almost intuitive sense that there is an unchanging and pure order of intelligible reality which can only be grasped by the mind and is merely imaged in the complexities of our actual world. One might call this a Platonic perception of an order of intelligibility which sense obscures, with an order of reality beyond that of transient coming into being and passing away.

To the pure mathematician, such an order probably seems impersonal and amoral. It has indeed a sort of supreme value, in its elegance and simplicity; but human feeling and desire seem far removed from it. Even Bertrand Russell, not renowned for his religious feeling, testified to an almost mystical feeling that pure mathematics aroused in him. It would certainly misconstrue such perceptions to call them apprehensions of a disembodied person. But would it be wrong to call them apprehensions of a supremely intelligible world, an order and beauty which lies at the heart of all things? And is the awed contemplation of that realm so far removed from worship, from the reverence for pure value which is unborn and indestructable, beyond the world of experience yet interpenetrating it at every point?

For the Aristotelian tradition, so important to Catholic Christianity, to say that God is good is to say that God is supremely desirable. So it is natural to claim that mathematicians actually sense the goodness of God in sensing the elegance of the structure of the world. However, a God who is only desirable to pure mathematicians is a little remote for most of us. The beauty of the divine being must, as Plato also suggested, be mirrored in the beauty of the natural world; so that, participating in the divine forms, material things may not only be the tombs of the soul (a distinctive thesis of the *Phaedrus*), but also the sacraments of the spirit (a view expressed in the *Timaeus*). It is this thought that Christians express in the doctrine that Christ is the logos, the rational intelligibility of God; and that Jesus is the material sacrament of that supra-human reality. Christ is said to be, in the scriptures, the visible image of the invisible God. And here is the thought of the divine intelligibility which underlies all things coming to expression in the human intelligence which can comprehend it.

It is possible for the mathematician, as for the scientist in general, to contemplate intelligible beauty without any great moral transformation of life. Religion sets out a practice of worship and prayer by which the individual can appropriate, to some extent, the creative power and wisdom of the being the mathematician contemplates dispassionately. Religion introduces the element of passion, both for good and ill; for it introduces a commitment to achieve union with the supreme value as an ultimate goal, and to express that value in personal life. Such an achievement requires passionate commitment, and its loss is seen as the loss of the true orientation of human life.

If God is a supreme intrinsic value, it is widely agreed that this value can be known only by self-renunciation and meditative introspection. It is not publicly verifiable, since it is not a finite entity which could be measured or controlled, and it does not manifest in accordance with predictable laws. Yet it is loosely and partly verifiable by experiences of freedom from passion, inner peace and joy; more rarely by visions or vivid feelings of an objective presence and by the occurrence of providential events. On the Christians view, it is manifested, though hardly verified, by the life and transfigured appearances of Jesus. For Christians living today, Jesus is no longer an accessible embodied person, but is known by an inward vision as the finite name and form of God. There is thus a form of participative knowledge by which a reality of supreme value becomes increasingly known as one adopts an appropriate approach to it, but which cannot be made a subject of experiment or measurement. In this sense, the supreme value, when it is regarded as an objective reality, is more like an ultimate subject than like an object; and as such it is knowable only in so far as it discloses itself to those capable and desirous of relating to it. For this view, faith is not so much a leap beyond reason as a commitment to a form of mental training and discipline which is inspired by a great spiritual teacher in the hope that it will lead to knowledge of supreme value.

As well as having a distinctive ontological postulate of a supremely valuable reality and a distinctive form of participative knowledge of it, religion has a characteristic form of explanation. This is not a matter of placing events under general laws or regularities. It is a teleological explanation, according to which one sees one's life in relation to a supreme goal of intrinsic value. Religious explanations interpret events by reference to a divine purpose or ultimate goal and to that which inhibits its manifestations. To understand the human situation is to see the value of the goal, to see the roots of sorrow in ignorance, attachment or pride, and to see what is necessary to overcome these restrictions and attain the goal. Thus the four holy truths of Buddhism teach that all conditioned existence involves suffering; that suffering is caused by selfish desire; that the way to end suffering is to eliminate such desire; and that the way to do that is to embrace the eightfold path taught by Gautama. In Christianity the creator's purpose is to bring all created life to share in the joy, creativity and fellowship of the divine life; this purpose is thwarted by selfishness and human pride; the way to regain this purpose is to turn from self to the power of divine love; and the way to do that is to accept the divine forgiveness and empowerment which is given by Christ. The form of explanation is structurally similar, though the precise content differs because of differences in general world-view, cultural frames of interpretation and histories of religious development.

The question of what place religion has in modern culture is the question of whether it is any longer found to be plausible to speak of one supreme value as the goal of human life, of participative knowledge as a genuine and distinctive form of knowledge, and of teleological explanation as an illuminating way of understanding one's own existence. The answer to these questions is not obvious, and consideration of it forms the heart of the study of religion, as an intellectual discipline. But in any case it is clear that to understand religion one must see it not as a set of peripherally eccentric rituals, but as a set of epistemic practices, claiming a form of knowledge which transforms the knower by requiring a moral and spiritual commitment as its precondition.

There is a conflict between a materialist approach and a religious approach, as here defined; and there is a conflict between any form of religious literalism and much of science. But there is no conflict between religion and science and such. They share a concern for truth, for what is ultimately the case. The sciences are concerned with publicly verifiable evidenced truth, whereas religion is concerned with personally apprehended self-transformative truth. They share a concern for explanation, postulating that there are reasons for things being as they are, that reality is intelligible, though religion seeks final causes whereas modern science typically seeks general non-teleological laws. They share a faith in the mind's capacity to attain truth progressively. They differ in that science is concerned very largely with the falsifying of hypotheses, whereas religion is concerned with the realization of a vision of supreme value. Science can afford to be and should often be dispassionate, critical and tentative; whereas religious visions require passionate commitment, affirmation of value and resolute purpose. It should be remembered, however, that this sort of passionate commitment is appropriate to science, too; not to specific scientific hypotheses, but to the practice of scientific inquiry itself, which must be passionately defended as the affirmation of truth which cannot be surrendered for the sake of expediency. Religion should defend that practice, but also claim its own distinctive and proper mode of inquiry, which is personal, participative and self-transforming.

It is a complete misunderstanding to think that the sciences deal in hard facts whereas religion is a sort of blind non-rational faith in completely untestable dogmas. The doctrines of religion arise out of a rational interpretation of important areas of human experience, areas to do with a growth in self-knowledge and in the personal and aesthetic dimensions of experience. Religions do appeal to authority, but it is to the authority of those who have seen further and experienced more deeply in these areas. And that authority is tested, often over generations of people who seek a transformation of life and a participation in a reality of supreme value by following their revealed path of worship, prayer and spiritual practice in a living community. Religion has a place in the intellectual life of humanity, as an exploration into the possibility of realizing a goal of supreme value, which places human life in its widest and most important context. It would indeed be strange if there were such a goal and it did not disclose itself at all to those who were prepared to seek it. It would be intellectually disreputable if the question as to the existence of such a goal was not pursued with as great an intellectual integrity and vigour as possible, in conversation with the best scientific knowledge and the widest social and artistic understanding.

I have spoken of 'religion' because that term, however unsatisfactory, denotes an area of human practice and experience which is distinctive and recognizable. It is also important to locate particular religions within the whole regime of faiths which constitute that set of human practices. Indeed, the third stage of religious development to which I have referred is precisely one in which it is no longer regarded as satisfactory to live with a set of competing claimants to ultimate truth, lying alongside one another but in almost total ignorance of each other. As long as one thinks of religions as making contradictory claims to some ultimate truth, the very idea of the religious quest as lying in the pursuit of one supreme objective value is weakened. Where the values in question seem to be bluntly opposed, one could hardly speak of a quest for the same sort of thing. However, because of the rise of critical consciousness, increased awareness of historical change and of the culturally affected character of human knowledge, we are now in a situation in which a number of developing scriptural traditions can come to new and wider understandings of themselves by consciously becoming part of a global religious outlook. Tribal religions can remain content with being the distinctive practices of one small group, ignoring all that goes on elsewhere. But to the extent they do that, they must fail to relate fully to the way the world actually is. They may fail to see the limitations of their own way and the aspects of truth that other ways may have perceived. In the modern world, the great scriptural faiths find themselves in a very similar situation. They can insist on a self-contained finality and completeness for their own scriptures. But if they do, they will fail to relate to the full range of contemporary scientific knowledge of the world. They may miss aspects of truth that other traditions have discerned. They may fail to understand themselves correctly, precisely because understanding requires a certain sort of distancing and critical analysis as well as empathetic participation. Not least, if they continue to make strident claims for finality and certainty without a proper knowledge of other traditions and how they have interacted with their own in the past, they are in danger of supporting chauvinistic, racist and intolerant attitudes which threaten the security of the world.

In this new situation of global religious awareness, it is not that one must give up what is distinctive in one's own tradition, and seek some minimal highest common factor in all religions. That would show a cavalier disregard for truth and for the importance of difference in human understanding. Rather, the task is to realize how provisional and incomplete the varied interpretations of one's own tradition have been, and to see how the interaction of differing conceptual schemes has been fruitful for growth in understanding in the past. If one believes that God has disclosed the divine nature and purpose in one tradition, one need not believe that this disclosure is so final that nothing can ever be added to it, in the way of understanding, or so complete that it stands in need of no interpretation when it is encountered in new cultural conditions. It is plausible to think – and it was certainly thought by many of the early Christian Fathers – that others may have seen patterns that we have missed, traced connections that we have overlooked, and can contribute to the understanding and interpretation of our own tradition, without threatening it. If the third stage may be called one of convergent spirituality, it is not one in which the different traditions will merge one with another. It is one in which each will accept the epistemic right of the others to exist and will accept that a comprehensive view will need to take into account their viewpoints; most importantly it will accept the inevitability of religious difference, and look for a positive role which such diversity can play in the growth of mutual understanding. There is thus a twofold task for religions as they move into this third stage, as I think they inevitably will. One is to reinterpret their outlook in terms of the provisional, but well-established, scientific view of a vast emergent and interconnected cosmos, to take scientific knowledge and its vision of a multi-billion year time-scale for the universe with full seriousness. The other is to extend their vision to take account of the insights of other religious traditions, to place their own tradition within a more global perspective.

If this can be done, then religions may be seen, not as reactionary defences against science, and not as legitimations of ethnic or racial separatism, but as vehicles for the acceptance of a wider spiritual unity of humanity, carrying a moral vision and a power for its implementation. Within such a perspective, the various faiths can celebrate their particularity while also contributing to a wider understanding of the human spiritual quest.

13 INTERFAITH PRAYER
Marcus Braybrooke

In December 1991, about two thousand clergy of the Church of England voiced 'theological, spiritual and indeed constitutional' objections to interfaith worship. The group affirmed support for appropriate co-operation with those of other faiths on community, social, moral and political issues. Interfaith worship, however, they held, conflicts with the Christian duty to proclaim the gospel and implies that 'salvation is offered by God not only through Jesus Christ but by other means', thus denying Jesus's uniqueness and finality as the only Saviour'.[1]

This is not the place to discuss the question of the uniqueness of Jesus Christ and the salvation offered through him, nor is this the place to deal with legal and constitutional issues. Rather, by looking more closely at occasions which might be described as 'interfaith worship', I hope to show the variety of such occasions and that they are based on different presuppositions. A more discriminating judgement is required instead of blanket condemnation.

The Open Letter particularly focuses attention on the Commonwealth Day of Observance at Westminster Abbey.

We should, however, not only be concerned with great public occasions but with more personal concerns. 'What sort of marriage service can we have?' asked a Christian engaged to a Jew. Or I recall being asked to take the funeral of a Christian whose widow was Jewish. She asked if her rabbi could take part. I happily agreed and he, after some hesitation, also agreed. Afterwards the widow said how much she appreciated this – but was sad that at their wedding neither a Jewish nor a Christian blessing was available. The dead are not so threatening as the living. But when I was asked to take the funeral of a Jew whom I had been visiting regularly during his last illness, and to whom I read the psalms, I demurred, but felt honoured to give the eulogy at his Jewish funeral. There has, as far as I know, been little research on such personal ceremonies. As to the public occasions, however, there is now nearly a hundred years of history.

History

The first organized attempt by members of different religions to share in prayer together seems to have been at the World's

Parliament of Religions in 1893, when each morning began with silence and the saying together of the Lord's Prayer, led on one occasion by a rabbi. The opening and closing sessions included some hymns, such as 'Lead, Kindly Light'. Already in the Brahmo Samaj, Hindu reformers such as Ram Mohun Roy and Keshub Chandra Sen had added readings from other scriptures of the world to the reading of Hindu texts. Subsequently in India in the 1920s Mahatma Gandhi included hymns and readings from many traditions at the ashram's evening prayers. In some Christian ashrams in India, Hindu scriptures were sometimes read while some missionary colleges broadened their daily worship to encourage participation by Hindu and Muslim students.

In Britain, Unitarians were probably the first to include in their services readings from other scriptures as well as from the Bible. Will Hayes, for example, as early as 1924, published a *Book of Twelve Services* later reprinted in *Every Nation Kneeling*. At the 1924 Religions of Empire Conference there were no devotional times, although the Revd Tyssul Davies independently arranged an interfaith gathering at the Theistic Church. At the 1936 World Congress of Faiths there were some readings from the sacred scriptures during the conference. Most members of the Congress also accepted invitations to attend as guests, services at St Paul's Cathedral and at Canterbury Cathedral; not that I am suggesting these were interfaith! One of the first large public services in which people of several faiths took part was the memorial service for Sir Francis Younghusband, the founder of the World Congress of Faiths, held at St Martin-in-the-Fields in 1942. On the occasion of the Coronation of Queen Elizabeth II, the World Congress of Faiths arranged a special service of prayer for people of all faiths and subsequently for several years arranged an annual All Faiths' service, until this was merged with the service held at the start of the Week of Prayer for world peace.

In 1965 an interfaith service was held at St Mary-le-Bow to mark the opening of the Commonwealth Arts Festival. In the following year a similar occasion was arranged for Commonwealth Day at St Martin-in-the-Fields. Because of some protests and concern voiced in Church Assembly and at the British Council of Churches about the use of a church for this, for a few years the ceremony was held at the Guildhall, a 'neutral' building, but now an Observance for Commonwealth Day is held each year at Westminster Abbey. Organized local services have become increasingly common, often linked to the Week of Prayer for World Peace. An interfaith civil service held in Wolverhampton in 1978, at the request of the Mayor, caught the public attention.

International interreligious conferences will often include devotional times led in turn by members of different religions and some joint ceremony at the end. The 1989 Assembly of the World Conference on Religion and Peace ended with a dawn meditation at Mornington Beach, near Melbourne. The 1984 Congress of the International Association of Religious Freedom held in Tokyo, for example, had daily devotions, each led by a different tradition in which sometimes a member of another religion was asked to participate. The closing ceremony, in which representatives of all religions took part, included a flower communion and an affirmation of allegiance to the church universal 'which recognizes in all prophets a harmony, in all scriptures a unity, and through all dispensations a continuity'.

Different Types of Service

It may be helpful to distinguish different types of service. The 1980 report of the Consultants to the Archbishops distinguished three different types of service:

1. Services of a particular religious community to which members of other faiths are invited as guests. If a group of Christians is present at Sikh worship in a Gurdwara, a Christian minister may be invited to read from the Bible, or to speak. If some Jews attend a Christian service, the rabbi may be asked to read from the scriptures to preach.

2. Interfaith gatherings of a serial multi-faith character. In these, each religious community represented – perhaps in chronological or alphabetical order – offers a reading or a prayer. These may be on a common theme, but no attempt is made to suggest corporate or united activity. Those present are in effect an audience listening to a religious anthology in which the distinctiveness of each tradition is clearly recognized.

3. Interfaith gatherings with a 'united order of service'. The occasion is planned so that all present may feel they are participants and there is likely to be an overall theme. There will, perhaps, be carefully chosen hymns or a 'universal' prayer such as: 'O God of many names. Lover of all nations, we pray for peace: in our hearts, in our homes, in our nations, in our world. The peace of your will'. The peace of our need. (From 'The Week of Prayer for World Peace', leaflet, 1983).

There may be a universal symbol, such as the lighting of candles or perhaps a common affirmation, as at the annual Multi-Faith Observance for Commonwealth Day.

We affirm our common faith in the dignity and unique worth of the human person, independent of colour, class or creed. We affirm our common faith in the need to establish justice between man and man, and, through common effort, to secure peace and reconciliation between nations. We affirm our common faith in the need to assert the supremacy of love in all human relationships. We affirm our common faith in the brotherhood of man and our concern to express it in service and sacrifice for the common weal.[3]

In these services it is always made clear that the distinctiveness of religious traditions are not compromised. Dr Howard Williams, welcoming the Dalai Lama to such a service said: 'It is obvious that I am a Welsh Baptist, not a Tibetan Buddhist.'

To this list three further types of services may be added.

4. Services which are clearly 'universalist'. Category 3 represented a coming together on a particular occasion of distinct traditions. There are those who affirm the oneness of religion under different outward manifestations, for example 'The Baha' is the Ramakrishna Mission, or the Theosophists.

5. Occasions to express repentance and reconciliation by one community of faith with another, for example some of the liturgies on the Holocaust in which Jews and Christians in the USA sometimes share or the ceremonies in York remembering the Massacre there in 1190.

Personal occasions – such as marriages or funerals, which I have already touched upon.

Our Theological Presuppositions

The different types of service presuppose different positions in the relations of religion to each other – as I have already hinted in distinguishing 3 and 4.

To attend the worship of another religion as a guest or to invite guests to our own religion need not imply 'legitimizing' their religion. It may be just an educational experience, designed to increase understanding and friendly relations. (Some would oppose even this countenancing of 'heathenism and idolatry'.) But do the hosts make any adjustments? My memory of the first Council of Christians and Jews Conference that I attended in the 1960s was that we all went to the Sabbath morning service at the Orthodox synagogue. It lasted an hour and a half and was all in Hebrew; many of us were little enlightened. One of the Jews muttered: 'It is a sin to weary the congregation'. I recall another so-called 'All Faiths Service' which turned out to be Anglican evensong. When the officiant turned to the congregation and said, 'We shall now all say the creed', the rabbi next to me muttered, 'A bit difficult for some of us.'

So do we adjust when others are present? It would not be appropriate to 'missionize' – or is that an example of the 'watering down' that critics mention? We might, if Christian, need to look at the lections. On one such occasion I was asked to preach when Jews had been invited to the communion and the gospel was Peter's confession 'You are the Christ...'[4]

And if we are guests do we adapt? Most Christians would be willing to cover their heads in a synagogue – although some Pentecostalists might object. In a Hindu temple do we greet the 'idol'?

Are we there just as observers – or does the occasion become an experience of worship for us? I recall one conference where an African was leading us in his traditional worship and we were invited to drink from the water which had been offered to the God. At the time, I was feeling rather depressed – and in taking part I had an experience of being welcome and accepted which was in tune with other deep religious experiences. It was, too, with a real sense of privilege that I shared in a Shinto rite – and felt something of the Shinto love of nature. (I discovered afterwards that I was asked because an Indian archbishop had declined.)

To what extent can we enter into the religious experience of another community of faith? I feel we have still much to learn from Swami Abhishiktananda and other pioneers in this field. I have taken part in some weekends of shared meditation with Swami Bhavyananda. Personally, if I am with Hindus meditating, I can, as in my own meditation, sense a oneness with the divine – but then I am at home in the mystical religious tradition which perhaps points to an underlying unity, or am I merely superimposing Christian meaning on other symbols?

I personally believe that we can share a little, at a religious and experiential level, the worship of another faith. Otherwise we have to say that religions, at their centre, are impervious to each other – and this has serious consequences for interfaith dialogue. But the experience of David Brown, former Bishop of Guildford, warns us of the difficulties:

> My distance from Islam came home to me in a sad but profound way one evening in Khartoum, when I went to the home of a Muslim religious leader. There were some 30 men sitting at ease in his courtyard,

and for an hour or more we enjoyed a good and open discussion about religious matters. Then the time came for the night prayer and they formed ranks to say it together. I asked if I might stand with them, but the Sheikh told me I could not do so, since I did not have the right 'intention'. I had to remain standing at the edge of the courtyard. Even though I have walked on the approaches of Islam for over 30 years, I can only speak of it as a stranger.[5]

Dr Shivamurthy Shivacharya has written: 'When we stand before a symbol of any tradition other than our own, we will all be spectators only and not the real participants... It will be a physical or mental participation out of curiosity and not an emotional participation or participation of the heart.'

The serial type of service accords to other faiths 'parity of esteem' (to use Peter Schneider's phrase), but need not imply any acceptance of their truth claims. If the gathering is, say, for the United Nations or human rights, then the coming together affirms our common humanity. This largely has been the basis of the World Council of Churches' co-operation with other faiths on peace and justice. It is on the basis of our humanity rather than our shared religiousness.

Officially, the World Day of Prayer for Peace at Assisi was in this category. Besides the prayer services of the different faiths, there was a time when we were 'together to pray', but did not 'pray together', i.e. we were physically in one place and listened to each others' prayers – but did we make those prayers our own? My feeling is that the Spirit made of the day a new Pentecost and others felt the same, but at no point did we join verbally in a prayer together.

Interfaith Services

The third category, interfaith services, assumes that to pray together is theologically appropriate.

Interfaith services which are prepared as a unity and in which all are invited to participate assume that beyond our differences we worship the One Eternal One – that all our religious dogma and ritual point to the Divine Mystery who can never be fully named. 'All names are given to you and yet none can comprehend you. How shall I name you then, O You, the Beyond all name', said Gregory of Nazianzen long ago; or, as Alan Paton said, our language and rituals are 'a net of holes to capture essence, a shell, to house the thunder of the ocean... a range of words to hold One Living Word'.[6]

As Bishop George Appleton said: 'We stand in worship before the mystery of the final Reality to whom or to which we give differing names, so great and deep and eternal that we can never fully understand or grasp the mystery of this Being'.[7] Others put less emphasis on such a mystical unity, and stress rather the common obligation of all people to work for peace, justice, the relief of suffering and the preservation of the planet.

While many Christians who take part will wish to maintain the uniqueness of Jesus Christ, they will wish to balance this by belief that God the Creator has made all people in the divine image and from common parents and that the Holy Spirit is active in the whole of human history.

In services of this type the distinctiveness of the great faiths is affirmed, it does not replace the regular liturgy and prayer of a faith community. In my view, it needs to develop appropriate new symbols rather than adapt existing symbols of particular faiths. Further, differences are seen to be enriching and God-given. Some Christians insist that all prayer should be 'through Jesus Christ Our Lord'. As a Southern Baptist leader has been quoted as saying: 'God does not hear the prayer of a devout Jew.' Is there one divine reality whom all seek to address or are the gods of other faiths 'false gods and idols'? I would hope all prayer is in the spirit of Jesus Christ, who endorses all that is good and true and lovely, that I did not feel that it must necessarily name him.

Universalist Worship

I feel more uncertain about the fourth category. This is because it may disregard differences – and while I accept a fairly pluralist position, my own faith commitment is to God through Jesus Christ. I do not seek to judge others' relationship with God, but my appreciation of other faiths is as a follower of Jesus. I am not clear that it is possible to transcend our particularity – such as our religion or our nationality – and wonder whether 'universalism' has not become a new particularity. Yet I share many of the universalists' aspirations: that that which unites is more important than what separates, and that there is a convergence of the great religions. But this, for me, is something still to be achieved and some 'universalist' services lack this sense of dynamism and growth.

Occasions of Repentance and Reconciliation

In March 1991, I attended a conference in Costa Rica, at which many of the indigenous people of Central and Latin America were present. The sense of hurt at the Christian conquest of 500 years ago was evident as well as their fear of a triumphalistic celebration of the 'discovery of America'. The need for some ceremony of Christian penitence was clear. Even more so is this the case in Christian–Jewish relations, but as the Chief Rabbi Dr Jonathan Sacks has written, almost every group has hurt some other group. Group penitence seems to me urgent if there is to be reconciliation. The liturgies on the Holocaust are an attempt to do this, but there is a danger that Christian theological presuppositions will be superimposed on Jewish suffering – if for example the remembering of the Shoah takes place in the context of the Eucharist, with its imagery of redemptive suffering.

Personal Occasions

As to personal occasions, we touch on a sensitive issue. I respect those who discourage marriage outside their faith community – especially where theirs is a minority in an oppressive society. Yet I feel that often we are pastorally insensitive and the needs of individuals are ignored. Marriage between people of different nationalities is likely to increase and may perhaps contribute to human unity.

It is possible in a mature relationship for two people each to affirm his or her faith and be fully respectful of the other. Indeed this is a model of interfaith relationships. But what of the children? What initiation rites are appropriate? Dual religious membership, unlike dual nationality, does not seem possible – although I have met someone who described himself as a Christian Hindu. Religious discipleship requires commitment; as we grow in faith our central commitment becomes clearer and more definite, but maybe we can incorporate into our faith values and beliefs from other traditions which are in harmony with our own. Is that possible in an 'interfaith' family, or is 'interfaith' as critics have suggested one step away from 'indifferentism'?

Conclusion

Just as most of these who have shared in interfaith dialogue would affirm that the experience has been deeply enriching, even if costly and risky, so I gladly recognize that my spiritual life has been enriched by praying with other faiths. To be a guest at another's worship is to come close to the spiritual centre of the tradition. In

Jerusalem I have visited the Western Hall several times – but as a tourist, until once I went late in the evening with a Jewish lady whose father was very ill. She pushed a little scroll between the great stones of the wall. It had become for me a holy place.

Many occasions of praying together will be informal responses to particular events, such as the time when some Jews, Muslims and Christians were arrested in South Africa during a civil rights demonstration. Locked together in a cell, in turn, those arrested recited from their holy scriptures. During the Gulf War, some Christians, Jews and Muslims felt it important to be able to pray together for peace.

Occasions for interfaith prayer are, even if carefully organized, *special*. They do not replace the regular prayer and liturgy of a faith community. They affirm, however, our God-given humanity and shared commitment to certain values or aspirations. They may be a fitting end to a weekend of dialogue, when the understandings and misunderstandings are offered to God. They may express our penitence for the past. They may be a creative response to personal situations.

In participating, I have felt myself to be sharing in the reconciling work of Christ, who seeks to break down all barriers and to make known the love of God for all people. Others who take part are inspired by other faith commitments. Together we believe that our deepest point of meeting is in the presence of God and that to pray or to be silent together in that presence is to know a divine blessing on all other work of interfaith dialogue and co-operation.

Interfaith dialogue is enriching, helping us to affirm our own religious identity while allowing it to grow as we respect and learn from those of other traditions. Interfaith worship, at its best, can be a symbolic expression of this and an eschatological sign of the harmony of faiths for which I pray. Interfaith worship, which should not be a substitute for the regular prayer of the faith communities, witnesses to the Oneness of God and the unity of the human family and can inspire us to break down all barriers and seek abundant life for all God's children.

14 THE CONCEPT OF INTERFAITH DIALOGUE
Bhikhu Parekh

Our age is characterized by two apparently contradictory religious tendencies. On the one hand religious fundamentalism is on the rise, not only in the developing countries of the Third World but also in the developed nations of the West, including and especially the USA. Fundamentalism is a response to a religious community's crisis of identity and integrity, and basically consists in reducing a complex and constantly growing tradition to a set of abstract, highly simplified and arbitrarily selected 'fundamentals' demanding total and uncritical allegiance.[1]

Alongside fundamentalism our age has also witnessed the fascinating phenomenon of interfaith dialogue. In stark contrast to the past missionary militancy and dogmatic certitude of the great world religions, especially Christianity and Islam, there is now a refreshing attempt on their part to understand one another and to develop common areas of interest and action. Since this is a recent development, the dialogue lacks a clear sense of direction and purpose. And since it is largely confined to a few well-meaning but generally powerless group of people marginal to the religious establishment, it lacks credibility and conviction. There is also the danger that rather than break down the barriers and counter fundamentalism, the dialogue might accentuate the sense of indifference and even become a cynical exercise in getting to know one's enemy better in order to fight him more effectively. The dialogue occurs against the background of centuries of suspicion and hostility and cannot avoid being shaped by this.

Since I greatly welcome the dialogue and consider it indispensable for the creation of a better and humane world, I intend in this paper to explore its nature, forms and presuppositions. Unless we are clear about what can be legitimately expected of an interfaith dialogue, the conditions under which it is possible and the reasons why it is necessary, we run the risk of conducting it in bad faith and of being disappointed with its outcome.

A dialogue is a structured and relatively open-minded conversation between people who think they have something meaningful to say to each other. They recognize that they have to live together and that they must therefore get to know each other. They also recognize that they have something to learn from each other and that talking would enrich and benefit them. A dialogue in this sense is possible only under four conditions.

First, the participants must respect and take each other seriously. They must accept each other as equals, not in the substantive sense of being equally good but in the formal and minimal sense of being capable of contributing to and benefitting from their discussion. If they think that the others are confused, misguided or fools with little capacity to learn and to teach, they will not take them seriously enough to engage in a meaningful conversation with them.

Second, dialogue presupposes shared concerns and a common language of discourse. Unless those involved are interested in asking common questions in a mutually comprehensible language, they are bound to talk past one another. It is, of course, true that dialogue *deepens* and *expands* the range of common concerns and helps *evolve* a shared vocabulary. However, it can do so only if the participants already share *some* common concerns, address *some* common questions, and share at least a *minimum* common vocabulary.

Third, dialogue presupposes that each participant brings to the discussion a distinct perspective and sensibility and a distinct body of insights. If the participants were all alike, they would have little to say to each other, and a discussion between them would have no point.

Finally, dialogue presupposes that one is prepared to learn from others and that one is not perfect. A person who thinks that he is in possession of the final and incorrigible truth necessarily has a closed mind. Since he is convinced that he has nothing to learn from others, the dialogue has no meaning for him. He might, of course, use it to explain himself to others or to win them over to his point of view. But this surely defeats the purpose of the dialogue and is hardly a dialogue in the sense of an open-minded conversation.

A dialogue properly so-called is difficult even for open-minded individuals discussing mundane matters; it is especially so for organized religions or what are loosely called faiths. A religion claims finality and is ill at ease with others making similar claims. Being based on faith, it is also uncomfortable with the rational process of dialogue. Since it is generally self-contained and self-sufficient, it has answers to all its questions and is unwilling to entertain different answers let alone new questions. Not surprisingly, interfaith dialogue has inherent limits and even a paradoxical character. So long as it is inter-*faith*, it cannot be genuinely open-minded. And if it is to be a genuine dialogue, it cannot view religion as *mere* faith. Religion rests on and is inconceivable without faith, but it cannot meaningfully converse with others unless it takes a more open-minded view of its fundamental beliefs. How this can be done, if at all, is the central question facing a theory of interfaith dialogue.

A historical example will illustrate how a dialogue can easily degenerate into an aggressive confrontation and defeat its own purpose. The Christian missionaries were given the freedom to propagate their faith in India in the third decade of the nineteenth century. Christianity had long known Judaism and Islam. Although critical and even intolerant of them, it had no difficulty accepting them as 'proper' religions. Hinduism was different. The Christian missionaries were convinced that a religion properly so-called must have a monotheist conception of God, a prophet, a single book revealing the will of God, a trained priesthood and an organized church. Since Hinduism did not satisfy any of these conditions, they insisted that it was not a religion at all and poured unmitigated scorn on it. It was, in their view, a crude mass of superstitions, polytheist, lacked 'a refined religious sensibility', and deserved to be condemned and consigned to the growing dustbin of history. The missionary criticism generated little-noticed public debates between Christians and Hindu pandits, from which the former learned little.

When the missionaries asked Hindu pandits if they believed in one God or many, the latter replied that the question was blasphemous and absurd. Even as colour, gender, height, size and such other qualities did not apply to God, the quantitive categories could not be applied either. He was both one and many, yet also neither. To insist that he *must* be one was to reduce him to the limited proportions of the human mind and thus to detract from his dignity. Furthermore, the question was predicated on the unsubstantiated assumption that God was a being or a person. If he was conceived instead as power or energy, the question made as much sense as whether air, energy or light was one or many. The Hindu pandits, many of whom were trained in the formidable Buddhist logic, went on to argue that since the universe was regulated and pervaded by God, *everything* in it was divine or informed or suffused by the divine presence. There was therefore nothing improper in calling it a *god*, a limited manifestation of the supreme being, and using it as a way of reaching up to him. Even the Christian view that the human soul represented a spark or a particle of God implied that every man was a god or godlike being.

When the missionaries asked the Hindus to show them their Bible, the latter asked why the divine self-revelation should be unique and exhaustive. Different historical epochs posed different problems and had different needs, and therefore God revealed himself in each historical epoch in a manner suited to it. When asked to name their prophet, the Hindus rejoined that rather than send his son or representative, God periodically came down on earth himself. When asked why they had no church, they replied that religion was ultimately a matter between a believer and God and required no mediation, and that the believers were free spontaneously to assemble to offer prayers without there being a formal church or trained priesthood.

Having disposed of the missionary criticisms as well as they could, the Hindu leaders questioned many a Christian belief and practice. They rejected the Christian conception of God on the grounds that it was relativistic and blasphemous, the former because it defined him from the narrow human point of view, the latter because it reduced him to the limited proportions of the human mind, attributed human emotions to him and detracted from his majesty. In their view the Hindu conception of the impersonal Brahman was free from these defects and infinitely superior.

The Hindu critics were not much impressed with the other aspects of Christian thought either. The concept of suffering God was unacceptably anthropomorphic and emotional. The doctrine of vicarious atonement violated the ideas of personal responsibility and just desert central to the Hindu doctrine of *Karma*. Crucifixion detracted from divine omnipotence and omniscience and involved an element of moral and religious blackmail. The concept of mediation between man and God was logically and morally unnecessary and a likely source of much religious corruption. The idea that Jesus was the sole mediator was arrogant and impertinent and the source of Christian intolerance. The figure of celibate, naturally innocent and unworldly Jesus bore no relation to the struggles of ordinary men and women and left them without a meaningful model. In this respect Rama and Krishna who led ordinary lives and showed how to cope with moral dilemmas and temptations were better. Being at the receiving end of imperialism, the Hindu leaders could not avoid commenting on the political role of Christianity. And they wondered how a religion of love and peace could acquiesce in slavery and other acts of inhumanity and brutality, sanction wars, even offer prayers for the victory of the State, and remain politically subservient.

Once the British consolidated their rule and used all the resources of the State to denigrate Hinduism, the Hindus lost their self-confidence and many of them begin to mimic Christianity. They turned Krishna into their equivalent of Christ, singled out the *Gita* as their Bible, presented Brahman as extra-cosmic God, defined it as a creator of the universe rather than as an all-pervasive intelligence inherent in the structure of the eternal universe, created church-like organizations in the form of the Ramakrishna Mission and Arya Samaj, and so on. Such Christianization of Hinduism led to considerable distortion and destroyed its authenticity. Our concern here, however, is not to trace the changes Hinduism underwent under colonial pressure but to uncover the assumptions that militated against a genuine Hindu–Christian dialogue. The missionaries approached Hinduism with a narrow and dogmatic conception of religion and were simply not prepared to admit that a religion could be structured differently. They mistook the familiar for the normal, and the latter for the natural, and made the all too familiar mistake of absolutizing their historically contingent form of religious consciousness. That is, they turned *their facts* into *others' values*. Furthermore, they kept asking Hinduism *their* questions. And when they found that it could not answer them, they dismissed it as intellectually shallow. They never had the patience and humility to listen to *its* questions and explore *its* answers to these. Not that they were wrong to ask questions developed within their own religious traditions; rather, they were wrong to think that these alone were worth asking. They were prepared to admit that their questions could have different answers, but not that other religions could ask different and equally legitimate questions. Such an approach foreclosed the possibility of a dialogue.

An interfaith dialogue might be inspired by two related but different impulses. First, it might spring from a desire to *understand* other religions and to explore how and why they arrive at their distinctive conceptions of God, religion, the universe, and man and his duties. Second, it might be inspired by a desire to *learn* from them, to acquire new insights into the nature of moral and religious life, and to deepen one's spirituality and enrich one's religious sensibility. Although the two approaches are related, for understanding and learning cannot be easily separated, they have different origins and consequences. In the first approach one seeks to understand others, but does not use that knowledge better to understand and critically evaluate one's own religion. A dialogue in the second case has a different thrust. It springs from a search for *critical self-understanding* and acknowledges that no religion is perfect and represents total truth about the nature of the divine. In such a view others do not remain separate but become part of oneself, and one's dialogue with them becomes an integral part of one's dialogue with oneself. In the first case interfaith dialogue springs from and encourages tolerance and mutual respect; in the second, it fosters a spirit of critical self-understanding and interreligious borrowing.

If I had to take an example of a religious man genuinely

engaged in the second kind of interfaith dialogue, I would point to Gandhi. I choose him neither because he was the only man in history to engage in it nor because he was the most sophisticated, for he was neither, but because I happen to know more about him than about the others. He struck up close friendships with Jews and Christians in South Africa, lived with them on his communal farm and made a close study of their scriptures. He went to South Africa to serve a Muslim patron and had close Muslim friends. And being a Hindu deeply influenced by the three great Indian religions, he had read widely in Hinduism, Buddhism and Jainism.[2]

For Gandhi every major religion articulated a unique vision of God and emphasized different features of the human condition. The idea of God as loving Father was most fully developed in Christianity, and the emphasis on love and suffering was also unique to it. As he put it: 'I cannot say that it is singular, or that it is not to be found in other religions. But the presentation is unique'. Austere and rigorous monotheism and the spirit of equality were 'most beautifully' articulated in and peculiar to Islam. The distinction between the impersonal and personal conceptions of God, the principle of the unity of all life and the doctrine of *ahimsa* (non-violence) were distinctive to Hinduism. For Gandhi every religion had a distinct moral and spiritual ethos and represented a wonderful and irreplaceable 'spiritual composition'. To a truly religious man all religions should be 'equally dear'.

Gandhi argued that since God was infinite and the limited human mind could grasp only a 'fragment' of him, and that too inadequately, every religion was necessarily limited and partial. Even the religions claiming to be directly revealed by God were revealed to men with their fair share of inescapable human limitations and communicated in necessarily inadequate human languages. To claim that a particular religion offered an exhaustive or even definitive account of the nature of God was to imply both that some men were free from inescapable human limitations and that God was partial, and thus to be guilty of both spiritual arrogance and blasphemy. Since no religion was final and perfect, each greatly benefitted from a dialogue with others. For Gandhi the purpose of an interreligious dialogue was threefold. First, it helped each religion understand the others better and encouraged it to feel relaxed enough to assimilate from them whatever it found worth accepting. Second, it helped each understand itself better and enabled it to appreciate both its uniqueness and similarities with the others. Third, it lifted each religion above the superficial levels of beliefs and rituals, deepened its spirituality and enabled it to catch a glimpse of the 'pure' or 'eternal' religion lying beyond all religions.

Since Gandhi believed that all religions charted the identical spiritual terrain from different directions, he thought that they had much to say to each other. Accordingly he made it a practice to read passages from different religions at his prayer meetings and encouraged his followers to make a 'reverential' study of their basic texts. When he was reading the New Testament with the students of Gujarat Vidyapith, there was a public protest. He replied:

> I regard my study and reverence for the Bible, the Koran and the other scriptures to be wholly consistent with my claim to be a staunch *sanatani* [orthodox] Hindu... My respectful study of other religions has not abated my reverence for and my faith in the Hindu scriptures. They have broadened my view of life. They have enabled me to understand more clearly many an obscure passage in the Hindu scriptures.

Gandhi found the idea of religious conversion profoundly irreligious and offensive. In his view it rested on three false assumptions. First, it assumed that a particular religion represented the final truth. We saw earlier why Gandhi considered such a view incoherent or blasphemous. Second, conversion consisted in changing a man's beliefs and assumed that religion was solely or primarily a matter of belief rather than of conduct. Gandhi rejected this view of religion on the ground that God was only interested in how a man *lived* and related to him and to other men, and not in what he believed. *Third*, conversion assumed that all men had identical moral and emotional needs so that a religion that was good for one group was necessarily good for all. Gandhi thought that such an assumption violated the central fact of human uniqueness.

For Gandhi, every man was born into a particular religion. Since no religion was wholly false, he should be able to work out his destiny in and through it. And if he felt attracted to some aspects of another religion, he should be at liberty to borrow them. Gandhi could not see why a man should ever need to give up his religion. That situation arose only when a religion was mistakenly understood in the image of the modern State in whose jealously guarded territory no one may settle without first giving up his old citizenship and acquiring a new one. When Madeleine Slade wished to become a Hindu, Gandhi advised her against it. She should, he insisted, live by her own Christian faith and absorb into it whatever she liked in Hinduism. Merely changing over to a new religion would not improve her conduct or way of life, the only thing that ultimately mattered. When they were overwhelmed with doubts, Gandhi encouraged his Christian friends to draw new inspiration and strength from their own religion. An American missionary,

Stanley Jones, spoke for many of them when he said that Gandhi had reconverted him to Christianity. In a different context he told his Jewish friend, Mrs Polak, that she need not 'become' a Christian in order to 'be' one. She could draw inspiration from Jesus's life and teachings and live *like* a Christian without ceasing to be a Jew. Hinduism gives its adherents and amazing degree of freedom to believe what they like so long as they conduct themselves in a socially required manner. Since the connection between belief and conduct is therefore looser than and logically different from that in almost all other religions, like most Hindus Gandhi had great difficulty understanding the phenomenon of religious conversion and the way changes in belief sometimes transformed conduct.

For Gandhi, a truly religious man should aim to live at three levels, representing increasingly higher levels of spirituality. First, his own religion was his necessary starting-point, and he should endeavour to live by its central values. Second, he should respect, enter into a dialogue with and assimilate from other religions whatever he found valuable. Third, he should eventually seek to go beyond all organized religions and practise 'pure' or 'eternal' religion in which prophets, priests, images, beliefs and rituals were all transcended and the believer lived in the constant and unmediated presence of God. Gandhi's own religious evolution followed this pattern. He was born and for a time lived as a traditional Hindu; he later generously borrowed from other religions and enriched his own; over time he evolved and practised a religion bearing a strong resemblance to what he called 'pure' religion. His first Christian biographer summed up his religious thought well:

> A few days ago I was told that 'He is a Buddhist'. Not long since a Christian newspaper described him as a Christian Mohammadan, an extraordinary mixture indeed. His views are too closely allied to Christianity to be entirely Hindu, and his sympathies are so wide and catholic that one would imagine he has reached a point where the formulae of sects are meaningless.

Religions are commonly thought of as closed worlds, almost like the sovereign nation-states zealously guarding their territorial boundaries. No one is allowed to belong to more than one religion, or to borrow the ideas and practices of another, without feeling guilty or threatened at the dilution of his or her religious identity. Interfaith dialogue is therefore expected to occur within and to do nothing to weaken the religious boundaries. Ghandi took a very different view. For him a religion was not a monolithic structure of ideas and practices, but a *resource* from which one freely borrowed whatever one found attractive and persuasive. As such, it was a collective property and a common human heritage. Every man was born into and deeply shaped by a specific religious tradition which as it were constituted his original family. He also enjoyed varying degrees of membership of other cultural and religious families, to whose achievements he enjoyed an unrestricted right of access. Gandhi said that as a Hindu he was an heir to its rich and ancient heritage. As an Indian he was a privileged inheritor of its diverse religious and cultural traditions. As a human being, the great achievements of mankind constituted a collective human capital to which he had as much right as their native claimants. While remaining firmly rooted in his own tradition, he therefore felt free to draw upon the moral and spiritual resources of the others. To express the two central ideas of rootedness and openness, he often used the metaphor of living in a house with its windows wide open. His house was protected by walls and gave him a sense of security, but its windows were wide open to allow cultural winds from all directions to blow into it and to enable him to breathe fresh air at his own pace and in his own way. *Ano Bhadra ritavo yantu vishvatah* (May noble thoughts from all over the world come to us) was one of his favourite classical maxims.

Gandhi took full advantage of his self-proclaimed intellectual freedom. He abstracted what he took to be the central values of Hinduism and set up a critical dialogue, even a confrontation, between them and those derived from elsewhere. Thus he took over the Hindu concept of *ahimsa* (non-violence), in his view one of its central moral principles. He found it negative and passive and reinterpreted it in the light of the activist and socially-oriented Christian concept of *caritas*. However, he felt that the latter was too emotive, led to worldly attachments and compromised the agent's self-sufficiency, and so he redefined it in the light of the Hindu concept of *anasakti* (non-attachment). His double conversion, his Christianization of a Hindu category after he had suitably Hinduized the Christian concept, yielded the novel idea of an active and positive but detached and non-emotive love. Again, he took over the traditional Hindu practice of fasting as a protest, combined it with the Judaic concept of representative leadership and the Christian concepts of vicarious atonement and suffering love, interpreted and reinterpreted each in the light of the others, and developed the amazing notion of a 'voluntary crucifixion of the flesh'. It involved fasting undertaken by the acknowledged leader of a community to atone for the evil deeds of his followers, to awaken their senses of shame and guilt, and to mobilize their moral and spiritual energies for redemptive purposes.[3]

For Gandhi a religion was not a sovereign system of authoritative beliefs and practices which its adherents may violate only on pain of punishment, but a great cultural resource which, like great works of art and literature, belonged to all mankind. One did not have to *be* a Christian in order to feel entitled to adopt Christian beliefs and practices. And a Hindu or a Muslim who did so did not *become* a Christian. Indeed, the very terms Christian, Hindu and Muslim were mistaken and a source of much mischief. They reified respective religions, set up rigid artificial boundaries, sanctioned false proprietary claims and created a psychological and moral pressure towards conformity. In the ultimate analysis, argued Gandhi, there were neither Christians nor Hindus, only whole and unfragmented human beings who freely helped themselves with the moral and spiritual resources of these and other religions. One could admire Jesus and even accept him as the son of God, but one could hold the Buddha, Moses, Mahavira, Zarathustra and others in equally high regard. Such men and women belonged to all religions, and hence to none alone. Whatever one may think of Gandhi, he offers the clearest possible antithesis of fundamentalism and demonstrates the creative potentialities of a genuinely open-minded interfaith dialogue.

Interfaith dialogue represented an important step in the right direction. As of now, it remains a fragile plant and could be easily snuffed out by the powerful forces of religious and political fundamentalism. It needs to be institutionalized and patiently nurtured, and that requires several things of which I wish to stress three. First, a new generation of men and women hospitable to interfaith dialogue needs to be raised, and therefore the spirit of interfaith dialogue should inform and permeate the teaching of religion in our schools. Second, interfaith dialogue remains abstract and formal unless constantly tested in and strengthened by concerted actions on common issues. There are many issues both in Britain and in the world at large on which no religious man can afford to remain silent. It is easy to get excited about such global issues as world peace and *apartheid* which require little sacrifice and courage. It is far more demanding to take a stand against an unfair immigration policy, racial discrimination, social and economic inequalities and injustices, the pervasive spirit of selfishness, and intellectual and moral intolerance that gravely damage the lives of thousands and about which one can really *do* something. The real test of the sincerity of interfaith dialogue lies in whether those belonging to the privileged and dominant faiths are prepared to stand up on behalf of the less privileged 'children of God'.

Third, although all religions have talked about human brotherhood, they have all defined and drawn the boundaries of brotherhood narrowly, and none has admitted *all* men and women *equally* within its fold. For Christians, Jesus is 'the way'. For centuries they have argued that those who accept him in this spirit are privileged; those who accept him as *a* way but not *the* way are at best stepbrothers; those not accepting him even as *a* way are doomed if not damned. Islam, too, has its hierarchy of brotherhood. It privileges Judaism and Christianity, but has little mercy on the so-called idolaters, apostates and atheists. Ethnic religions find it difficult to accommodate the universalist notion of brotherhood, whereas the universalist religions grant brotherhood on a highly selective basis. In our increasingly interdependent world, every religion needs to take a careful look at the sources of narrowness, intolerance and violence within it.

15 CHRISTIAN–MUSLIM DIALOGUE IN THE TWENTIETH CENTURY
Shabbir Akhtar

What kind of attitude should one have while engaged in a dialogue with someone from a different religious persuasion? Why should a Christian or Muslim engage in dialogue? Should he seek to demonstrate the superiority of his faith? Is the posture of responsible exchange a good one? Why would a religious person seek to terminate dialogue? Would he be justified in doing so?

There is nowadays, beneath the surface, much genuine tension and disquiet in the area of Islamic–Christian exchange. Though both Christians and Muslims continue, at religious conferences, to talk very enthusiastically about the need for eschewing polemical critique in favour of eirenic exchange, it would be no exaggeration to say that neither party trusts the other.

Muslims do sometimes suspect the motives of their Christian counterparts. And there may be grounds for suspicion. Why, after all, should Christians whose forefathers have opposed Islam root and branch, by means fair and foul, for well over a thousand years, suddenly wish to effect a peaceful reconciliation? This is an important worry. For the current liberal attitude towards Islam prevalent among some Christians is either the result of a betrayal of a principle held tenaciously for centuries or else it is a realization of past errors. Neither of these possibilities is sinister: nations can sometimes owe allegiance to false ideals and do so for centuries; to realize one's errors or those of one's ancestors is an act of humility and, as such, worthy of respect. What is troubling, however, is the possibility that dialogue is merely part of a new strategy to deal with an old enemy. (Remember that Islam has been, remains, and will remain, far and away Christianity's most successful religious rival.) Could it be that some Christians are merely putting a different bait on the old hook? Could it be that dialogue is sometimes undertaken in deference to the maxim 'Know thine enemy?'

These are not meant to be rhetorical questions; and I do not wish to impugn the motives of all Christians engaged in dialogue with the Muslim faithful.[1] My own answers, to be given here without regard for the rules of professional diplomacy, will, I fear, seem rather harsh and unpleasant, especially to a people who regard the demands of politeness as overriding those of truth. It seems to me that the practice of Christian institutions by and large gives the lie to the claim about desiring a genuinely impartial or sympathetic study of Islam. There are grounds for this accusation, though I do not expect Christian readers to agree with me. It cannot be a coincidence that in western universities Islam is rarely if ever taught by someone who embraces its inspiration. Christianity is taught often enough by Christians, Buddhism by Buddhists, and so on. There is, notwithstanding the liberal ethos of western intellectual culture, a strong operative bias against the hiring of Muslims, especially well-informed Muslims, to teach Islam.[2] The motives for this are fairly easily identified: a vigorous Islam poses a great threat to the historical and religious foundations of an apparently disintegrating western Christianity. But while this fear is understandable enough, it cannot constitute a defensible ground for disallowing Muslims to teach Islam – or even Judaism and Christianity.

To refuse to see unfairness in the present arrangement, deliberate as it clearly is, requires some degree of sophistry. Nor will it do to retort that, for purposes of teaching, adherence to a faith prejudices one's outlook. For while that is usually true, it is equally the case that rejection often prejudices one's outlook in a different direction. And, in any case, it is indefensible to single out Islam for special, indeed prejudicial, treatment. One could argue that Christianity should be taught more or less exclusively by Christians in a seminary just as Islam is always taught by Muslims in an Islamic seminary (*madrasah*). But it is odd to prohibit Muslims from teaching their own religion in 'liberal' western universities while allowing Christians to teach Christianity. Indeed, Christians often each Islam in such institutions, while it is difficult to find a Muslim teaching Christianity or Judaism alongside his non-Muslim colleagues.[3]

There are, to widen our discussion, certain attitudes that tend to cause friction between Christians and Muslims engaged in dialogue; and some of these threaten the continuation of organized exchange. Christians, to focus on one particular attitudinal issue, frequently accuse the Muslim protagonists of 'triumphalism': Muslims, it is alleged, complacently pretend that a good few of the problems facing Christianity are peculiar to that religion and have no relevance to Islam. Thus, modernity is to most Muslims, Christians contend, simply a Christian problem.

This is a partly just accusation. Many Muslims do boast that Islam is immune to the many challenges of secular modernity. This is indeed triumphalism (in the pejorative sense) and ought to be abjured. It is an attitude nourished by an ignorance (or at least an inadequate understanding) of the nature of the modern sceptical reservation about *all* transcendent religions. Islam may well have to consider seriously the possibility of making concessions, albeit minor ones, to the secular temper. (One good result of Muslim obscurantism here has been that Islam remains Islam: there are no revised versions, no 'neo-Islamic' doctrines or trends.) To refuse resolutely to recognize even the need for any such concessions in the case of Islam while recognizing, even emphasizing, such a need in the case of Christianity is tantamount to a species of triumphalism, though to be fair, Muslims are rarely guilty of this particular variety of it. Their attitude is often simpler; Christians are having problems controlling the subversive sceptical developments within their own culture; Islam can take care of these developments if only Christians will hand over their difficulties to the Muslims.

Such a pretension is, of course, to put it minimally, quite silly. When it comes to the challenges of a secular reason fully emancipated from age-old theistic structures, all the theists are in the same – and, as it happens, currently rather leaky – boat. To make concessions to secular modernity, however, is one thing; to make concessions to Christianity quite another.[4] And it is here that the charge of triumphalism becomes problematic. We can easily see this when we note that 'triumphalism', like 'reductionism' or 'revisionism', is a term of opprobrium, and one that readily finds its place in the polemical lexicon. What, then, is triumphalism? And what is wrong with it? Now, surely to mention one's strengths, to argue that Christianity may have weaknesses absent from its great religious rival, is not in itself culpable. Perhaps, Islam is, when all is said and done, genuinely superior to Christianity (and Judaism). Perhaps, just perhaps, Islam has all the strengths of Christianity and none of its weaknesses. In fact, of course, all of us, Christians no less than Muslims, talk of our strengths. Could it be that when the other party does it, it is tempting to call it 'triumphalism'?

The charge of triumphalism is an interesting and revealing one. It offers us an insight into the evolution of Christian attitudes towards Islam. In many ways, this accusation may actually be the residue of that much older, much more crass, charge of fanaticism – a charge still in vogue in popular and intellectual western culture. Muslims have been, and still are, accused of fanaticism sometimes solely on account of the fact that they, unlike many Christians, refuse to compromise on matters of principle. And yet if adherence to principle be fanaticism, then fanaticism is an admirable trait – and one in rather short supply among modern Christians.

Fanaticism is of course other people's passion. (What the English newscaster calls suicide may still be martyrdom in God's eyes.) All nations are fanatical about one thing or another, whether it be elevated matters such as religion and honour or trivial matters such as football and sensuality. We can all live with some prejudices – but not with others.

To get back to our theme, not all Muslim claims about the alleged relative superiority of Islam *vis-à-vis* its great religious rival can reasonably be dismissed as triumphalist in a derogatory sense. We must allow conceptual room for the possibility of recording one's strengths just as we should allow room for recording one's weaknesses. And Muslims are, I believe, perfectly justified in seeking to argue that Islam has a relative strength, for example, in the areas of canon and intellectual appeal. Christianity has in the region of canonical formulation a weakness well documented even by its adherents. Many Christians have been attracted to Islam's exceptionally powerful intellectual foundations. Why should a believer be prohibited from mentioning the strengths in his vision?

Christians, particularly those committed to the proselytization of Muslims (and Jews), are naturally disturbed by Islam's powerful hold on the minds of many Muslims. But the dexterity with which committed Christian apologists and missionaries continue to mix poison and praise with respect to Islam simply has not produced the required results. The rate of conversion from Christianity to Islam is relatively high, often attracting highly distinguished Christians; the rate of conversion in the opposite direction is very low indeed, often attracting only undistinguished Muslims. It is true that conversion from Islam to Christianity is usually fraught with dangers: Islamic societies have strong disincentives, formal and informal, against conversion.[5] But in the modern secularized West most Muslims can convert to Christianity, and do so usually with relative impunity. And yet in spite of that liberty, few Muslims of any distinction have gone over to join the Christian Club. The stock Muslim claim, that *all* Muslims who convert are merely insincere opportunists rescued from poverty by the missionary's dangerous gift of financial assistance, is unconvincing. It is indeed unfair to doubt the sincerity of most of these conversions, especially when one notes all the isolation and suffering often entailed.

Sincerity aside, one can safely say that most conversions from Christianity to Islam are based on some measure of intellectual reasoning; often reasoning about Christianity's glaring weakness in the area of scriptural canon. Conversions in the opposite direction are almost always based on subjective religious experience, itself often inspired by the wish for a kind of guarantee about the attainment of salvation.[6] Islam, it is thought – and this is a correct understanding of Islam – offers no guarantees of success in the religious life; Christianity famously offers a kind of 'insurance policy' for sinners. The attractions of the Christian view, deceptive though it clearly is, are not difficult to discern.[7]

To record facts, such as these in the sociology of conversion, is not in itself either polemical or triumphalist. Indeed, it seems to me, we *should* record unpleasant facts. (Or is honesty in religious dialogue – as in business – the worst policy?) Certainly there are grounds for genuine disquiet here generated by the current circumstance of rivalry. Christians and Muslims are both in the same business: that of religious success. And it would be absurd to pretend that such a circumstance is not often radically divisive.

There is a tendency among educated Christians and Muslims to sail under false colours in order to keep afloat a liberal ecumenical enterprise. And yet such a strategy is religiously unacceptable, for it sacrifices, sells short, the virtue of truth merely for the sake of attaining a false if comforting sense of community. Of course, dialogue (or, in the latest fashion, 'trialogue', with a few liberal Jewish thinkers lending a helping hand) does achieve genuinely educational ends if only for a handful of academics. But one should put in the balance the fact that Christianity and Islam co-exist in an atmosphere of fundamental and native anxieties about questions of moment. The gulf between the faiths, like the gulf between the dualist's mind and matter or the conservative politician's East and West, is not likely to be bridged merely by dialogue undertaken by a handful of expensively educated academics.

I do not wish to deny the importance of responsible exchange between members of different faiths. But it must be responsible: well-informed, cognisant of the tensions, ready to acknowledge rift and difference, concerned to record realities.[8] And this is indeed a tall order. Will Christian–Muslim dialogue endure into the next decade? My own view about the future of such dialogue – a view denigrated by some as unduly pessimistic – is, I believe, surely realistic. I myself find it difficult to attend an interfaith conference without thinking that religious exchange will indeed endure into the next century – but merely as a fashion. It could be that religious liberalism of the kind exhibited in dialogue may not survive the currently widening ideological rift between the Crescent and the Cross in many parts of the globe. If it does survive the trial, it is most likely to do so, like modern optimism, by relying on increasingly unclear generalities.[9]

It is not recent scholarship alone that has noted the deep, perhaps irresolvable, doctrinal incompatibility between Islam and Christianity. The problem had already been felt and recorded as early as the seventh century. In fact the Qur'àn itself invites Christians to a prayer duel (*mubahilah*) in the larger attempt to break the deadlock. According to this arrangement, sometimes known as 'trial by imprecation', the contending parties invoke the wrath or adverse judgement of God expecting it to `fall' immediately and visibly on the dishonest, guilty or otherwise misguided party. The trial by imprecation can also be invoked by one individual against an alleged religious imposter or heretic; and it was invoked in the nineteenth century by orthodox religionists against Mirza Ghulam Ahmad, the founder of the Qadiani sect, now expelled from Islam. The results of this procedure are difficult to interpret.

Muhammad had set out, in accordance with Qur'ànic instructions (Q:3:55–61), to meet his Christian dectractors in a large open space. The Christians, according to the Muslim account,[10] arrived on time, but were deterred by the sight of Muhammad and his party's sincerity and confidence. The Christians declined the challenge.

That method of imprecation is, whatever its merits in the age of revelation, clearly unsuited to our current circumstance. Given the silence of God today, the deadlock between any given faith, such as Islam, and its rivals, is not so easily broken. To be sure, there may well be any intellectual process transpiring beyond death in which the ambiguities and doctrinal stalemates of this life are finally resolved and broken just as the moral imbalance of mortal existence will, according to ethical theism, be eventually and satisfactorily rectified in a world yet to come.[11] But this view, even supposing it to be coherent and true, still leaves all the important theological puzzles on our hands. Why does God allow many large portions of mankind to remain in doubt, hesitation, or even outright error concerning matters of moment? The Qur'àn sternly warns us that confession of the monotheistic credo *after death* may not suffice to escape damnation: we had better find out while we are still living. If so, isn't God morally obliged, so to speak, to make clear, especially in an age of confusion, his existence, will and purpose for men on earth?

As the various doctrinal deadlocks in Christian–Muslim debate become increasingly prevalent, the critique of the religious rival is likely to become purely moral. Each faith has an associated normative outlook; Christians and Muslims naturally argue that the ethical scheme associated with their faith is superior to all other such schemes. It is felt that religions can sometimes be ranked for plausibility in terms of their moral, as opposed to purely metaphysical, appeal. Such a shift of focus is, it might be argued, a welcome one indicating the direction in which a possible resolution of the Christian–Muslim deadlock lies.

The theme of interreligious dialogue is likely to occupy the centre of theological concerns in this and the coming century. Many characteristically modern religious puzzles are generated by a growing realization that the doctrinal elements in any one given faith cannot reasonably maintain a universality of normative claim upon modern human allegiance. The presence of authentic religiosity outside one's own tradition of faith seems undeniable if religiously disconcerting. Indeed, enlightened opinion among theists – Jews, Christians and Muslims – is more or less unanimous that scripture contains irresolvable puzzles with respect to the existence of plural pieties.

Once upon a time it was reasonable to say: 'Every religious controversy is due to someone's ignorance.' No longer though. It is possible now to understand various faiths in a comprehensively cross-cultural way; there has been a spectacular recent growth in our knowledge of rival views and ideologies. But there is currently a stalemate among ideological opponents. And the Christian–Muslim deadlock is an especially intractable one that is likely to endure for a long time. In the end, we may all do well to take Father Robert Caspar's characteristically charitable advice, deriving from the Qur'ān (Q:2:148; 5:48): instead of being rivals in the negative and harmful mode, Muslims and Christians should cultivate rivalry in good works.[12]

16 RANKING RELIGIONS
Dan Cohn-Sherbok

Over the last few years there has been considerable debate about the relationship between the religions of the world; in particular Christians have been anxious to formulate a theology of other religions which transcends the traditional Christian belief that God's revelation and salvation are offered exclusively in Jesus Christ. In this context a number of theologians have questioned the finality of Christ and Christianity.

Christianity and Religious Pluralism

Professor John Hick, for example – the leading proponent of this view – speaks of a revolution in theology which involves a radical transformation of the concept of the universe of faiths. He claims that 'the great world religions [are] different human responses to the one Divine Reality, embodying different perceptions which have been formed in different historical and cultural circumstances'.[1] Similarly, the Roman Catholic priest, Raimundo Panikaar, argues for a revised form of ecumenism which strives for unity without harming religious diversity. Panikaar argues that the fundamental religious fact of the world's religions is the mystery known in every authentic religious experience. For Panikaar, this mystery within all religions is both more than and yet has its being within the diverse experiences and beliefs of the religions:

> It is not simply that there are different ways of leading to the peak, but that the summit itself would collapse if all the paths disappeared. The peak is in a certain sense the result of the slopes leading to it... It is not that this reality has many names as if there were a reality outside the name. This reality is the many names and each name is a new aspect.[2]

Thus he claims that no one religion can claim to be the ultimate truth.

Panikaar and Hick are not unique in their views. Similar positions are put forward by such theologians as Dr Stanley Samartha, formerly director of the World Council of Churches Programme on Dialogue[3] and Professor Paul Knitter of Xavier University.[4]

Criteria for Grading Religions

The acceptance of such a theocentric model of the universe of faiths does not imply, however, that all religions are equally valid. Addressing himself to this point, Professor Hick in an extremely valuable discussion of this issue asserts that religious concepts and practices are not all on the same level of value or validity.[5] This is so among the different religions and even within individual religious systems. Indeed, he points out, throughout history the most significant religious figures have been critical of various ideas and attitudes: Gautama rejected the notion of the eternal atman; the Hebrew prophets criticized mere outward observances and practices; Jesus attacked the formalism and insincerity of the scribes and Pharisees; Muhammad rejected the polytheism of Arabian society; Guru Nanak and Martin Luther were critical of the traditions into which they were born.[6] Thus Hick maintains that assessing religious phenomena is a central feature of religious seriousness and openness to the divine. It is legitimate to grade aspects of religions and place them in some order of merit. No one, he believes, is going to think that all the features of the world's religions are on the same level of value or validity: different aspects 'have to be regarded as higher or lower, better or worse, Divine or demonic'.[7] Yet Hick emphasizes that while it is proper to assess religious phenomena, it is not realistic to grade the world's religions as totalities. 'Each of these long traditions', he writes, 'is so internally diverse, containing so many different kinds of both good and evil, that it is impossible for human judgement to weigh up and compare their merits as systems of salvation.'[8] Commenting on this view, Paul Griffiths and Delmas Lewis des-cribe Hick as a nonjudgemental activist who is unwilling to make judgements about his claims of the world's religions,[9] but this is a mistake. Hick makes it clear throughout his discussion that it is the theologian's proper task to ascertain what aspects of a tradition are 'belief-worthy, revelatory, plausible, rightly-claiming allegiance'.[10]

The difficulty with Hick's position is not, as Griffiths and Lewis maintain, that he refuses to make judgements about the truthclaims of religions, but rather than the evaluative framework he outlines is open to serious criticism. The first criterion Hick proposes is theological coherence: 'We can try to assess such a system in respect of its internal consistency...'[11] Yet there is no self-evident reason why internal consistency should necessarily be regarded as a central virtue of a religion. It may well be that religious experience transcends ordinary categories of logical reasoning; furthermore, even if it were shown that a religious system is coherent in terms of belief and practice, this would not necessarily imply that it was in fact based on a true encounter with divine reality. Allied with this notion of internal coherence is a second criterion of religious adequacy – 'its adequacy both to the particular form of experience on which it is based and to the data of human experience in general'.[12] Here, however, it is unclear how one is to determine whether a theology or philosophy within a religious tradition is adequate to the originating religious vision or successful in interpreting that vision to a new age. There is no doubt that the theologies of Thomas Aquinas, al-Ghazali, Maimonides, Shankara and Buddhaghosha are intellectually impressive, but are they true to the original vision on which they are based? Are they successful interpretations for subsequent believers? There is no obvious way to deal with these questions, and any answers will inevitably be based on subjective reactions and interpretations.

The third criterion Hick suggests is spiritual in nature. Here the test consists in ascertaining how far religious ideas promote or hinder the aims of salvation and liberation. 'And by salvation or liberation', Hick writes, 'I suggest that we should mean the realization of that limitlessly better quality of human existence which comes about in the transition from self-centredness to Reality-centredness.'[13] In explaining this principle, Hick gives examples from several religions: Christians give themselves to God in Christ in a total renunciation of the self-centred ego and its concerns; Muslims give themselves in total submission to God; Hindus strive for union with the Ultimate through meditation and selfless action. While it is true that within the world's religions this theme of selflessness in different forms is an important feature, there are other central motifs as well. Whether this aspect should be the touchstone of religious validity is open to debate. Religious systems provide different and varied spiritual fruits – it is certainly plausible that other spiritual attitudes and concerns are of equal or even superior value than ego-renunciation and self-giving to the real.

The final criterion Hick proposes is moral assessment.[14] In recommending this standard Hick extols the lives of various saints of the world's religions, yet he emphasizes that the actual histories of religious traditions frequently fall short of moral ideals. In this context he catalogues what he considers modern moral evils engendered by religious faith: the lethargy of eastern countries in relation to social and economic problems; the West's exploitation of natural resources; Hindu and Buddhist otherworldliness in retarding social, economic and technological progress; the unjust caste system of India; the burning of widows in India; the cutting off of a thief's hands under Islamic law, and so forth.[15] In making these judgements Hick wishes to illustrate that in the history of all religious traditions there is both virtue and vice. Nevertheless, what is absent from this list is a systematic framework for ethical decision-making. Moral attitudes are notoriously difficult to assess. Does Hick recommend we adopt a teleological or deontological stance? When considering the viability of religious claims concerning the multifarious dimensions of human behaviour, what is to be the basis for making a correct judgement? These central questions are unfortunately left unanswered despite Hick's assurances that certain aspects of the world's faiths are morally inadequate, thereby rendering them religiously less viable.

A similar criticism applies to Hick's consideration of the moral character of religious leaders. What is important about such individuals, he writes, is the coherence between their teaching about God and the ways in which such teaching is reflected in their own lives. Taking the example of Jesus, Hick asserts that if Jesus had taught hatred, selfishness, greed, and the amassing of wealth by exploiting others he would never have been regarded as 'Son of God'. The same, Hick argues, applies to each of the great religious figures; on this basis, he believes it is possible to identify 'the operation of an ethical criterion in the recognition of a mediator of the Divine or the Real'.[16] Yet while it may empirically be the case that Jesus's followers would not have accepted him as Christ if his ministry had not conformed to his teaching, it does not necessarily follow that when such coherence is found in the life of a religious leader, that person has in fact had a true encounter with God. Nor for that matter should one necessarily conclude that a lack of coherence demonstrates the falseness of a religious leader's claims – when such a figure does not live out his message, this may well be the result of human weakness, temptation and sin.

Similar criticisms made of Hick's criteria can be levelled at the bases for grading religious faiths delineated by Paul Knitter in a study of Christian attitudes toward the world's religions. According to Knitter, there are three guidelines for determining the truth-value of any religion or religious figure:

1 Personally, does the revelation of the religion or religious figure – the story, the myth, the message – move the human heart? Does it stir one's feelings, the depths of one's horizons?

2 Intellectually, does the religion also satisfy and expand the mind? Is it intellectually coherent? Does it broaden one's horizons of understanding?

3 Practically, does the message provide for psychological health of individuals, their sense of value, purpose and freedom? Does it promote the welfare, the liberation of all peoples?[17]

As in the case of Hick's criteria, the answers to these questions will inevitably involve subjective interpretation and personal judgement. For example, the life and teachings of Jesus evoke a spiritual response on the part of Christians but have little meaning for Jews. Similarly, the Buddha is of profound significance for Buddhists but has little relevance for Muslims. Again, the legal system of Islam has no significance for Hindus. In all these cases, it is simply impossible to make an objective evaluation of the truth claims of the world's religions on the basis of an existential response. The same applies to the intellectual coherence of religious traditions: Jews, for example, find the Christian doctrines of the Trinity and Incarnation irrational and incoherent. For Christians the Theravada Buddhist's rejection of a supernatural deity undermines the spiritual life. Muslims regard Hindu polytheism as religiously abhorrent. Thus, Knitter's second criterion also fails to provide a firm foundation for evaluative judgement. The third criterion is equally problematic: how is one to assess whether particular religious beliefs promote psychological health and liberation? Orthodox adherents regard liberal movements within their own faiths as misguided; liberals on the other hand argue that certain traditional elements of their faiths are psychologically constraining and hinder personal and communal growth. We can see therefore that Knitter's suggestions, like Hick's, fall short of providing a satisfactory basis for ranking religions.

The Criterion of Viability

These proposals for evaluating religions and religious figures are ultimately unsatisfactory because they fail to provide clear-cut and generally accepted bases for evaluation. Yet this should not be a surprising conclusion. In the past adherents of a particular religion judged all other religions by the criteria of their own faith; the eclipse of such an exclusivist stance by a theocentric picture of the world's religions leads inevitably to a relativistic conception of the universe of faiths. Within such a framework, as we have seen, grading religions – whether on the basis of theological coherence, religious adequacy, spirituality, morality, existential response, psychological health, or liberating capacity – involves subjective, personal decisions grounded on fundamental presuppositions about divine reality and the human condition. Given such a situation, is it possible in any way to grade religions objectively? Hick is certainly correct that religious systems as totalities cannot be ranked since they are themselves composed of different streams of traditions. Nevertheless, it should be possible to evaluate separate movements within the world's religions on the basis of their viability, namely, their capacity to satisfy the spiritual demands and animate the lives of adherents. Within such a context there would be no need to appeal to an alleged universal standard of judgement; instead the criterion of viability could serve as the sole guideline for rating religions. If a movement within a particular religious system were seen to be effective in the lives of its followers, it would rank higher than another religious system which did not in fact satisfy the spiritual needs of adherents. Such a guideline would not yield judgements about the truth-claims of the various faiths yet it would furnish important information about the religious adequacy of the world's religions and enable one to place them in some hierarchical order on the basis of ascertainable evidence.

Modern Judaism furnishes an illuminating example of the possibilities of this means of grading religions. Through the centuries traditional Judaism has maintained that God revealed the Pentateuch to Moses on Mt Sinai. This belief implies that the whole Torah, including theology, history and law, is of divine origin – everything contained in these books was revealed by the Almighty. This principle guarantees the validity of the legal system and serves as the foundation of the theological tenets of the faith. Yet, it has become increasingly difficult for most Jews to accept this fundamentalist belief in the origin of scripture. The main challenges to the doctrine of Pentateuchal infallibility have united to produce a convincing picture of the Pentateuch as a work with a human history and coloured by human ideas, including human errors.[18] This shift in understanding has had far-reaching consequences for modern Orthodoxy. There is still a small segment of Orthodox Jews who hold fast to the traditional conception of the origin of the Torah. For them Orthodox Judaism is in every way a viable religious system, but in practice the majority of Jews who affiliate to Orthodox Judaism have set aside not only the central belief in Torah from Sinai but also its attendant notions. These lapsed Orthodox Jews no longer subscribe to the conviction that each and every word of the Pentateuch was dictated to Moses, nor do they accept that the ancient rabbis were infallible interpreters of the law whose decrees are perfectly in accord with God's will. Consequently they do not feel bound to observe the 613 scriptural commandments nor the thousands of rabbinic laws based on these precepts as recorded in the Code of Jewish Law. Instead lapsed Orthodox Jews observe only those segments of the legal tradition which they find of importance. It is not uncommon, for example, for such Orthodox Jews to insist on a strict observance of the food laws while neglecting the laws of ritual purity in other spheres.

Similarly, lapsed Orthodox Jews no longer feel bound to accept many of the theological beliefs inherent in the Torah, nor the principles of the Jewish faith as enshrined in Maimonides' formulation of the thirteen cardinal beliefs of Judaism. Doctrines such as belief in the resurrection of the dead, final judgement, and reward and punishment in the hereafter have been largely ignored or discarded. Thus, Orthodox Judaism as a system of belief and practice has ceased to be a viable religious system for the majority of those who describe themselves as adherents. Here there is an example of a religious system which has ceased to be effective for those who regard themselves (and are regarded by the Jewish community generally and the outside world) as Orthodox Jews. For these lapsed Orthodox Jews – as opposed to authentic Orthodox Jews who are firmly committed to the faith – traditional Judaism is no longer tenable as a religious system since its theological tenets preclude significant adaptation and change. Thus, in grading the world's religions on the basis of viability, it is clear that contemporary Orthodox Judaism in its lapsed phase would rank lower than any religious system which is fervently adhered to by a substantial majority of its followers.

In contrast to modern Orthodoxy (where there is a striking discrepancy between the demands of traditional Judaism and the lifestyle of lapsed Orthodox Jews) contemporary Reform Judaism is more consonant with the needs and expectations of its followers. Unlike Orthodox Judaism, the Reform movement is open to fundamental change since it has rejected the belief that the Pentateuch was given by God to Moses. This movement within world Jewry has broken ranks with Orthodoxy by declaring that the Pentateuch is a post-Mosaic, composite work – the product of a divine encounter with Israel but with a strong human component. Laws as well as religious beliefs are thus seen to be the product of historical circumstances. On this basis Reform Jews have largely rejected the halachic aspects of traditional Judaism. Reform Judaism is conceived essentially as a prophetic faith, emphasizing moral conduct combined with prayer and worship. Within this context, Reform Jews feel free to dismiss the legal and theological features of traditional Judaism which they no longer regard as tenable. Without the theological constraints of Orthodoxy, Reformers maintain that it is legitimate to adapt the tradition to meet modern needs and concerns. At the centre of Reform belief is the conviction that the Torah – as understood in its widest sense – must be open and developing. God's revelation is seen not as a series of theoretical absolutes, but as progressive in character. Within this framework, the role of the Reform rabbi is to search the classic Jewish sources for guidance for everyday living as Jews in contemporary society.

Such openness inevitably leads to confusion about which aspects of the tradition should be retained and which discarded. Yet there is no doubt that the majority of those who identify as Reform Jews find Reform Judaism viable as a religious system. Its very flexibility and diversity enable its adherents to shape the tradition to meet their spiritual needs. One could argue that Reform Judaism as a polymorphous entity is not internally coherent and consistent, yet its pliable character does enable it to adapt easily to individual needs. In a ranking system then, Reform Judaism – whatever its intrinsic merits – would receive high marks as a viable system of belief and practice. Unlike Orthodoxy, which presents a theoretical framework of belief and practice which is largely neglected by so-called adherents, Reform Judaism offers a loosely-knit structure which is amenable to personal choice and individual taste. Its viability consists in its effectiveness as a religion to influence and shape the lives of its followers according to their existential needs.

The Application of the Viability Criterion

These two examples from the Jewish world illustrate how the principle of viability can be used as a criterion for grading religious systems. Again, it must be emphasized that in evaluating a religion according to this standard, no judgement is being made about the validity of its truth-claims, nor is one attempting to ascertain whether the religion is in fact based on a true encounter with the Divine. All that is being judged is whether the religious system is practised and believed in by the majority of its so-called adherents. The process of grading religions is therefore essentially a sociological rather than a philosophical or theological exercise. The concern is not with inherent value, truth or validity, but with the capacity of a religious system to function effectively in the lives of its adherents: to do so there must be a correspondence between the tenets and practices of a religion and the way of life of those who allegedly subscribe to it. Ranking religions thus involves a comprehensive investigation into the present state of religious beliefs and practice in the world's religions.

One would need, for example, to examine the current state of affairs in the Muslim world. Do present day Muslims in fact accept the Qur'àn as a perfect revelation from God? Is the Shar'ia an active force in shaping the lives of the Muslim community? Are both Sunnis and Shi'ites true followers of their separate traditions? How universal is the revival of Islamic fundamentalism in the Arab world? The answers to such questions should help to clarify the extent to which Islam as a religious system is a vibrant and active force in Muslim life. Similar questions could be posed regarding Christianity. Here one would need to examine the extent to which

Christian beliefs and values are incorporated into the lives of members of the various branches of Christendom: Eastern Orthodox, Roman Catholic and Protestant. These groups obviously have different views of the essential features of the Christian life – what is at stake in a test of viability is the degree to which followers have incorporated the teachings of their respective traditions into their lives. A parallel case of religious diversity is found within Hinduism. With neither founder, creed, nor fixed pattern of observance, it is more difficult to measure the viability of the Hindu faith than in most traditions. Nevertheless, Hinduism embodies a certain ethos and a number of underlying conceptions (such as samsara, karma and moshka). Thus, as with other faiths, it should be possible to discover the degree to which Hinduism as a philosophy and way of life is meaningful for those who consider themselves Hindus.

Turning to other religions of the East, one could attempt to ascertain the extent to which the teachings of the Buddha serve as the focus of the lives of those who describe themselves as Buddhists. Do they truly accept the Four Noble Truths as valid? Does the Noble Eightfold Path serve as the blueprint for living? Is the belief in Nirvana widely accepted? To take another example of an eastern religion, is there for Jains a general acceptance of the doctrine of transmigration and rebirth? Is non-violence a characteristic of the lives of most Jains? Are they scrupulously vegetarian? Again, in this process of grading religious systems one would need to consider the effectiveness of new religions and quasi-religious cults to fulfil the spiritual needs of their followers. Are the adherents of such groups as Hare Krishna, Divine Light Mission, Unification Church, Transcendental Meditation and the like deeply dedicated? Do they actually accept the teachings of their various spiritual leaders? In all these cases the answers to these and similar questions would provide a basis for drawing up a hierarchical list of the world's religious systems based on the principle of viability.

Conclusion

It might be objected that grading religions in this way does not reveal what is of crucial importance – the relative inherent merits of the world's faiths. In one sense this is a fair criticism: the criterion of viability does not provide a touchstone for testing the truth-claims of a particular faith. But, as we have seen, ranking religions in terms of truth appears to be an impossible task since the criteria for judging religions in this manner are ultimately based on subjective judgement and personal predilection. Ranking religions on the basis of viability, however, would overcome this impasse by providing an objective procedure for evaluating religions on the basis of effectiveness. Drawing up such a viability map of the universe of faiths might well provide illuminating information in a number of important spheres: first, from a phenomenological standpoint, knowing about the realities of belief and practice in the world's religions could provide invaluable insights for the student of religion. All too often introductions to a religious heritage as well as more advanced studies offer only theoretical accounts of the elements of a tradition without indicating whether adherents actually accept the doctrines of their faith or attempt to infuse its teachings into their daily lives. Ranking the world's religions according to viability would help to fill this gap.

Secondly, such an investigation might well illustrate (as in the case of Orthodox Judaism) that some of the world's religions have today ceased to play a major role in the lives of so-called adherents. In the face of increasing secularism, this would not be a surprising situation, yet it is significant that the new cults seem to have attracted followers who are deeply committed. These modern movements appear to meet the spiritual needs of their disciples more successfully than mainstream traditions. In many cases converts to these cults have rejected the religions into which they were born because they find them spiritually bankrupt – in their place the cults offer them a discovery of the holy and experience of a transcendental reality. Such a development raises a number of serious questions about the effectiveness of the world's major religious traditions in contemporary society. Finally, in the same connection, ranking religions according to viability would help to illustrate whether Orthodox or liberal traditions have a greater hold on adherents. In the case of Orthodox Judaism, it is clear that the theological rigidity of Orthodoxy has undermined its vitality as a living faith, yet the opposite might be the case in other religions, such as Islam. This kind of information could contribute to an understanding of the dynamic of faith in a scientific age. These areas of concern are simply suggestive of the ways in which a test of viability could be of benefit. Though it would not determine the relative truth of the world's religions, such an approach is entirely consistent with a theocentric conception of the universe of faiths and could provide a sympathetic framework for appreciating and understanding the religious experience of humanity today.

Notes

Setting the Scene
1 Leaflet accompanying the booking form.
2 *Daily Express*, 16 April 1990.
3 Keith Ward, *A Vision to Pursue – Beyond the Crisis in Christianity*, SCM Press, London, 1991, p. 176.

Chapter 1 Toleration
The Archbishop of Canterbury's Morrell Address on Toleration was given at the University of York on 22 November 1991. The Memorial Address is part of a programme of studies in toleration based in the Department of Politics at the University of York, and supported by the C. and J.B. Morrell Trust.

1 John McManners, ed., *The Oxford Illustrated History of Christianity*, OUP, Oxford, 1990, p. 267.
2 See the Writings of Herbert Butterfield.
3 Mgr Ronald Knox, *The Belief of Catholics*, Ernest Benn, London, 1927, p. 241.
4 Richard McBrien, *Caesar's Coin*, Macmillan, London, 1987, pp. 114-27.

Chapter 2 Christianity and World Religions
The Sir Francis Younghusband Memorial Lecture was delivered by Robert Runcie, then Archbishop of Canterbury, at Lambeth Palace on 28 May 1986.

Chapter 3 Christianity and Other Religions
Gavin D'Costa's article previously appeared in *Dialogue & Alliance*, Vol. 2, No. 2, Summer 1988.

1 Cited in Yves Congar, *The Wide World: My Parish*, Darton, Longman and Todd, London; 1961, p. 116.
2 Cited in Wm. Theodore de Barry, ed., *Sources of Indian Tradition* Vol II, Columbia University Press, New York and London, 1958, p. 26.
3 See Gustavo Gutierrez, *A Theology of Liberation*, SCM, London; 1974, ch. 11.
4 Karl Barth, *Church Dogmatics* Vol 1/2, T & T Clark, Edinburgh; 1970, section 17.
5 D. Freeman Niles, 'Karl Barth: A Personal Memory', *The South East Asian Journal of Theology*, Vol. 11, pp. 8–12.
6 See John Bowden, *Karl Barth: Theologian*, SCM, London; 1979, p. 19

7   For a discussion of Barth's theology see my article "The Absolute and Relative Nature of the Gospel", in John Miller, ed., *Religion and Canadian Pluralism: An Ongoing Dialogue*, Waterloo University Press, Canada, 1988.
8   Barth's own stance was complicated and changed in his later life. See Paul Knitter, *Towards a Protestant Theology of Religions*, N. Elwart, Marburg; 1974, pp. 32-6.
9   Edward Percy, ed., *Facing the Unfinished Task: Messages Delivered at the Congress on World Mission*, W. Eerdmans, Grand Rapids, 1961, p. 9. See also the "Frankfurt Declaration" in *Christianity Today*, 19, June 1970; "The Lausanne Covenant" in Gerald Anderson and Thomas Stransky, eds., *Mission Trends Number 2: Evangelization*, W. Eerdmans, Grand Rapids; Paulist Press, New York, 1975, pp. 239–52; Hendrick Kraemer, *The Christian Message in a Non-Christian World*, Edinburgh House Press, London, 1938, and *Religion and the Christian Faith*, Lutterworth Press, London, 1956; Paul Knitter, *No Other Name? A Critical Survey of Christian Attitudes Towards Other Religions*, SCM, London, 1985, ch. 5; and my book *Theology and Religious Pluralism*, Basil Blackwell, Oxford & New York, 1986, ch.3.
10   I shall use the masculine personal pronoun for God, without intending to denote any gender.
11   See Wisdom 8:1; Acts 14:17; Romans 2:6–7; I Tim. 2:4. See also Hick and Rahner cited below.
12   See Rosemary Ruether, *Faith and Fratricide*, Winston Press, Seabury, 1985 and Franz Mussner, *Tractate on the Jews*, Fortress Press, London & Philadelphia, 1984.
13   I have developed these and other criticisms in *Theology and Religious Pluralism*, ch. 3.
14   This tension is present in Barth's work in as much as he was an exclusivist while being a universalist (the belief that *all* men and women are ultimately saved)!
15   See John Hick, *God and the Universe of Faiths*, Fount, London, 1977, chs. 9 and 10; and *God Has Many Names*, Macmillan, London, 1980, (US edition 1982). See also pluralists such as Knitter, op. cit., 1985, chs. 8–10; Alan Race, *Christians and Religious Pluralism*, SCM, London, 1983, chs. 4–6; and Alastair Hunter, *Christianity and Other Faiths in Britain*, SCM, London, 1983.
16   Hick, 122.
17   Ibid., 140.
18   I have dealt with Hick's theology of religions and its development over the years in some detail in *John Hick's Theology of Religions: A Critical Evaluation*, University Press of America, Lanham, New York and London, 1987.
19   Hick, op. cit., 1977, p. 464. My brackets.
20   See Sarvepalli Radhakrishnan, *The Hindu View of Life*, George Allen & Unwin, London, 1927, ch. 2.
21   See William Christian, *Opposition of Religious Doctrines*, Herder and Herder, Macmillan, London and New York, 1972.
22   See also Heinz Schlette, *Towards a Theology of Religions*, Questiones

Disputate Series, Burns and Oates, London, 1966; John Robinson, *Truth is Two-Eyed*, SCM, London, 1979; Hans Küng, *On Being a Christian*, Collins; Doubleday, London; New York, 1976, pp. 89-116; and Knitter, op. cit., 1985, ch. 7.
23 Karl Rahner, *Theological Investigations,* Vol. 5, London; Darton, Longman & Todd; Seabury, New York, 1966, p. 122.
24 For further discussion see D'Costa, op. cit., ch. 4.
25 See Karl Rahner, op. cit., Vol. 6, which appeared in 1969.
26 See Alan Race, 'Christianity and Other Religions: Is Inclusivism Enough?', *Theology*, 89, 1986, 729, pp. 178-86.
27 John Henry Newman, *An Essay on the Development of Christian Doctrine*, Longmans, Green & Co., London, p. 373. See also Robert Schreites, *Constructing Local Theologies*, SCM, London, 1985.
28 See for instance Hick, op. cit., 1980, chs. 2, 6.
29 See Hans Küng and Jürgen Moltmann, eds., *Christianity Among World Religions: Concilium 183*, 1986, pp. 22-30; 67-74.
30 See Vatican II 1965a, ch. 1 art. 2, and Vatican II 1965b.
31 See Christopher Lamb, *Belief in a Mixed Society*, Lion Books, London, 1985.
32 Some issues that I have not inspected concern the impact of biblical criticism regarding the centrality of Christ, the place of mission, the status of the Church, the value and meaning of particular religious traditions and the methodological assessment of the phenomenon of religion. I can only plead lack of space, rather than lack of importance for their omission.

Chapter 4 Christ and Interfaith Worship

1 'An Open Letter to the Leadership of the Church of England', Open Letter Group, *Church Times*, 6 December 1991.
2 Karl Barth, cited in Eberhard Busch, *Karl Barth: His Life from Letters and Autobiographical Texts*, trans. John Bowden, SCM Press, London, 1975, p. 411.
3 C.F.D. Moule, *The Birth of the New Testament*, A. & C. Black, London, 1971, p. 17.
4 See Moule, op. cit., pp. 11–32.
5 Ibid., p. 17.
6 Ibid.
7 C.F.D. Moule, *The Phenomenon of the New Testament*, Studies in Biblical Theology, second series, 1, SCM Press, London, 1968, p. 21; see also his *The Origin of Christology*, CUP, Cambridge, 1977, pp. 47–106.
8 Moule, *The Birth of the New Testament*, op. cit., p. 71.
9 Karl Barth, 'The Revelation of God as the Abolition of Religion' (extracts from *Church Dogmatics*, Vol. 1, Part 2, ET 1956) in John Hick and Brian Hebblethwaite, eds, *Christianity and Other Religions: Selected Readings*, Collins, London, 1980, pp. 36–7. I have tried to show how it is possible to construct a pneumatology – based on this missing link in Barth's theology – which embraces theological diversity in my 'On Theology' in P.A.B. Clarke and Andrew Linzey,

eds, *Theology, the University and the Modern World*, Lester Crook Academic Press, London, 1988, pp. 29–66.
10 Barth, in Hick and Hebblethwaite, op. cit., p. 49.
11 Barth, ibid., p. 45.

Chapter 5 Evangelization and Other Faiths: the Motivation for Mission

Michael Barnes's lecture was given to the Living Theology course, Glasgow, in July 1991, to celebrate the 500th anniversary of the birth of Ignatius of Loyola and the 450th anniversary of the foundation of the Society of Jesus.

1 From the Roman Catholic perspective, a useful account of the different terms used in describing mission is to be found in the recent document from the Vatican's Pontifical Council for Inter-religious Dialogue, *Dialogue and Proclamation: Reflections and Orientations on Inter-religious Dialogue and Proclamation*, published in the Bulletin of the PCID, 77, 1991. Hence it is worth noting a certain ambiguity in the way the term 'evangelization' is used. Evangelization, it is said,

> refers to the mission of the Church in its totality. In the Apostolic Exhortation *Evangelii Nuntiandi* the term evangelization is taken in different ways. It means 'to bring the Good News into all areas of humanity, and through its impact, to transform that humanity from within, making it new' (para 18)... Yet in the same document, evangelization is also taken more specifically to mean 'the clear and unambiguous proclamation of the Lord Jesus (para 22)... In this document the term *evangelizing mission* is used for evangelization in the broad sense, while the more specific understanding is expressed by the term *proclamation* (para 8).

2 Filippo Filippi, ed., *An Account of Tibet: the Travels of Ippolito Desideri, S.J., of Pistoia, 1712–1727*, with an introduction by C. Wessels, S.J. Routledge, London, 1931.
3 Ibid., pp. 99–100.
4 The translation of the Exercises which I have followed is that of Elder Mullan, S.J., from the edition of David Fleming, S.J., contained in *The Spiritual Exercises; a Literal Translation and a Contemporary Reading*, Institute of Jesuit Sources, St Louis University, 1978.
5 From the 'Autobiography' of Ignatius, *St Ignatius' Own Story*, as told to Luis Gonzalez de Camara, trans William J. Young, S.J., Loyola University Press, Chicago, 1980, p. 67.
6 The pattern of the Exercises follows a sequence of four periods, roughly equivalent to weeks, the whole making up some thirty days in all. For an excellent modern introduction to Ignatian spirituality and the Spiritual Exercises see David Lonsdale, *Eyes to See, Ears to Hear*, Darton, Longman & Todd, London, 1990.
7 Spiritual Exercises, para 98.
8 Ibid., para 139.
9 St Ignatius of Loyola, *The Constitutions of the Society of Jesus*, trans

George E. Ganss, S.J., Institute of Jesuit Sources, St Louis University, 1970, para 288.
10 Spiritual Exercises, paras 234–7.

Chapter 6 Christ and the Scandal of Particularities

This chapter has been published in German in a book entitled *Horizontüberschretung: Die Pluralistische Theologie der Religionen*, edited by Reinhold Bernhardt, published by Gütersloher Verlagshaus Gerd Mohn, Gütersloh, 1991.

1 Larry Hurtado, *One God, One Lord*, SCM Press, London, 1988.
2 J.A.T. Robinson, *The Roots of a Radical*, SCM Press, London, 1980, p. 65.
3 J. Moltmann, *Der Weg Jesu Christi: Christologie in messianischen Dimensionen*, Christian Kaiser Verlag, Munich, 1989.
4 Karl Barth, *Church Dogmatics*, Vol. 1/2, T. & T. Clark, Edinburgh, 1956, p. 297.
5 Ibid., p. 327.
6 Theological Advisory Commission of the Federation of Asian Bishops' Conferences, 'Seven Theses on Interreligious Dialogue: an Essay in Pastoral Theological Reflection', printed in *International Bulletin of Missionary Research*, Vol. 13, No. 3, July 1989.
7 From an extract by Karl Rahner in *Concise Theological Dictionary*, Herder–Burns & Oates, London, 1967.
8 *Theological Investigations*, Vol. 4, p. 112.
9 J.A.T. Robinson, *Truth is Two-Eyed*, SCM Press, London, 1979, ch. 5.
10 See my *Christians and Religious Pluralism*, SCM Press, London, 1983, for a more detailed account of what is propounded here.

Chapter 7 Dialogue in an Age of Conflict

This chapter was originally an address at St. John's College, Nottingham, Autumn, 1991.

1 George Steiner, *Real Presences*, Faber, London, 1989.
2 R.D. Sider, *The Gospel and its Proclamation: Message of the Fathers of the Church*, Michael Glazier, Delaware, 1983, pp. 60ff. For a theological evaluation of the material in Justin and Clement see Kenneth Cracknell, *Towards a New Relationship: Christians and People of Other Faith*, Epworth, London, 1986, pp. 98ff.
3 It is, presumably, on passages such as these that the Augustinian and Reformation view of prevenient grace is based.
4 On the question of the diversity in the biblical material, as well as its underlying unity, see John Goldingay, *Theological Diversity and the Authority of the Old Testament*, W. Eerdmans, Grand Rapids, 1987.
5 W. Brueggmann, *Trajectories in Old Testament Literature and the Sociology of Ancient Israel*, JBL 1979, No. 98, pp. 161–85.
6 See further my *Culture, Conversation and Conversion* in V. Samuel and C.M.N. Sugden, eds, *AD 2000 and Beyond: a Mission Agenda*,

Regnum, Oxford, 1991, p. 29.
7   Norberto Saracco, *The Liberating Options of Jesus*, in V. Samuel and C.M.N. Sugden, eds, *Sharing Jesus in The Two-Thirds World*, PIM, Bangalore, 1983, pp. 49ff.
8   Otto Kaiser, *Isaiah 1–12*, SCM, London, 1983, pp. 204f.
9   D.J. Sahas, *John of Damascus on Islam*, Brill, Leiden, 1972.
10 David Hume, *Dialogues Concerning Natural Religion*, in R. Wolheim, ed., Hume on Religion, Fontana, London, 1963.
11 Eric J. Sharpe, *The Goals of Inter-Religious Dialogue*, in J. Hick, ed, *Truth and Dialogue*, SPCK, London, 1974, pp. 77ff.
12 Pontifical Council of Inter-Religious Dialogue and the Congregration for the Evangelization of Peoples, *Dialogue and Proclamation*, reflection and orientation on Inter-Religious Dialogue and the proclamation of the Gospel of Jesus Christ. The Bulletin issue 26/2, May 1991. p. 42f.
13 *The Challenge of the Scriptures: The Bible and the Qur'àn*, Orbis, New York, 1989.
14 British Council of Churches, Committee for Relations with People of Other Faiths, *Relations with People of Other Faiths: Guidelines on Dialogue in Britain*, BCC, 1981.
15 See my *Islam: a Christian Perspective*, Paternoster, Exeter, 1983, p. 148. More recent documents continue to display this ambivalence. See report on CWME San Antonio Conference, Frederick R. Wilson, ed, *The San Antonio Report, Your Will be Done: Mission in Christ's Way*, WCC Publications, Geneva, 1990.

Chapter 8 The Case for Religious Pluralism

Inaugural Lecture given by The Reverend Professor Paul Badham, Professor of Theology and Religious Studies at St David's University College, Lampeter, in the University of Wales, 6 December 1991.

1   Peter Brierley, *'Christian' England: What the English Church Census Reveals*, Marc Europe, London, 1991, p. 203.
2   Conference on Culture and Religion, Institute of Philosophy of the Russian Academy of Sciences, Moscow, 21–23 November 1991.
3   Open Letter Group, 'An Invitation to the Clergy of the Church of England', 20 September 1991.
4   Cf. John Hick, *God and the Universe of Faiths*, Macmillan, London, 1973, p. 122.
5   Karl Rahner, 'Christianity and the Non-Christian Religions', in G.A. McCool, *A Rahner Reader*, Darton, Longman & Todd, London, 1975, p. 217.
6   H.J.D. Denzinger, *The Church Teaches: Documents of the Church in English Translation*, Herder, New York, 1965, p. 165.
7   D. Freeman Niles, 'Karl Barth: A Personal Memory', *The South East Asian Journal of Theology*, Vol. 11, pp. 8–12.
8   W. Cantwell Smith, *The Faith of Other Men*, New English Library, London, 1965, p. 101.
9   John Paul II, *Redemptor Hominis*, 1979, para 14. (The Pope is usually

translated as saying 'Every man'. I have translated it 'Every one', because His Holiness did not intend to exclude women from salvation when he said this.)
10   J. Neuner, *Christian Revelation and World Religion*, Burns & Oates, London, 1967, p. 7.
11   A. Flannery, 'The Relation of the Church to Non-Christian Religions', *Vatican II: the Conciliar and Post-Conciliar Documents*, Dominican Publications, Dublin, 1975, p. 739. This particular translation wrongly referred to 'worship' of Jesus. I have altered this to 'venerate', both as a more correct translation of the text, and as corresponding to actual Muslim practice.
12   'Dogmatic Constitution on the Church', 2.16. Flannery, op. cit., p. 216.
13   Rowland Williams, *Parameswara-jnyana-gosthi A Dialogue of the Knowledge of the Supreme Lord, in which are compared the claims of Christianity and Hinduism and various questions of Indian Literature Fairly discussed*, Deighton Bell, Cambridge, 1856.
14   John Hick, 'Rational Theistic Belief without Proofs', in Paul Badham, *A John Hick Reader*, Macmillan, London, 1990.
15   Rowland Williams, *Rational Godliness*, London and Cambridge, 1855, Sermon 19.
16   Rowland Williams, 'Bunsen's Biblical Researches', in B. Jowett, *Essays and Reviews*, Parker & Son, Oxford, 1860, p. 78.
17   John Hick, *God has Many Names*, Macmillan, London, 1980.
18   John Hick, *An Interpretation of Religion*, Macmillan, London, 1989, p. 1.
19   Ibid., p. 236.
20   Ibid., p. 269.
21   Ibid., p. 11.
22   Keith Ward, *Images of Eternity*, Darton, Longman & Todd, London, 1987.

Chapter 10 Models of Interreligious Communication: Reflections on Interfaith Dialogue

Bibliography

Anderson, G.H. and Stransky, T.F., eds., 1981, *Christ's Lordship and Religious Pluralism*, Orbis Books, New York.

Anglican Consultative Council, 1988, *Towards a Theology for Inter-Faith Dialogue*, London, Church of England Board for Mission and Writing.

Barnes, M., 1989, *Religions in Conversation: Christian Identity and Religious Pluralism*, SPCK, London.

Berger, P.L., 1980, *The Heretical Imperative: Contemporary Possibilities of Religious Affirmation*, Collins, London.

British Council of Churches, 1983, *Relations with People of Other Faiths. Guidelines for Dialogue in Britain*, London, rev. ed.

Chatterjee, M., 1967–68, 'The Presuppositions of Inter-Religious Communication: A Philosophical Approach', *Religious Studies*, 3, pp. 391–400.

Coward, H. ed., 1989, *Hindu–Christian Dialogue. Perspectives and Encounters*, Orbis Books, New York.
de Souza, A., 1986, *Relevance of Religion and Inter-Religious Dialogue in Modern Society*, Indian Social Institute, Delhi.
Eck, D.L., 1985, 'Inter-religious Dialogue as a Christian Ecumenical Concern', *Ecumenical Review*, 37/4, pp. 406–19.
Forward, M., ed, 1989, *God of all Faith: Discovering God's Presence in Multi-Faith Society*. The Methodist Church Home Mission Division.
Hick, J. and Hebblethwaite, B., eds, 1980, *Christianity and other Religions*, Collins, Fount Paperbacks, London.
Hooker, R.H., 1989, *Themes in Hinduism and Christianity. A Comparative Study*, Peter Lang, Frankfurt.
Hughes, E.J., 1986, *Wilfred Cantwell Smith: A Theology for the World*, SCM Press, London.
King, U., 1980, *Towards a New Mysticism: Teilhard de Chardin and Eastern Religions*, Collins and Harper and Row, London and New York.
King, U., 1986, 'Darshan – Seeing the Divine: The Meeting of Hindu and Christian Experience', *The Fifth Lambeth Interfaith Lecture*, Centre for the Study of Religion and Society Pamphlet Library, University of Kent, Canterbury.
Knitter, P., 1985, *No Other Name? a Critical Survey of Christian Attitudes towards the World Religions*, SCM Press, London and New York.
Lochhead, D., 1988, *The Dialogical Imperative: a Christian Reflection on Interfaith Encounter*, SCM Press, London.
Nirmal, A.P., 1980, 'Some Theological Issues Connected with Interfaith Dialogue and their Implications for Theological Education in India', *Bangalore Theological Forum*, XII/2, pp. 107–29.
Panikkar, R., 1978, *The Intra-Religious Dialogue*, Paulist Press, New York.
Race, A., 1983, *Christians and Religious Pluralism: Patterns in the Christian Theology of Religions*, SCM Press, London.
Ruether, R., 1981, *To Change the World: Christology and Cultural Criticism*, SCM Press, London.
Russell, L.M., 1974, *Human Liberation in a Feminist Perspective*, Westminster Press, Philadelphia.
Sargant, J. and Sugden, E., 1986, *Unfamiliar Journey: Christians and Interfaith Dialogue*, British Council of Churches Committee for Relations with People of other Faiths, London.
Smith, W.C., 1981, *Towards a World Theology: Faith and the Comparative History of Religion*, London; repr. New York, Macmillan, 1989.
Sundarajan, K.R., 1978-79, 'The Hindu Understanding of the Christian Doctrine of the Trinity', *Insight: A Journal of World Religions*, 3, pp. 34–47.
Teilhard de Chardin, P., 1969, *Human Energy*, Collins, London and New York.
Teilhard de Chardin, P., 1975, *Toward the Future*, Collins, London and New York.
Thomas, M.M., 1970, *The Acknowledged Christ of the Indian Renaissance*, The Christian Literature Society, Madras.

Chapter 11 A Religious Understanding of Religion: a Model of the Relationship between Traditions

1. Quoted by Shinran, *Notes on 'Essentials of Faith Alone'*, Hongwanjii International Centre, Kyoto, 1979, p. 5.
2. *De Vera Religione*, 36, 67.
3. *Summa contra Gentiles*, I, 14, 3.
4. *In librum de Causis*, 6.
5. *Ascent of Mount Carmel*, 310.
6. *Guide to the Perplexed*, I. 58.
7. *Qur'àn*, 6: 101; 23:91; 37:180.
8. *Kena Upanishad*, I. 3.

Chapter 13 Interfaith Prayer

1. 'An Open Letter to the Leadership of the Church of England', Open Letter Group, *Church Times*, 6 December 1991.
2. See my article 'Inter-Faith Worship', in J.G. Davies, ed., *A New Dictionary of Liturgy and Worship*, SCM Press, London, 1986.
3. From 'An Observance for Commonwealth Day' at Westminster Abbey, March 1983.
4. *Discernment*, Vol. 1, No. 3, Winter 1986/7, pp. 31–3.
5. British Council of Churches, *Can We Pray Together*, 1983, p. 1.
6. For a translation of St. Gregory of Nazianzen's hymn, see *World Faiths*, Summer 1976. Alan Paton's words are from a letter written to a boy about to be confirmed.
7. George Appleton, in a sermon at an All Faiths Service, King's College Chapel, London, 1970.

Bibliography

Other literature on the subject besides that mentioned above includes:

Akehurst, P.R., and Wootton, R.W.F., *Inter-Faith Worship?* Grove Booklet 52, 1977.
Braybrooke, M., ed, *Inter-Faith Worsnip*, Galliard, 1974.
Multi-Faith Worship? Questions and Suggestions from the Inter-Faith Consultants of the Board of Missions and Unity, Church House Publishing, 1992.
Puthanangady, P., ed., *Sharing Worship*, National Biblical Constitutional Liturgical Centre, Bangalore 1988.
'Report to the Archbishops', *Ends and Odds*, No. 22, March 1980.

Chapter 14 The Concept of Interfaith Dialogue

1. For a further discussion see my *the Concept of Fundamentalism*, University of Warwick Press, 1992.
2. This is discussed at length in my *Gandhi's Political Philosophy*, Macmillan, London, 1989.
3. Gandhi is a standing refutation of the kind of traditionalist relativism

recently made popular by Alastair MacIntyre. For Gandhi a tradition is a resource not a closed body of ideas, and it is possible and indeed necessary both to remain rooted in a tradition *and* to enrich it by borrowing from others. Like many others MacIntyre derives his view of tradition mainly from religion, especially Catholic Christianity, and misses out its other forms.

Chapter 15   Christian–Muslim Dialogue in the Twentieth Century

An earlier version of Shabir Akhtar's article appeared in *A Faith for All Seasons*, Bellew Publishing, London, 1990.

1   Hans Küng's sincerity and honesty surely deserve recognition. Küng is one Christian writer who has not tried to evade criticisms of the predominant Christian attitude towards Islam. It is because the Church manages to produce men like Küng that opponents are forced to recognize the humility of the Christian clergy. See Küng's 'Christianity and World Religions: the Dialogue with Islam as One Model', in *The Muslim World*, Vol. LXXVII, No. 2, April 1987, pp. 80–95. Hussein Nasr has a good response to Küng in the same issue of the journal, pp. 96ff.

2   Much the same applies to interfaith centres set up to serve multicultural communities in the United Kingdom. These centres are essentially missionary organizations. A Christian policy-maker directs the centre; people of other faiths, including a few Muslims, are hired to fill subordinate positions. Strategically significant positions of influence remain in Christian hands; and this is justified in a Christian country. But, if so, how are such centres religiously liberal?

3   I recognize that Islamic universities in most countries would not countenance Jewish or Christian teachers of Islam. But such closed societies make no claim to being liberal in their religious attitudes. Christians sometimes complain that despite the presence of Muslims in large numbers in the liberal West, there is no school of religious or philosophical thought, reared in western ethos, that may be labelled 'Islamic' in perspective. If my observations are near to the mark, this state of affairs is to be expected.

4   Certainly, to recognize the integrity of religiously plural perspectives, as we all must in the modern world, may require a general concession to other faiths – a concession at applies *inter alia* a concession to Christianity.

5   For further discussion of apostasy in Islamic thought, see my *Be Careful with Muhammad! The Salman Rushdie Affair*, Bellew Publishing, London, 1989, ch. 4.

6   Many conversions to Roman Catholicism have, however, also had a markedly strong element of intellectual reasoning. There are probably few instances of Muslims converting to Catholic Christianity.

7   The fact that a religion offers one precisely what one desires is not in itself a reason for thinking it true (or false). The Qur'an fiercely condemns all unduly optimistic assessments of the likelihood of success

in the religious life.

8 In this respect, the scripture of Islam is far superior – in its honesty and directness of mood – to the papers presented at interfaith conferences. In the Qur'ān, friendly references to the Jewish and Christian societies co-exist along with hostile remarks about some of their members – a feature that has baffled Jewish and Christian commentators, leading some to conclude, wrongly and hastily, that the Qur'ānic stance is self-contradictory. In fact, of course, this circumstance of tension is only to be expected in an area of more or less sectarian disagreement itself underlined by native anxieties about issues of moment.

9 In the Muslim camp, Hasan Askari deserves mention as a *Shi'ah* scholar committed to the attainment of a genuine community of sentiment and doctrine among adherents of the three theisms. His attempts to have trialogue and, more ambitiously, a global theology, both strike me as being wildly naïve. See *Inter-Religion: Journal of Spiritual Quest*, edited by Hasan Askari, Vol.2, No. 1, July 1987, for the usual diet of poorly argued claims about 'universal mysticism' mixed with inferior poetry. For somewhat more realistic hopes, see the recent writings of Hossein Nasr. My own view, like that of the Qur'ān, is, predictably, pessimistic. The Qur'ān does not encourage dialogue beyond a certain point, recognizing the fact that deadlocks created by dogma cannot easily be broken. There is a hint in the sacred volume that men will carry these disputes beyond the grave and contend in front of 'thy Lord on the Day of Resurrection who will decide touching their differences' (Qur'ān 2:113). The Qur'ān regards debate between Jews and Christians as being entirely baseless: 'And the Jews say the Christians have nothing to stand on and the Christians say the Jews have nothing to stand on; and yet they both read the same scripture!' (Q:2:113).

10 No Christian account of this event has been traced.

11 This is of course a version of John Hick's famous view known as 'eschatological verification'. The claim is that death is, as it were, an argument: it serves to prove or disprove a given faith. For details, see John Hick, 'Theology and Verification', in Malcolm Diamond and Thomas Litzenburg, eds, *The Logic of God: Theology and Verification*, Bobbs-Merrill, Indianapolis, 1975, pp. 188–208.

12 See Robert Caspar's thoughtful remarks in 'The Permanent Significance of Islam's Monotheism', in *Concilium*, special issue entitled *Monotheism*, edited by Claude Geffre and Jean-Pierre Jossua, T. & T. Clark, Edinburgh, 1985, pp. 67–78. Caspar's piece is translated by Francis McDonagh.

Chapter 16 Ranking Religions

An earlier version of this chapter appeared in Dan Cohn-Sherbok's *Issues in Contemporary Judaism*, Macmillan, London, 1991.

1 J. Hick, *God and the Universe of Faiths*, St. Martin's Press, New York, 1973, p. 131.
2 R. Panikaar, *The Unknown Christ of Hinduism*, Orbis, New York,

1981, pp. 24, 19.
3. S. Samartha, *Courage for Dialogue*, Orbis, New York, 1982.
4. P. Knitter, *No Other Name*, Orbis, Mary Knoll, 1985.
5. J. Hick, 'On Grading Religions', *Religious Studies*, 17.
6. Ibid., p. 451.
7. Ibid.
8. Ibid., p. 467.
9. P. Griffiths and D. Lewis, 'On Grading Religions, Seeking Truth and Being Nice to People – A Reply to Professor Hick', *Religious Studies*, 19, pp. 75–80.
10. J. Hick, 'On Grading Religions', p. 457.
11. Ibid., p. 462.
12. Ibid.
13. Ibid., p. 467.
14. Ibid., pp. 462–3.
15. Ibid., pp. 465–6.
16. Ibid., p. 459.
17. Knitter, op. cit., p. 231.
18. See L. Jacobs, *Principles of the Jewish Faith*, Vallentine Mitchell, London, 1964, p. 219.

Contributors

The Most Rev. John Habgood is Archbishop of York
The Rev. Canon Christopher Lewis is Residentiary Canon, Canterbury Cathedral
The Most Rev. George Carey is Archbishop of Canterbury
The Rt. Rev. Lord Runcie was Archbishop of Canterbury
Dr. Gavin D'Costa is a Lecturer in Theology and Religious Studies, University of Bristol
The Rev. Dr. Andrew Linzey is Director, Centre for the Study of Theology, University of Essex, Colchester
Fr. Michael Barnes is a Lecturer in the study of Religions, Heythrop College, London
The Rev. Alan Race is Director of Studies of the Southwark Ordination Course
The Rt. Rev. Michael Nazir-Ali is the General Secretary of the Church Missionary Society
Professor Paul Badham is Professor of Theology and Religious Studies, St. David's University College, University of Wales, Lampeter
Professor Geoffrey Parrinder was formerly Professor of the Comparative Study of Religions, King's College, London
Professor Ursula King is Head of the Theology Department, University of Bristol
Professor John Hick is Danforth Professor of the Philosophy of Religion, Claremont Graduate School, California
Professor Keith Ward is Regius Professor of Divinity, University of Oxford
The Rev. Marcus Braybrooke is Vicar of Christ Church, Bath
Professor Bhiku Parekh is Professor of Politics, University of Hull
Dr. Shabbir Akhtar has worked in Bradford race relations and is an independent member of the Bradford Council of Mosques
Rabbi Dr. Dan Cohn-Sherbok is University Lecturer in Theology, University of Kent, Canterbury